Southern Waters

Southern Waters

THE LIMITS TO ABUNDANCE

CRAIG E. COLTEN

LOUISIANA STATE UNIVERSITY PRESS

BATON ROUGE

Published by Louisiana State University Press
Copyright © 2014 by Louisiana State University Press
All rights reserved
Manufactured in the United States of America
LSU Paperback Original
First printing

Designer: Laura Roubique Gleason
Typeface: Warnock Pro
Printer and binder: Maple Press

Mid I-Main
Stacks
TD
223.
.5
.C65
2014

All original maps created by Mary Lee Eggart and Clifford Duplechin.

Library of Congress Cataloging-in-Publication Data
Colten, Craig E.
  Southern waters : the limits to abundance / Craig E. Colten.
    pages cm
  Includes bibliographical references and index.
  ISBN 978-0-8071-5650-6 (pbk. : alk. paper) — ISBN 978-0-8071-5651-3
(pdf) — ISBN 978-0-8071-5652-0 (epub) — ISBN 978-0-8071-5653-7 (mobi)
  1. Water-supply—Management—Southern States. 2. Water conservation—
Southern States. 3. Water quality—Southern States. 4. Water quality manage-
ment—Southern States. I. Title.
  TD223.5.C65 2014
  333.9100975—dc23

                                                              2014007935

Contents

Figures and Tables

FIGURES

TABLES

Acknowledgments

As a graduate student at LSU in the 1970s, I recall driving out of Baton Rouge along Scenic Highway—the road with the currently inappropriate name that passes through a dense concentration of petrochemical refineries—and seeing a rural home with a large pond in front. On subsequent outings across the South, ornamental fish ponds increasingly caught my attention, and I considered making these features the focus of my dissertation. In many ways they represented an idealized landscape. Countless rural residents could cast a line into their very own private pond without even firing up their pickups. To my mind, these diminutive impoundments offered the ultimate in convenience for the committed southern angler. However, today they seldom serve as fishing holes. Too tiny to satisfy the quest of the southern fishermen, who favor outings complete with big bass boats at remote camps where spirits flow and manly behavior escapes the spousal gaze, these ponds are largely decorative and not ideals. Furthermore, they are not the product of the southern imagination. Federal programs promoted them around the country, and they dot the landscape across this land. As time passed, my fascination with these ponds faded, but in many respects this work returns to ideas about the value that southerners see in water, even though I have not waded into the fish pond topic.

Water looms large in the South. Growing up in north Louisiana, on numerous occasions I was coerced into fishing expeditions that yielded little more than a hook imbedded in my finger and perhaps a string of scrawny bream. While I never gained the same passion for fishing as many of my boyhood friends, the lure of the mighty bass runs deep across the region and provides the substance for exaggerated accounts. Water's significance goes back much further than the twentieth-century bass fisherman. It was also prominent in Indian lore and geosophy. It dominates many elements of the region's settlement history, both prehistoric and historic, and it infuses the arts and imagery of the region. From Huck Finn's escapades on the Mississippi to the lyrics of "Swanee River," to the stage name of the Blues master McKinley Morganfield, or Muddy Waters, to the professional bass-fishing tournaments, water courses through the region's history, geography, and iconography.

I had started this project before Hurricane Katrina delivered devastating floods to the Gulf Coast in 2005. That defining event forced me to place the project on the back burner for several years as I became immersed in several waves of poststorm projects. I kept it alive in fits and spurts. The irregular investigations allowed me to rethink the larger endeavor, and I finally returned to it full time in 2012. That year, the Louisiana Board of Regents, through the Board of Regents Support Fund, bestowed on me one of the greatest gifts a scholar can ever hope to receive. An ATLAS grant (ATLAS 38635 LEQSF (2012–13)-RD-ATL-01) provided me with the luxury of dedicating a year to completing this volume. It relieved me of my classroom teaching responsibilities and funded a concluding round of archival and field research that took me from Florida to Virginia. During that pleasant year, I was able to write several new chapters and polish a number of previously composed drafts. All in all, it was one of the most satisfying years of my academic career, and I am extremely grateful to the Board of Regents for its generous support. I hope this volume lives up to the Board's expectations.

On my gonzo research forays from collection to collection, countless librarians and archivists lent a hand as I inflicted my manic requests on their orderly holdings. Patient professionals in state libraries, state archives, and national archive facilities guided me to an abundance of historical material, and I am deeply indebted to them. I spent time working in the state libraries and archives of the following states and want to acknowledge the valued assistance of the staffs in each: Virginia, North Carolina, South Carolina, Georgia, Florida, Kentucky, Tennessee, Alabama, Mississippi, Louisiana, and Texas. I also received valued assistance at National Archives facilities in Maryland, Texas, and Georgia. Forays into the stacks of University of Texas Library, Texas State University Library, and University of South Carolina Library round the list of my out-of-state research destinations, and the Rosenberg Library in Galveston assisted with its online photographic collection. And I must also recognize the archivists at Hill Memorial Library at LSU and also Stephanie Braunstein and her helpful associates in the Government Documents section of LSU's Middleton Library, as well as the efficient staff at the LSU Law Library.

Research assistance came from a number of graduate students at LSU and Texas State University as well. Notably, Amy Sumpter, John McEwen, Louise Cheetham, Alexandra Giancarlo, Reno Cecora, and Rita Setser assisted me at various points along the way. I could not pinpoint their precise contributions, but they all were vital to the completion of this project.

Kent Mathewson, Andrew Sluyter, and Dydia DeLyser have been splendid and supportive colleagues. My longtime geography collaborators Lary Dilsaver, Terry Young, and Geoff Buckley offered insight into topics when I was breaking new ground and motivation to press ahead by corraling me to present preliminary findings in some wonderful forums.

The Rachel Carson Center and its director, Christof Mauch, offered me a fellowship to continue looking at the international dimension of this project, for which I am extremely grateful.

As my gray hairs begin to outnumber the darker strands, I find myself thinking about the mentors, both official and informal, who helped guide me into this fluid topic. I want to thank those individuals who provided me with guidance, support, and most importantly with the opportunity to pursue this privileged scholar's life. Sam Hilliard, who steered me through my master's thesis, pointed out the many wonders in "this rich land," showed me that you could have fun as a geographer, nurtured my interest in the American South, and encouraged me to continue graduate studies. Don Meinig was magnificently patient with me as I stumbled into the frosty drumlin fields of Syracuse and consistently supported me as I launched into my vagabond career. His dedication to fine prose helped me refine my own writing, although mine never rose to the caliber of his polished prose, and he instilled in me a dedication to and appreciation for stories rooted in the landscape. Two environmental historians also stand out as informal mentors. Joel Tarr and Martin Melosi welcomed me into the field, strengthened my work through their constructive critiques, and allowed me to join them on the paths that they blazed. Bruce McMillan of the Illinois State Museum and Shelley Bookspan of PHR Environmental Consultants brought me onboard when academic employers were uninterested and provided essential support to carry out research that ultimately defined my career. John Tiefenbacher and Julie Tuason at Texas State helped convince me to leap back into the academy and proved to be splendid colleagues. Bill Davidson finagled a way for me to return to my alma mater and settle into a remarkable phase of my career, while Bob Kates invited me into the realm of community resilience and sustainability after Hurricane Katrina. There are so many others—teachers, colleagues, and students—who contributed to accomplishments that bear my name, but in reality deserve to be shared.

LSU Press supported this project from the day I proposed it, and I am especially grateful to Alisa Plant for her interest and efficiency in moving the project forward. The editors at the press help enliven my sometimes tiresome prose. I also need to thank the several reviewers who suggested improvements to chapters published elsewhere—the journals and presses receive acknowledgment in the Notes. Finally, the reader who offered insightful recommendations on ways to improve the final manuscript earned my gratitude. Even though authors are not inclined to embrace suggestions that require a bit more research, these suggestions deserved the effort.

And as always, I am indebted in so many ways to my family and my lovely wife, Marge. My family instilled in me a curiosity about what lies around the next bend, and Marge has allowed me to chase the many dreams that have shaped our lives together.

Southern Waters

Introduction

Drought and shortage do not spring to mind when considering water in the American South. Classic accounts of the region are replete with tales of watery abundance. In literary and scholarly works, floods and swamps emerge as two of the most prominent regional symbols. Mark Twain used the meandering Mississippi River as a centerpiece for his acclaimed literary works, and John Barry's blockbuster *Rising Tide* showcases the great flood of 1927.[1] Notions of widespread saturation, fostered by such places as the evocatively named Great Dismal Swamp, have infused the imagination of generations. Abundance, bordering on excess, resides at the core of our thinking about southern waters.

European explorers and settlers launched this conceptualization of the region's fluvial riches. Hernando de Soto, while looking for gold, found freshwater pearls and a Mississippi River in flood. The French brothers Iberville and Bienville probed an intricate and dense network of rivers and bayous in the Mississippi River delta. And much later, Thomas Jefferson reports on the plentiful waterways flowing across Virginia from the Blue Ridge to the sea. Their accounts of ample water have coursed through popular understanding of the region over the ensuing centuries. Abundance provided ample opportunities for waterborne commerce and hydropower. Yet it also presented environmental risks in the form of floods and disease. This contrast between resource and hazard is a fundamental part of the southern landscape.

Regional studies published in the 1930s reported prominently on the South's hydraulic fortunes (fig. I.1). Geographer Almon Parkins observes that "the South has by far the greatest mileage of waterways, whether we consider natural or improved waters," while sociologist Howard Odum contrasts the drought-parched Great Plains with the South's abundant rainfall and hundreds of miles of rivers that stand as "natural wealth of the first order."[2] It is useful to begin this work with the impressions of these regionalists. They wrote at a time when the nation was in the midst of a major drought that was sending dust clouds across the parched landscape of the Great Plains and driving folks from their farms. Meanwhile the South was recovering from the floods of the 1920s and trying to eradicate malaria—a disease associated with ill-drained topography.

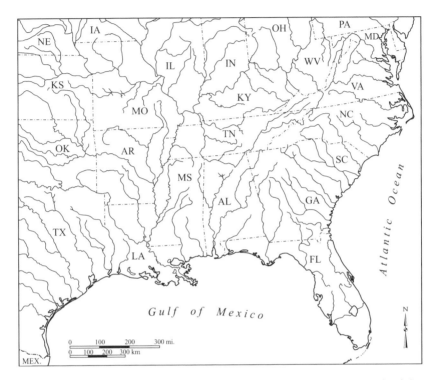

FIG. I.1. A dense network of surface streams is a fundamental characteristic of the South. Cartography by Mary Lee Eggart.

These contrasting conditions prompted massive efforts at large-scale regional planning, and this involved taking stock of water resources. Driven by a desire to identify the limits to the country's natural resources and to guide more prudent use of them, the federal government launched a series of river basin studies in 1936. Reports emanating from this effort represent the first attempt at comprehensive river basin management in the United States. They considered a wide range of water issues—including flood control, navigation, water supplies, hydroelectric power, pollution, drainage, wildlife conservation, and recreation.[3] Among the principal concerns in the southern basins were issues aligned with abundance, not shortage: flooding, power, drainage, disease, and recreation. But while these reports did not identify water shortfall as a pressing concern in the humid portions of the South, it has certainly become a prominent concern in recent decades.

Urban and industrial growth since the mid-twentieth century has fundamentally transformed the South from its predominantly rural, agricultural pattern of the 1930s. Highly engineered waterways serve multiple users, and these many users have come to expect dependable supplies that sometimes cannot all be delivered simultaneously. Cities like Houston, Miami, and Atlanta have placed unprecedented demands on water supplies, and their experiences have exposed some of the limits to abundance. As they continue to grow, their water use will only expand. Coupled with climatic vagaries, water has become a contentious commodity in the twenty-first century. This complex situation calls into question the sustainability of southern water supplies, particularly in the face of climate change.

Current thinking on the impacts of climate change suggests numerous impacts on the South's water situation. Increasing temperatures will increase demands for urban water consumption—for watering lawns and cooling power plants that provide electricity for air conditioning—and for agricultural irrigation. More intense, although erratic, rainfall events will trigger localized flooding, even though the intervals between major downpours is expected to increase and make drought a more common occurrence. Sea-level rise will increase risk of both riparian flooding, as rivers achieve higher flood stages, and littoral inundation from hurricanes and tropical storms. These fluctuations, coupled with growing urban and rural demands, will continue to intensify competition for increasingly irregular water supplies.[4]

This volume will address how the U.S. South has undergone the transition from a region of surplus to one of emerging shortages. It will relate how a society that values water, while living in an environment fraught with inconsistencies and affected by tinkering with natural processes, strives to eliminate both excess and shortage. The actions taken to manage water are much larger than the reconfiguring of flood-control policy after the 1927 Mississippi River flood or the late twentieth-century water wars over the Chattahoochee River. Attempts to control water include practices that have been unfolding over decades. By looking at the long-term process we can identify how society has grappled with emergent deficits. In doing so, I hope to address one of the core research questions of sustainability, that is, how to identify long-term trends in order to address future needs.[5] To provide that prospective outlook, I will consider water issues that have demanded public attention over the course of the past two centuries. Additionally, I consider the fact that, although many small, local water dramas have played out across the region during that time, the region's climatic and cultural cohesiveness offers a unifying framework that distinguishes it from neighboring territories. When we step back from the local water issues and consider the region as a whole, broader patterns of water use and management emerge, and they reflect shared political foundations, similar economic underpinnings within a warm and moist climatic zone. This vantage point provides a valuable perspective on adjustments made when surplus grades into shortage. Hence, I will employ a regional framework to shape my narrative.

Water in Geographic Context

A river basin, the territory drained by a principal stream and its tributaries, provides a logical geographic basis for water management and for the study of human-environment relations. There is a comforting fluvial logic when one can follow water from the headlands to the sea and trace human interactions with the hydrological system within the bounds of a watershed. Riparian legal principles adhere to the river basin logic—an upstream user cannot interfere with the quantity and quality of water a downstream user expects to receive. The 1930s National Resources Committee reports followed this format, as have subsequent river management efforts.[6] And it is no surprise that most of the fine scholarship on rivers also conforms to the basin as a geographical framework.

The most prominent works that explore the long-term intersection of human activity and water in the United States have focused on the water-poor West and in some respects use basins to characterize the larger region. In this region with several prominent rivers that flow from the Rockies or Sierras across an arid territory, water shortage and conflicts have provided the grist for compelling environmental history. Donald Worster has traced the increasing scale of water collection and distribution. He provides a powerful account of determined efforts to wrest every possible drop of water from the lowly irrigation canal. In his own words, the true West is "a culture and society, built on and absolutely dependant on, a sharply alienating, intensely managerial relationship with nature."[7] The sprawling Colorado River and the rivers of California's Central Valley provide the focus for his study. To the north, Richard White examines nature-society interactions made evident by the replumbing of the Columbia River. By bounding his study in alignment with the river's watershed, he is able to highlight the linkages between a river that persists despite human efforts to capture hydroelectric power, fight floods, improve navigation, store water for irrigation, and sustain habitat for aquatic life.[8] The basin provides cohesion and documentary consistency for the researcher, and the water conflicts that arose in these arid western basins provide high drama. The human quest to tap the meager supplies for economic development pushed these basins to their environmental limits. To cope with inadequate supplies, western water policy—known as prior appropriation—evolved. It elevated water to a commodity, much like timber, minerals, and land.[9] As a commodity, water entered into interbasin commerce and thus escaped the confines of the basin of origin. Thus, there has emerged a wider western water history, one shaped by particular policies that gave priority to those who first made claims to water—at least among the European-American settlers to the region. By studying the western water situation basin by basin, regional insights have emerged.

Splendid environmental histories of the Rhine, the Liri, and the Rhone follow the basin logic as well.[10] Treatments of the Fraser, the Bow, the St. Francis, and the Assiniboine rivers in Canada further emphasize the basin as the obvious conceptual container for studying waterways.[11] Basin studies are able to encompass the full range of environmental and human issues, even those that may impinge on the fluvial setting from distant political or economic centers. These European and Canadian examples exemplify the overlap between local and larger geographical contexts.

The basin still largely frames discussion of waters in the humid East, but not exclusively. In New England, for example, Ted Steinberg and John Cumbler both examine the use of riparian legal principles to police the impacts of an increasingly urban and industrial society on streams in the region. Steinberg considers how industrial capitalism fundamentally altered the human ecology of New England's rivers and how riparian law evolved to support the "maximization of economic growth."[12] While this process played out in particular basins, water law of the region enveloped multiple basins. John Cumbler, who takes his study into the early twentieth century, argues that New England reformers pushed for citizens' rights to clean water. Using the Connecticut River basin as his study area, he argues that a broader understanding of emerging water policy can be found in a single basin.[13] Richard Judd uses the "Northeast Frontier" as the territorial frame for his examination of fisheries conservation. He argues that "understanding the complicated relation between folk thinking, ecological change, and conservation trends is best accomplished through a regional approach."[14] By casting his investigative net across multiple river basins, he treats the region as a biologically and culturally cohesive unit. The modest scale of the region makes this a bit more manageable, although the fragmented record found in multiple states complicates documentation.

Historians have discovered water policy innovation in both the West and New England, while the American South has been presented as lagging in initiatives to manage its environment.[15] Political scientists, however, provide studies of the emergence of recent environmental policy in the South that reveal both regional characteristics and a certain degree of innovation.[16] Their work also highlights variation within the region in terms of political solutions. I would add that at a regional scale, the South presents some complexities not found in either the West or New England. It is a water-rich region, like the Northeast, but also has legal foundations in English, Spanish, and French traditions. It grades from areas of abundance—the southern Appalachians—to areas with meager precipitation—west Texas—to areas with distinctly seasonal rainfall—south Florida. Despite the climatic range, discussions of what defines the South often start with climate.[17] Temperature, more than moisture, often rises to the top of historical accounts of plantation agriculture, public health, and regional culture. Nonetheless, abundant water remains a key ingredient of the climatic component of the South's distinctiveness that has not been displaced by the rejection of environmental determinism in academic discourses or by the introduction of air conditioning in daily life.

There has been a sizable body of recent research on southern waters, largely framed either by river basins or particular wetlands. Notably, Jeffrey Stine considers environmental concerns and social confrontations that accompanied the construction of the Tennessee-Tombigbee Waterway; Marty Reuss details the complex transformation of and political struggles over the management of the Atchafalaya Basin; Richard Bartlett focuses on the interstate pollution battle along the Pigeon River; and Chris Morris offers a sweeping portrait of the conflicting impulses that drove management of the lower Mississippi.[18] By relying on a particular geographic frame, these authors are able to illuminate the nature-society relationships played out on navigable or interstate waterways. Likewise, discussions of the Great Dismal Swamp, the Okefenokee, and the Everglades offer comparable analyses of discretely defined waterbodies.[19] Far from being provincial, these studies link broader land-use decisions, economic practices, and political policies to particular places. Yet none tries to offer an overarching perspective on the South.

Geographers largely have abandoned the regional approach. No texts on the South have appeared in decades, although the region continues to garner ample attention.[20] In an appeal for a critical geography of water in the American South, Chris Meindl makes the case for a regional approach that addresses some of the prevailing inequities that remain and the need to confront the challenges of increasing strains on a water supply that has its limits. Social and racial issues that remain from the Old South and the push for continued economic growth embraced by proponents of the New South intersect in the water arena.[21] Across the core of states of the old Confederacy, plus Kentucky, there is an obvious surplus to the water balance. These states share a similar conservative political culture that resists national influences while readily accepting federal financial assistance. This political culture has shaped the region's approach to water management. Regional boosters have pushed for economic and urban growth for much of the last century, which has propelled many urban centers to the limits of their water supplies. It is this relatively recent growth, while water seemingly was plentiful, and the sudden encounters with the limits to abundance that provide a basis for this particular treatment of the South. These states have awakened to periodic deficits and their experiments with managing shortage and adjustments to newly discovered limits offer an extraordinary example for examining adaption to changing circumstances. By considering the South as a whole, this work will be able to tease out common patterns and also reveal subtle distinctions that emerge from local efforts to cope with water shortages.

Water management is a prominent topic in the geographic literature. While environmental historians have been drawn to the American West, geographers have tended to focus on international water issues—often at a basin scale.[22] William Graf has offered observations on management of U.S. rivers. In 1992 he explored the relationship of science and policy and selected the arid West as the framework for his investigation. In this water-limited region, he observed that during the Progressive Era and during the period from 1950 to 1970, scientific input increased in importance in shaping public policy related to western rivers, but that during the post-1970 period, despite the passage of numerous environmental statutes, science lagged in providing guidance for public policy.[23] More recently, he offered prescriptions for restoring the integrity to America's rivers. In that appeal, he noted the complexity of crafting public policy that balances the numerous scientific perspectives used to address river management.[24] Martin Doyle questions whether historical management practices will satisfy future water demands at the national scale, but he concludes that despite its messiness, American river management has been remarkably resilient and adaptable.[25] Both these geographers recognize the intricate linkages between science and policy and the value of a historical perspective. They also have taken on the ambitious goal of considering river management at the national scale. In doing so, however, they reduce the resolution at the local scale. By honing in on the American South, I hope to sharpen the resolution within a region with decided similarities that yet also encompasses a range of environmental and social diversity.

Sustainable Directions?

Managing water resources in the South has followed a path of maximum exploitation to meet short-term needs rather than one of sustainability. This should come as no surprise and is not a criticism of past water users. Colonial explorers and settlers saw an abundance of water in the region and sought to tap it for transportation, power, and food. Given their assessment of water resources and prevailing social attitudes, their approach was reasonable. After all, one of the first key steps toward pursuing sustainability is the discovery of limits. During the early colonial period, when there were no extensive European settlements in the arid or seasonally dry margins of the South, abundance seemed pervasive and unending.[26]

This work will trace the discovery of the limits to abundance. It will begin with a series of chapters that explore coping with abundance and excess. Wetlands covered sizable tracts of territory along the eastern seaboard and the gulf coast. In the minds of European settlers these areas impeded orderly agricultural development. Projects to drain and reclaim them began during the colonial era and continued into the twentieth century. Driven by economic impulses, drainage was among the first techniques to deal with excess water. Floods along the many southern rivers presented another example of fluvial surplus. Fending off high water, from river floods and hurricanes, became a regional obsession and one eventually funded largely by the federal treasury. Investments in flood control across the South have been massive and have contributed to several long-term environmental concerns, particularly in Louisiana and Florida where the most extensive levee systems exist. The fourth chapter deals with water excess and examines the struggles to eliminate diseases that watery environments nurture. Insect-borne diseases like yellow fever and malaria were prominent in the South, and mosquito eradication efforts in the twentieth century shaped water management policies and targeted small wetlands and also the management of large reservoirs.

A second set of chapters will highlight the emerging recognition of shortages. Early inklings of the limits to abundance appeared even in the colonial era as mill dams impeded fish migrations and prompted policies to protect aquatic life. But for most states in the South, early policy prioritized navigation and public access to navigable rivers. Federally financed navigation works after the Civil War dedicated waterways to specific activities and placed limits on other uses, and twentieth century hydropower projects embraced multiple-use principles but were not sustainable in design. The underlying legal tradition that privileges navigation continues to influence current management and sometimes comes into conflict with late twentieth-century environmental laws. Conservation of wildlife, including fish, rose in importance in the early twentieth century and its practitioners sought to offset declines in aquatic life by creating sustainable yields of fish, not to be confused with the concept of sustainability. Adoption of conservation practices in southern states reveals a willingness to accept federal guidance and also an adjustment to longer-term goals in ways that have been colored by issues of class and race particular to the region. Pollution of southern waterways became pronounced in the second half of the twentieth century and accentuated another form of water shortage—not in supply, but in terms of quality. Adjusting to pollution control while promoting industrial development created tensions between policy makers and citizens. The most profound conflict-engendering demands have come from urban populations, demands which become most obvious during irregular droughts. Limits to abundance have appeared during much of the South's post-colonial history. The Conclusions section will contrast large-scale water transfer with efforts to promote water conservation. It will attempt to frame future water management through past initiatives and will highlight the tendency to seek grand technical fixes, while ultimately discovering that conservation practices are more effective and also bode well for sustainability.

Management of southern waters has relied on sizable and costly engineered works. Levees and hydroelectric projects are the hallmarks of twentieth-century projects. While most have performed satisfactorily much of the time, although not perfectly, they demand constant surveillance, maintenance, upgrading, and retrofitting. These projects are hardly sustainable. And almost without exception, these human interventions in natural processes send out ripples through the environmental systems that they are inserted in. They may fix one problem, but they often contribute to others. Some consequences are unintended, while some are foreseen as unavoidable in the quest of a project's principal, limited objectives. Long-term sustainability was not part of the planning. A shared challenge to their managers is how to fold less disruptive and more sustainable elements into these existing fixtures.

These chapters will be built on a series of case studies largely framed by the most convenient territorial unit—the river basin. Yet, by attempting to offer case studies from across the South, coupled with a thorough review of court cases, state agency records, and historical sources, I will expand this treatment to the regional scale. The range of case studies is not exhaustive, nor are the topics of water management. Nonetheless, when it is taken together with the many fine river basin studies, this volume, with its historical gaze, will, I hope, offer a geographic synthesis and add insight to the fluvial future of the South.

Water managers in the South, as in other locations around the world, are beginning to consider water planning in light of sustainable supplies for multiple users. Climate change, which has gained acceptance in the hydrological sciences, forecasts increasing conflicts among water consumers—both locally and across the region. By considering over two centuries of time, I aimed this work at exposing the modest adjustments made to diminishing water resources. In doing so, it will demonstrate that adaptations have been made, some have worked and some have been less effective, and most were not really made with an integrated, adaptive, long-term sustainable human-environment system in mind. Yet, the modest adjustments in the past can offer guidance as we continue to grapple with water issues across the region. As water managers seek sustainable solutions, this long-term perspective should help them avoid the more unsustainable fixes of the past.

1

The Meanings of Water

Introduction

On April 9, 1682, LaSalle claimed all the "seas, harbors, ports, bays, adjacent straights" of the Mississippi River basin, plus the inhabitants, their settlements, and the mineral and aquatic resources, for King Louis XIV of France.[1] His assertion of sovereignty revealed a fundamental European concept, and one particularly aligned with French traditions, that river basins provided a means for unifying territory. The claims of LaSalle and other explorers who planted their national flags in the Americas assumed that watersheds provided one basis for the social organization of space, and they highlight a key component of European thinking about the meaning of water.

Indigenous cartography, in turn, revealed to Europeans the central role waterways played in the spatial organization of Native Americans. The many rivers, large and small, provided an abundant set of reference points that indigenous people used to navigate. Waterways were critical in the choices native people made for settlements and offered vital route ways for long-distance travel and exchange. Streams and bayous were ubiquitous in how native societies organized their landscapes and elements of their belief systems.

In the course of their journeys, French explorers tapped indigenous knowledge and came to appreciate the abundance of waterways and riparian resources. They marveled at the size of fish in the rivers, commenting in wonder on the one giant specimen that fed twenty of LaSalle's troops.[2] Within a few years of declaring possession of the Mississippi River basin, the French replicated native practices in organizing their settlement system to conform to the dendritic pattern of the mighty river and its tributaries, and they charted their imperial ambitions along the arc of the Mississippi and St. Lawrence rivers. On the eastern seaboard, English colonists too relied on the dense network of streams for shaping their advancing settlements. From Jamestown to Savannah, river mouths provided multiple features that accommodated colonial outposts. Spanish coastal attachments also appeared where fresh water met the sea. Settlers in the new land came to realize not only the opportunities of waterways but also the dangers inherent in riparian settings. Floods, another form of abundance, punctuated the establishment of the European footholds and made apparent the tenuous nature of the sites that offered harbors for the incipient cities. Yet, strategic considerations, useful resources from the rivers and their nearby coastal wetlands, and the dream of riches from the interior eclipsed concerns about hydrologic disadvantages.[3]

Throughout the southeastern portion of North America, some Europeans' concepts about the meaning of water coincided with notions already held by native peoples. Native people also utilized water for basic survival and established settlements where adequate supplies were available. They too navigated streams and rivers to interact and trade with neighbors both near and distant. Waterways supplied important aquatic food sources to indigenous Americans and to Europeans. Both societies relied on water in religious ritual and ceremony. But while there were similarities, preference for aquatic resources, means of navigation, and religious significance differed in fundamental ways. In short, water played an unquestionably significant role within indigenous and European societies who chose to inhabit the riparian settings and because of this parallel appreciation the colonial settlement process offers a means to consider the transatlantic blending of ideas about the abundance of water.

There were overlapping meanings of water, but Europeans arrived with distinct concepts about it.[4] Beyond initial appraisal, common law and technological expectations created very different frameworks for managing water resources. Europeans brought with them notions about deriving power from watercourses and legal principles to regulate access to and the just use of water. In addition, the colonists arrived with ideas of wetlands as undesirable and even dangerous places that demanded transformation for improved usage. This transformative impulse to drain wetlands for agriculture also arrived with Africans.

This chapter examines the intersection between the contrasting transatlantic views of water and how they influenced interactions between original inhabitants in the southeastern corner of North America and new arrivals from Europe and Africa. It also considers early accounts of water that added an ominous element to its meaning that was previously unknown. Further, early legal constructs illustrate the overlay of ancient European notions about use and protection of water in ways unanticipated by native customary practices. Throughout, the assumption of an abundance of water in the Southeast tended to downplay any concerns with coping with shortages.

Frameworks for Transatlantic Encounters

Donald Meinig provides a useful framework for considering the transatlantic encounters between Europeans and native people. He points out three stages of "transatlantic interaction." His "prelude" phase produced limited impact on both sides of the Atlantic, but yielded initial understanding of coastal areas by Europeans and formed the basis for native comprehension of foreign visitors. His "fixation" phase included initial settlements and more extensive changes in the Americas, while also producing greater effects as European ports began to feel the impact of transatlantic intercourse. More expansive settlement networks characterized the colonial phase. Further, his three colonial types emphasize interactions with native peoples and differentiate between the northern colonial impact (expulsion and articulation) and the tropical model (stratification). Articulation, mixed to some degree with expulsion and eradication (due largely to disease), was common in the American Southeast. There was sufficient interaction in the Southeast for Europeans to learn about routes and resources and to develop trade with native peoples. The Spanish sought to extend their "stratification" model to the southeastern littoral. Meinig's model offers an effective temporal and geographic framework.[5]

Andrew Sluyter's presentation of the "colonial triangle" is critical of Meinig's work but to my mind adds to it by emphasizing the mechanisms for interactions that produced both conceptual and material transformations between transatlantic societies. In his analytical framework, Sluyter considers the reciprocal relationships among European, native, and landscapes as colonial societies encountered new lands and people. In addition, he emphasizes the need to move beyond the material elements of European encounters with native peoples as has often been the tendency and to incorporate the biophysical dimension—water in this case.[6] Water constitutes one critical element of the biophysical dimension that Sluyter does not address specifically in his study of Mexico. By merging Meinig's temporal and spatial model with Sluyter's colonial triangle and emphasizing water (fig. 1.1), this chapter provides a glimpse into how previously distinct societies dealt with an essential biophysical resource and how the transatlantic contact modified appraisal and management of this essential fluid.[7]

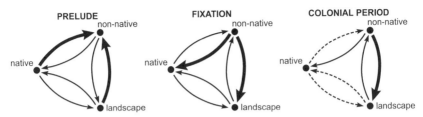

FIG. 1.1. Sluyter's model of material and conceptual exchanges in Meinig's stages of transatlantic contact. Graphic by Clifford Duplechin.

Indigenous Meanings

In coastal marshes near the Mississippi River, water and the resources it contained were vitally important to the prehistoric Tchefuncte people about two thousand years ago. They relied heavily on a local mussel, the *rangia,* for subsistence and built middens from the discarded shells. Since transporting mussels long distances was not feasible, settlements had to be close to the resource. Mounds built of the refuse from this subsistence pattern have enabled archaeologists to date the seaward advance of the great river's delta, identify people who lived there, and trace their reworking of a wetland environment in ways to escape regular inundations. Water-based resources in what became Louisiana provided the means of survival both in terms of diet and flood avoidance. Archaeologist Tristram Kidder argues that prehistoric manipulations of the landscape with refuse, plus indigenous knowledge of local geography, made the site of what became New Orleans desirable to colonial settlers.[8] Thus, water-based resources helped define the settlement pattern.

Well beyond the moist environs of the Mississippi delta, prehistoric settlement sites commonly were oriented toward water and its resources. From the earthworks at Poverty Point in north Louisiana to Mississippian mound builders across the South, terraces above flood plains were the location for ceremonial structures and lasting settlements.[9] Access to diverse foodstuffs in these settings enabled pre-agricultural people to sustain fixed settlements. As agriculture gained a place in food production, floodplain settlements defined the preferred environments for Choctaw at the time of European contact.[10] Water ran directly through decisions about where to live.

Water also yielded essential foodstuffs. Shellfish were important to pre-contact societies beyond the Tchefuncte in Louisiana and have survived in archaeological remains. Mussel shells are abundant in east Tennessee prehistoric sites and likely were an important element of the diet. Although fish bones are not well preserved, archaeologists have concluded that fish were seasonally important food items to upland Indian groups.[11]

Colonial observations indicate fish and aquatic life remained critical foodstuffs after contact. James Adair's eighteenth-century account notes several fishing methods near the Atlantic seaboard: shooting with bow and arrow, stone weirs, basket traps, spearing, and poisoning. Fishing on the north shore of Lake Pontchartrain, Indians used trot lines with bone hooks, and during the spring flood season, lower Mississippi natives used nets and poisons to catch fish in backwater lakes. Such a diverse toolkit suggests fish played an important role in subsistence activities and colonial observers had ample opportunity to witness the pursuit of fish. One archaeological investigator reported that at least a quarter of faunal remains were from aquatic species, suggesting a corresponding level of effort procuring these foodstuffs.[12]

John Lawson, an Englishman who traveled through the Carolinas in the early eighteenth century, noted that Indians caught sturgeon and oldwives. The latter they dried by "barbakue" to preserve them for transport and consumption in the future. Naturalist William Bartram reported that in the interior of Florida was a "vast lake, or drowned swamp, well known, and often visited both by white and Indian hunters, and on its environs the most valuable hunting ground in Florida." Water bodies, as reported by European chroniclers, served as bountiful food sources for indigenous inhabitants. Native people employed simple technologies to improve their ability to secure resources from the rivers. Robert Beverley's colonial history reports that, in addition to weirs (fig. 1.2), Virginia natives built stone dams in streams and set traps for fish at narrow openings in their structures. They used basic technologies to manipulate the fluid habitat to enlarge their catch.[13]

Waters also yielded precious objects. Hernando de Soto, and somewhat later the French explorer Jean Ribaut, observed that native peoples obtained pearls from oysters and freshwater mussels.[14] Chroniclers traveling with de Soto reported that southeastern Indians treasured pearls and used them in jewelry and in making decorative figures. In addition, some tribes honored the dead by placing pearls in burial sites. One indigenous female leader presented de Soto and his men with a pearl necklace in an effort to placate the invaders. De Soto's troops also plundered pearls from ossuaries in a desperate attempt to gather treasure, which they apparently could

FIG. 1.2. "Their manner of fishynge in Virginia." From Thomas Hariot, illustrated by John White and translated by Richard Hakluyt, *A Briefe and True Report of the New Found Land of Virginia,* 1588 (New York: Sabin & Sons, 1871). Used with permission of the University of North Carolina Library.

not collect themselves from the waterways they explored. Later, LaSalle encountered ample supplies in the Natchez and Tensas temples and observed children of Natchez nobles wearing pearls around their necks. Not only were pearls decorative; they symbolized status. In Virginia, Indians demonstrated to John Smith how they dove for marine mussels to obtain pearls.[15] Additionally, conk shells taken from marine waters were highly valued and were "the richest Commodity amongst the Indians" according to one colonial chronicler.[16] From the waters came objects of value and status, which native people had the skills to gather.

John Lawson also notes that native inhabitants were well versed in poison and introduced toxins into water bodies. The common use of placing poisons in water was for fishing. Indians in the Southeast used the practice, likely diffused from South America. By dumping certain roots or nut hulls that contained natural neurotoxins behind barriers placed in streams, they could stun or intoxicate fish. When the impaired fish floated to the surface, they were easily collected. After collection, the fish could be moved to clean water and revived and with no apparent impact on those consuming them.[17] Knowledge of the power of poisons in water could have been used against enemies, but Lawson reports that anyone caught poisoning a spring to kill others would be subject to the "most cruel Torment imaginable, his body burned to ashes that would then be cast into the river." Use of water as a means to deliver death to enemies, while apparently understood, was not tolerated, but poison was a viable tool for harvesting fish.[18]

Numerous chroniclers report on native people's use of waterways for transportation.[19] Often trails followed streams inland, and indigenous travelers used canoes to navigate downstream. Well-known trade routes followed eastern seaboard streams. While streams did not serve as territorial boundaries, strategic positions along water routes and their use by particular tribes produced an indigenous political geography strongly associated with watersheds. Place names inherited from the native trade routes during Meinig's "prelude" period, especially rivers, became cartographic fixtures that lasted beyond initial contact.[20]

Canoes, large and small, enabled native travelers to move throughout the Mississippi River system and along the many rivers draining the Piedmont along the eastern seaboard (fig. 1.3). Dugout canoes were nearly universal on the inland waters of the Southeast, and Spanish explorers reported large numbers of canoes along the gulf coast. In a dramatic encounter, de Soto and his troops met an armada of one hundred canoes that sought to impede the Spaniards' passage across the Mississippi River. This attempted blockade indicates a notion that waterways were not commons for all to traverse—even though that might have been the case for indigenous travelers. Apparently tribes recognized territoriality in terms of fishing rights, and they attempted to impose those limits on the plundering horde of Europeans accompanying de Soto.[21]

Indigenous travel was not limited to inland waters. Archaeological

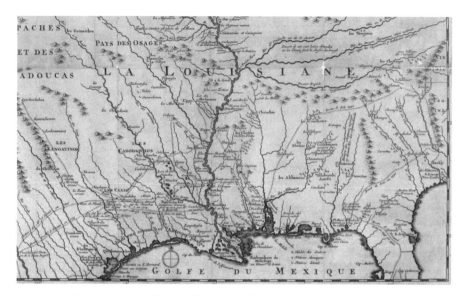

FIG. 1.3. Major rivers as depicted in 1718. Guillaume de L'Isle, Carte de la Louisiane et du cours du Mississipi [i.e. Mississippi]: dressée sur un grand nombre de mémoires entrautres sur ceux de M. le Maire. Paris: Chez l'auteur le Sr. Delisle sur le quay de l'horloge avec privilege du roy, 1718. Library of Congress.

evidence confirms trade and interaction around the Gulf of Mexico and Caribbean. Travel was likely coastal and relied mainly on human-powered canoes. There are some suggestions of precontact sailing vessels and even speculations of transatlantic voyages in small craft that took advantage of the Gulf Stream current.[22]

Water held religious meanings for indigenous people of the Americas. Within the expansive Mississippian world, indigenous cosmology envisioned a "Below World." This spiritual space was an underwater realm that could be entered through caves, lakes, springs, and streams.[23] Thus, rivers served as important settings in the sacred beliefs of Native Americans. Cherokees considered rivers as a powerful spirit known as either "Long Man" or "Long Snake." They believed that its head was in the highlands and its foot in the coastal lowlands. Thus a hydrologic spirit flowed through the landscape. Priests could comprehend the murmurs of the waters and use their understanding of this spiritual communication to divine the future. People sought to avoid offending the Long Man spirit for fear of reprisal. Springs, in their belief system, served as gateways into the underworld and were thus important links to numinous territories.[24]

Indigenous mythology was infused with elements of water. Lore contained tales of people who lived beneath the surface of water. There were tales of wagering all the water and losing it—suggesting encounters with drought. An Alabama Indian origin myth told of migration across the ocean. Some lore narrated encounters with alligators and other water-based creatures.[25] Water was a common and rich element in Native American mythology.

Many tribes employed ritual bathing to purify themselves. At the new moon, for example, Cherokee would go to the water and bathe. After giving birth, women would wash their newborn infants in water in the belief that this would both strengthen and extend their lives. As part of the ceremonial practices for initiating a new chief, Creek men would bathe in a river after a sweat lodge ceremony. Additionally, there were important spirits like the Cherokee Uketna and the Seminole water cougar that posed a threat to humans and thus lent an ominous element to waters. Water could also be used by native doctors to effect cures. In many ways, water had an important supernatural role in native religion and provided a positive force to native people. Belief in water as a substance infused with spiritual value shaped all other notions about this basic liquid. Thus, religious beliefs tinged other water-related activities such as travel or collecting aquatic resources.[26]

Wetlands and pests found there did not inspire dread among native peoples. Malaria and yellow fever arrived in the Americas with the Old World populations and only posed a threat after contact. While native mosquitoes could torment humans throughout the Southeast, people took refuge in smoky dwellings or covered their bodies with oils to find modest relief from these airborne pests.[27]

The apparently fluid nature of tribal affiliations and hierarchy and the oral traditions lessened the formulation of rigid "legal" rights to water and the use of waterways, but traditional practices sought to ensure access to resources associated with water. And water infused all aspects of native life.

Naming Waterways

Transatlantic blending began with place names. To an extraordinary degree, Europeans adopted native names for waterways—Mississippi, Potomac, and Chattahoochee. While there are major exceptions, in a sphere of overlapping appraisal, indigenous names frequently prevailed. At the same time, Europeans affixed imported names to settlements and political units—New Orleans in Louisiana, Jamestown in Virginia, and St.

Augustine in Florida. Waters and waterways were part of a natural endowment that was thoroughly identified by name in a well-developed indigenous geography.[28] European settlements, in contrast, constituted material expressions of the colonial societies and names reflected their actions. While critical discussions of place naming emphasize how imperial invaders impose control on the landscape by replacing indigenous terms with words from their own language, the persistence of indigenous river names suggests a concession to local geographic expertise.[29]

A review of the names of waterways emptying into coastal waters indicates the prominence of indigenous names. Using an 1856 map to capture names settled upon by the close of the colonial era, I tallied names of rivers (bayous) and creeks (table 1.1).[30] Only in Texas and Florida, long-time Spanish territories, were European names prevalent. In former English and French colonies, European names were not uncommon, but native words were prominent. Some, like the Pearl River (Mississippi-Louisiana) and Black Warrior River (Alabama) may have been European translations of indigenous terms. In addition, many smaller inland waterways illustrate to the tenacity of native languages on the landscape.

While much has been written on the contribution of indigenous knowledge to the development of European understanding of the new world

TABLE 1.1 River Names along the Southeastern Seaboard, 1856

State	River–E	River–I	Creek–E	Creek–I
Maryland	10	9	6	3
Virginia	2	2	0	1
North Carolina	4	6	0	0
South Carolina	5	8	0	0
Georgia	3	3	2	0
Florida	9	7	2	0
Alabama	1	2	0	0
Mississippi	2	3	0	0
Louisiana	3	9	0	0
Texas	12	3	0	0

Note: River–E = European; River–I = Indigenous.

Source: Based on state maps in G. H. Colton, *Colton's Atlas of the World* (New York: J. H. Colton & Company, 1856).

geography, little has been said about the reason for the powerful persistence of native stream names.[31] Granted, some rivers during the period
of exploration acquired European designations (such as the Mississippi-
Fleuve St. Louis) only to lose them in the long run. It was also common for
one colonial power to name a stream and subsequent conquering powers
to translate that title to their own language.[32] Attaching names to landscape features was a fluid and ongoing process. Yet somehow, river names
from largely forgotten indigenous languages have survived. When Europeans attached their own names to waterways that they had not adequately
explored, confusion sometimes ensued, suggesting a rationale for retaining indigenous names.[33]

Europeans learned to navigate the complex system of river, bayous, and
lakes of the lower delta of the Mississippi River from native guides. LaSalle
and others who traveled downstream on the Mississippi applied the Al-
gonquin term meaning "great water" to the entire course of the waterway.
When Iberville sailed up the Mississippi in 1699, he returned to the sea via
the Bayou Manchac-Lake Pontchartrain route (fig. 1.4). His native guides
passed the bayou's name to the Europeans, who retained the indigenous
appellation. The native name for Bayou Manchac means "rear entrance,"
suggesting its use as an alternative route that enabled paddlers to avoid
fighting the Mississippi's current.[34]

European explorers, and later traders and settlers, frequently adopted
indigenous names for waterways as part of the process of assembling their
own knowledge of local geographies. Early explorers, who merely sailed
along the coast, commonly attached European words to landmarks. In
contrast, de Soto's early interior settlement designations followed indigenous terminology. He did not conquer or establish settlements of his own
and thus merely plotted existing place names.[35] In the southeastern corner of the continent, the dense network of waterways provided route ways
and access to the interior, and Europeans seeking greater knowledge about
the interior typically conferred with indigenous people. Through this direct contact, in anticipation of inland penetration, indigenous terminology prevailed. Even as existing societies were pushed aside and other place
names expunged from the maps of European cartographers, a multitude
of waterways retained their indigenous titles. This represents a clear exception to the hegemony of colonial powers in renaming the landscape.
In some cases, rivers received the name of prominent tribes along their
course, such as the Alabama.[36] In other situations, the Europeans merely
adopted existing terms, and there are abundant examples across Georgia.[37]

FIG. 1.4. French depiction of Louisiana waterways. Detail of Carte particulière d'une partie de la Louisianne ou les fleuve et rivierres [i.e. rivières] onts etés relevé à l'estime & les routtes [i.e. routes] par terre relevé & mesurées aux pas, par les Srs. Broutin, de Vergés, ingénieurs & Saucier dessinateur/Demarigny. 1743. Library of Congress.

Not infrequently, names assigned by early colonial explorers fell by the wayside to be replaced by indigenous terms. In the absence of political or social power, it is remarkable that streams names either persisted or resurfaced. This suggests local adoption and a potent influence on local geographic understanding from indigenous knowledge, particularly in terms of water routes.

Some place-name scholars suggest that colonists in Virginia found indigenous names repugnant for cultural and religious reasons, while

Catholics in Maryland were more accepting. Indeed in Maryland, stream names of Indian origin constitute the highest percentage of named landscape features, although native names are affixed to a lowly 6 percent of all streams.[38] Nonetheless, the prevalence of native stream names in the eastern portion of the state underscores the importance of waterways to indigenous travelers and the lasting influence of these names during initial encounters with Europeans. Tabulations of Indian place names by linguists, although idiosyncratic, reveal both the prominence and the persistence of names attached to streams (table 1.2). In Louisiana and Alabama, town names frequently represent post-colonial designations, often late nineteenth-century railroad town names. The remarkable tenacity of stream names from initial contact into modern official toponymy exposes a perplexing counter-argument to the hegemonic erasure of native terms.

TABLE 1.2 Native American Place Names for Selected Southern States

State	Water Body	Town	Other
Mississippi & Alabama[a]	70	16	4
Alabama[b]	189	100	30
Louisiana[c]	49	47	14

Notes:

[a] Henry S. Halbert, "Choctaw Indian Names in Alabama and Mississippi," *Transactions of the Alabama Historical Society* 3 (1898–99): 64–77.

[b] William A. Read, *Indian Place Names of Alabama* (1937; Tuscaloosa: University Press of Alabama, 1994). Commercial railroad companies assigned many Alabama town names during the nineteenth century.

[c] William A. Read, "Louisiana Place Names of Indian Origin," *University Bulletin: Louisiana State University*, new series, 9, no. 2 (1927): 1–71. Railroad companies assigned many Louisiana place names during the nineteenth century, and many were indigenous names imported from outside the South.

Appraisals and Settlement

Europeans bent on establishing settlements in the Americas had to include water in their appraisals of sites for outposts—or "fixations." The French explorer Jean Ribaut traversed the southeastern coast in the 1560s in search of a suitable site for an outpost; he searched diligently for a sheltered harbor that also contained a freshwater outlet. Upon discovering a protected harbor behind the barrier islands, he initiated forays to the shore. This initial contact represents Meinig's "prelude" and the appraisal of water resources reflects considerations tied to Ribaut's mission with its intent to plant future "fixations" (fig. 1.5). He observes a multitude of fish near the mouth of the freshwater river; he spies one indigenous inhabitant wearing an acorn-size pearl suggesting other riches could be secured from the waters; and he comments on the suitability of the location for a French settlement. Although the harbor offered sufficient depth for modest vessels, Ribaut notes that the harbor could accommodate larger ships "if there were Frenchmen dwelling there that myght scoure thentree [sic] as they do in France." With an eye to colonization, drinking water, food resources, harborage, and potential riches became the keys to Ribaut's appraisal of water resources—albeit human modification of the harbor might be necessary. Despite the presence of abundant fisheries, the French and later the Spanish had difficulty securing adequate provisions in the Florida frontier. From the time of de Soto's initial exploration, the Spanish attempted to extract tribute in the form of food from indigenous peoples. This "stratified" colonial system yielded meager stores however.[39]

Food exchanges between the French and indigenous groups became a

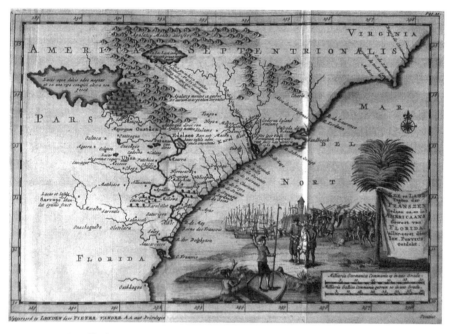

FIG. 1.5. Detail of Carolina and Florida Coast. French forts built by Ribaut are labeled "Karel Slot." Zee en Land Togten der Franszen Gedaan na, en in't Americaans Gewest van Florida, allereerst door Ioh, Pontius Ontdekt. Van der Aa, Netherlands, 1707. Used with permission courtesy of the William P. Cumming Map Society, www .cummingmapsociety.org.

fundamental part of diplomatic protocol in Louisiana and later in provisioning urban dwellers. While fish were included, they were not the primary object of exchange. By the end of the colonial period, Louisiana Indians participated in the market economy, selling in urban markets waterfowl, fish, and other animals associated with watery habitats.[40] Indigenous aptitude for gathering these resources sustained their importance in European appraisal of aquatic resources.

More than a century after Ribaut's voyage, Robert Beverley continued the appraisal of waters in terms of harborage, navigation, and fisheries. About the Chesapeake Bay he notes that "from one end to the other, there is good anchorage," and he continues, "these rivers are of such convenience, that for almost every half dozen miles of their extent, there is commodious and safe road for a whole fleet." He adds the rivers are fed by "an infinite number of crystal springs of cool and pleasant water." His assessment expands the value of streams to include their hydropower. Among the benefits of the springs was that they could supply power "for as many mills as they can find work for." Some of the springs, according to Beverley, "send forth such a glut of water, that in less than a mile below the fountain head, they afford a stream sufficient to supply a grist mill." He also comments on the abundance of herring and sturgeon found in the rivers. Not all features associated with the waterway were beneficial, however. He also reports that the rivers sustained worms that prey on ships' hulls during the summer if the watercraft are not adequately protected with pitch and tar. To guard against a potential hazard, human technology could assure continued use of the safe harborage. Likewise, technology could capture the power of the streams flowing to the sea. An overlay of technological concepts was necessary to deal with one of the limiting factors of water and to secure new benefits.[41]

John Smith selected a site in Virginia where his ships could "lie so neere the shoare that they are moored to the Trees in six fathom water." An account of the river's resources was filled with superlatives. Not only could it safely harbor large ships; springs were abundant, lush forests lined its banks, and many fruits grew beneath the trees. Additionally the chronicler noted that "there are many branches of this River, which runne flowing through the Woods with great plentie of fish of all kindes." Despite this bounty, within weeks of establishing a fort, Smith's men were dying of famine. Only after indigenous people supplied them with fish, corn, and bread did they begin to express hope of surviving the coming winter. While the English observed plenty, they were unable to avail themselves of it. In fact, reconstruction of the climate during the stressful period indicates a serious drought compounded the colonists' dire situation.[42]

Bienville argued that the site of New Orleans offered superior strategic access to both upriver and coastal transportation for French settlement in the early eighteenth century. Thus, the place, which native people used as a portage between the river and nearby Lake Pontchartrain, blended inland and marine navigation opportunities. Ocean-going ships could navigate to the site across the placid waters of Lake Pontchartrain without sailing against the river's considerable current. Goods from upstream could arrive at the riverfront, and those destined for export could be portaged to ships anchored at the lakefront. Lending credence to Bienville's assessment, one French observer wrote that "trying to take barges up the St. Louis [Mississippi] is like trying to catch the moon with your teeth." It was the combination of marine and inland navigational options that gave New Orleans its advantage over higher and drier locations upriver. It also offered a strategic position in terms of protecting the site from British interlopers.[43]

Much later, Thomas Jefferson's *Notes on the State of Virginia* (1785) continued to appraise his home state's waters in terms of transportation possibilities. His discussion of rivers itemizes the inland extent of ocean-going ships and the feasibility of canoe transportation along the upper courses of the eastern seaboard rivers. He also reports on the Mississippi and other trans-Appalachian waterways. European assessments of biophysical resources added a dimension little appreciated by indigenous appraisals—namely marine transportation.[44]

Europeans subscribed to belief systems that assigned ritualized cleansing power to water. Christian baptism, whether full immersion or the more ritualistic daubing, employs water to cleanse adherents of sin. Obviously Europeans would have recognized native water rituals as having a parallel in their own religion. And conversely, native people whom Europeans sought to convert would have also found a familiar element in Christian ritual. Nonetheless, the meanings of the water-based ceremonies remained distinct and were not interchangeable, at least in the eyes of Christians. Beyond water's purifying power, European understanding of the hydrologic cycle remained thoroughly influenced by religious beliefs into the eighteenth century.[45] As long as the movement of water from the oceans to streams and back again remained couched in religious terms water retained a mystical quality beyond either a strictly scientific substance or a basic resource. As Europeans sought to convert native peoples, their own concepts supplanted indigenous ones. And as native populations declined so too did their traditional beliefs.

The French, more so than the British or Spanish, made imperial claims based on hydrologic territories. LaSalle claimed the entire Mississippi River basin for France in 1682.[46] With almost no knowledge of the territory, he assumed a cohesiveness formed by the mighty river's watershed and sought control over any potential routes to the western sea. Contemporaneous French advances in the hydrologic sciences perhaps contributed to their use of waterways to define their territorial claims.[47] Despite proclaiming possession for a European sovereign and some initial use of European names, the French eventually adopted indigenous names for the river and its tributaries. After referring to the Mississippi as the "Colbert" and the "St. Louis," the French ultimately accepted the preexisting indigenous terminology for the upper course, which they applied to the lower river as well (fig. 1.4).[48]

English colonies staked out territories based on lines of latitude that often overlapped with other imperial claims (fig. 1.6). The small river basins of the eastern seaboard were insufficient to satisfy the audacious intent of the British. Yet, John Smith's 1612 map of Virginia represents his

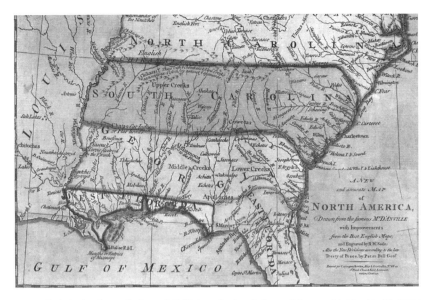

FIG. 1.6. Interior boundaries of British colonies followed lines of latitude. "A New and Accurate Map of North America, Drawn from the Famous Mr D'Anville with Improvements From the Best English Maps," engraved by R. W. Seale, printed for Carrington Bowles. London, 1771. Library of Congress.

knowledge of the territory based on river basins rather than on the geometric depictions made by colonial cartographers (fig. 1.7). In this case, British authority extended no further than the territory as presented to them by indigenous inhabitants and reflected a strong watershed orientation during the "prelude" phase.[49]

FIG. 1.7. Virginia as discovered and described by Captayn John Smith, 1606; graven by William Hole, London, 1624. Library of Congress.

At the same time, Europeans also used waterways as boundaries. The sluggish Bayou Manchac separated the Isle of Orleans, of French dominion, from the area to the north, which was, at different points in time, Spanish, British, and U.S. territory (fig. 1.4). Other waterways provided boundaries between colonies.[50] The Potomac separated Maryland from Virginia, while the Savannah River served as part of the boundary between Georgia and South Carolina (fig. 1.6). As direct knowledge of the actual landscape decreased with distance from the coast, geometric boundaries supplanted rivers as territorial markers. Unity by way of watershed was not a constant. When Europeans applied their concepts of rivers as boundaries, they introduced legal notions of exclusive use or control over a fluid resource.[51] Where the boundary actually ran—down the center line or along one bank or the other—determined who could navigate the waterway or exploit its resources.

In Louisiana, French along the lower Mississippi found watery excess a situation demanding environmental transformations. To protect the incipient colonial capital from river floods, settlers at New Orleans began erecting levees. By 1728, the colony required individual land owners to erect earthen barriers between the river and their plantations.[52] During the 1720s, Le Page du Pratz reported that those who arrived near New Orleans before him had cleared the land and erected a levee to reduce the site's dampness. Indeed, he observed that the ubiquitous crawfish mounds, an indicator of wetland conditions, were less common since dikes reduced standing water near the colonial capital.[53] Nonetheless, transforming the soggy terrain surrounding New Orleans was a project that continues to the present.[54] Floods posed just one of the watery hazards that could be dealt with using long-established European techniques for controlling water.[55]

Early assessments of New Orleans reflect Europeans' association of wetlands with insalubrious conditions. French investigators back in Europe were reporting that marshy areas contributed to poor health in the eighteenth century.[56] Arriving from Europe with this idea, Jean Baptiste Bernard de la Harpe reported in 1720 that New Orleans occupied a site within a satisfactory latitudinal belt for good health according to European experience, but that the true geographical situation was not being conveyed to potential settlers. He explained that the "land is flooded, impractical, unhealthy, unfit for cultivation of rice."[57] Only two years later Pierre de Charlevoix provided a contrasting opinion when he noted that the climate was wholesome.[58] Yet, Le Page du Pratz, the oft-cited and sometimes untrustworthy colonial chronicler, reported upon arriving at his temporary residence on Bayou St. John near New Orleans that "I have room to believe, that the situation was not of the healthiest, the country about it being very damp."[59] He relocated after only a short stay near New Orleans to the better-drained loess bluffs at Natchez. Near the end of the colonial period, traveler James Pitot discusses the annual summer outbreak of "pestilential fever" arising from the local swamps.[60] Early observers concluded that New Orleans's site was unhealthful, but some like de Charlevoix opted to conceal this fact from potential investors and settlers who might support the colonial enterprise.

With the arrival of old-world diseases such as malaria and yellow fever, Europeans, while not fully appreciating the etiology of the insect-borne diseases, associated them with environmental conditions. These threats were previously unknown to native peoples. Malaria was common in Europe and gave rise to the miasmatic theory of disease—which held that putrid emanations from stagnant water and decaying vegetation spawned disease. Wetlands such as swamps and marshes, in the view of Europeans, were the source of such miasmas.[61] Thus waterlogged locations, which also served as habitat for disease-delivering mosquitoes, acquired an old-world reputation as unhealthful.

Early assessments of Charleston, South Carolina, associated the low country with insalubrity. In directions to settlers, the proprietors stated "wee would have you as much as you can to direct and perswade ye people to plant as far up in ye countrey as may be to avoyd ye ill aire of ye low lands near ye Sea wch may endanger theire health at theire first comeing." A further warning reinforced this view: "Above all things let me recommend to you the making of a Port Town upon the River Ashley and to chuse such a place as may [be] healthyest and seated upon the highest Ground, and as far up the River as shipps of burden will goe. The Place where they are now planted in is so Moorish that it must needs be unhealthy and bring great Disrepute upon our new settlement."[62] Thomas Ashe in 1682 also noted the regular arrival of "agues and fevers" (likely malaria) in Carolina during the summer months.[63] Malaria became prevalent throughout the southeastern colonies and over time was one of the most fatal colonial afflictions.[64]

By the 1690s, yellow fever began making its appearances in North American ports. Unlike malaria, it required considerable population density to unleash an epidemic.[65] While it became a threat in New Orleans by the late eighteenth century, the saffron scourge became prevalent in New Orleans, Charleston, and Savannah only after their populations reached sufficient size in the nineteenth century to sustain its spread.[66] Yellow-fever epidemics merely reinforced miasmatic theory, which associated wetlands with disease.

Numerous accounts of Louisiana after statehood in 1812 reinforced the notion that wetlands were unhealthy. William Darby in 1817 noted that "it must be observed, that there are two evils, arising from the surplus water, to be remedied on the Mississippi; one, the incumbent waters in the river; the other the reflux from the swamps. It is in most instances very difficult to remove one inconvenience without producing the opposite."[67] By fending off river floods, levees diverted water into the back swamps, where it contributed to insalubrious conditions. Timothy Flint in 1826 noted the one "dreary drawback" to New Orleans's site: its insalubrity. Undaunted,

Flint, like others of his day, contemplates how to alleviate the undesirable situation: "Could the immense swamps between it [New Orleans] and the bluff be drained, and the improvements commenced in the city be completed; in short could its atmosphere ever become a dry one, it would soon leave the greatest citys [sic] of the Union behind."[68] Drainage of the wetlands had long been an unobtainable quest of European settlers in the lower Mississippi delta, and the persistence of swamps and marshes presented an ominous environment to Europeans that demanded manipulation. The introduction of old-world diseases produced this effect, and European wetland drainage techniques did not offset the disease threat to any substantial degree by the close of the colonial period.

Africans, who Europeans thought were less susceptible to many of the supposedly "miasmatic" diseases, had their own view of the coastal wetlands. In South Carolina they introduced planters to rice cultivation and agricultural techniques that reworked coastal marshes into productive fields. By 1713, South Carolina planters were growing rice in water. Geographer Judith Carney argues that this cultivation method required thorough knowledge of the complex wetland cultivation techniques, and it is unlikely that Anglo merchants who traded with China acquired sufficient understanding of the practices in their limited encounters with Chinese cultivators. Rather, enslaved Africans from locations with established rice-growing traditions introduced the techniques to the Carolina low country, where it expanded rapidly after 1750.[69] In Louisiana, African knowledge, along with French experience, figured into the establishment of rice as an important staple crop.[70] Africans would have seen the wetlands, not as an ominous threat, but as a setting suitable for cultivating an essential foodstuff. Relying on African expertise and labor, rice became the export staple of coastal Carolina and a favored food in Louisiana. Transformation of the biophysical setting using African technologies made this agricultural production possible.

Enslaved Africans across the South also turned to swamps and marshes for food and sanctuary. Fishing and hunting during times when they were not laboring provided slaves with supplements to a meager diet.[71] The abundant streams, sloughs, and lakes in coastal areas provided sites for acquiring fish with hook and line, traps, and weirs. Slave owners tolerated this activity since it enabled their workers to extend their rations and also won the master a bit of good will. Nonetheless fishing also contributed to subversive opportunities. Knowledge gained in fishing and hunting provided those who escaped with some familiarity of how to survive in surrounding wetlands.[72] Gwendolyn Hall reports that "maroons" quite effectively adapted to swamp life in Louisiana. They established remote settlements, subsisted on wildlife they hunted and fished and crops they raised, and sold their labor to the cypress cutters during the eighteenth century. Solomon Northrup, a freeman who was placed in slavery during the nineteenth century, also took shelter in the Louisiana swamps when he escaped.[73] With less to fear in terms of disease, people of African descent could evade recapture in the wetlands they had come to know and the Europeans increasingly dreaded.

Water also played a central role in religious ritual among enslaved African Americans. Enslaved Africans in Catholic Louisiana commonly entered the church through the custom of baptism.[74] Full body immersion baptism has been a fundamental ritual in Baptist congregations in the American South and has roots in Africa. For enslaved residents of the region, the symbolic ritual of a sinner's death and resurrection offered a brief experience that paralleled dreams of freedom. Dunking in a stream or pond, which stood for the River Jordan, made that biblical water body even more important symbolically in the quest for freedom. Celebrated in lore and song, the River Jordan became the watery landmark associated with liberation.[75]

Initial European interest in water resources in the New World focused on marine resources and produced little conflict with native populations, who were more interested in freshwater or estuarine life. Whales and cod drew fishing fleets to the northern waters, and not to the southern Atlantic or gulf coasts. When John Lawson compiled his natural history of the Carolinas in the early eighteenth century, he offered an extensive discussion of the larger marine species such as whales, sharks, and porpoises from which oil could be obtained. He surveyed the principal inland fishes relied on by native populations, but concluded that "what more are in the fresh Waters we have not discover'd, but are satisfied that we are not acquainted with one third part thereof; for we are told by the Indians, of a great many strange and uncouth shapes and sorts of Fish, which they have found in the Lakes laid down in my Chart." Despite abundant fish resources, French and Spanish settlements in Florida persistently remained short of locally produced food stuffs and relied on imports.[76] Eventually fish became a featured part of the French cuisine in Louisiana. In the Carolinas and Virginia, English colonists initially suffered from an inability to tap abundant aquatic resources; however, over time they mastered techniques that allowed them to exploit the freshwater fisheries. Indeed, aggressive

English fisher folk in Virginia contributed to declining fish populations by the mid-eighteenth century. Herring provided an abundant source of seasonal food, taken by commercial and subsistence fishermen during their annual spawning runs. The value of this resource is reflected by increased real estate values for land adjacent to migratory streams. The importance is also underscored by the pressure placed on fish by overfishing and subsequent passage of colonial statutes to protect fish populations. Laws outlawed wasteful harvesting practices such as "gigging" and required mill owners to install fish slopes to enable migration around dams.[77]

Legal Overlay

Ted Steinberg, who has looked closely at the legal transformation of water rights in the Northeast, claims that Native Americans had a nonexclusive concept of property. While they actively hunted and fished from local land and water, they did not assert formal hunting or fishing rights. Their notions of the right to use land, and thereby the natural resources associated with it, did not stem from concepts of ownership.[78] Allan Greer has argued that "common property was, in fact, an fundamental feature of landholding in both the New World and the Old in the early modern centuries." He adds, "Generally, North American territory was claimed and controlled by specific human societies (usually in cooperation with animal and spiritual entities), and these societies determined how they would be managed."[79] Tribal claims of hunting and fishing territories likely did not have precise boundaries and thus did not accord with European notions of political borders. Furthermore, early European interpretations of indigenous cartography assumed stable social and territorial boundaries, while in all likelihood those boundaries were not as fixed as supposed. Indigenous "sociograms" depicted social relations more than geopolitical territories, and they underscore a fluidity in territorial assertions.[80]

In terms of water resources, southern Indians claimed fishing rights, but such views were likely more flexible than the common-law notions brought from Europe. Construction of dams to facilitate fish catches attached certain priority of use to those who constructed the dams.[81] Yet, such modest impoundments would have had minor impact on other riparian activities, and we find no record that they prompted disputes. Likewise, poisoning of fish conferred rights to the stunned fish, but the impacts were temporary and the claims ephemeral.

The prevailing English theory of water rights during the colonization of the eastern seaboard held that water was a common resource, and use conferred rights of access. Unlike terrestrial property, water was fluid and moved, and so it did not have the same exclusive ownership qualities as land—thus European and native notions about water resources were not entirely antithetical. According to European concepts, a senior water user who had established rights through long-established fishing or other activities had priority over a junior user. Yet, under basic principles of nuisance, one user was not entitled to diminish another user's enjoyment of the resource. In the event one user diverted water from the stream, interfered with navigation, or constructed a dam that flooded another's land, the party sustaining loss of use could sue for damages. Rights were earned by use, not by ownership of land. As a common resource, navigation, fishing, and even power production from a waterway were considered part of the public domain. Nonetheless, one user could not infringe on another's use.[82]

Intruding colonists may have negotiated with local populations for land, but not for water rights. And indeed, there appears to have been an assumption that when the colonial power acquired land through treaty or other means, water rights followed. In effect, sovereign ownership of water and common use presaged the nineteenth-century riparian notions that attached water rights to riparian landowners. France claimed the lands and waters of the Mississippi River basin, and French legal concepts in the eighteenth century shared the English common-law concept that rights accrued through use.[83] Spanish water law also held that rivers were commons, available to the public for navigation and fishing. In New Spain, the Crown owned all property and waters which it could dispose of to the public, individuals, or to municipalities. For the most part, water remained a commons under the sovereign law in Florida and Texas.[84]

Colonists put traditional European water-rights concepts to use when it came to water resources, but in some cases they were insufficient to handle complex situations. The colonists viewed waterways and the resources they contained as commons that all could use, as long as one individual's use did not infringe on others. As grain rose in importance in the Virginia economy by the mid-eighteenth century, entrepreneurs erected mills in increasing numbers. Mill dams blocked the migration of herring and other fish and led to noticeable declines in the valuable fish population. To protect a significant commercial fishery, the colonial legislature passed laws in 1759 and 1761 requiring dam owners to include openings in the dam for the passage of migratory fish. Shortly thereafter, they bolstered their attempts to conserve the public fisheries by requiring fish slopes, similar to fish ladders, that could be closed except during the principal fish runs. These measures proved more effective, but ultimately the increasing number of mill dams throughout the region depleted the migratory fish stocks. Across the Carolina piedmont sawmills were becoming numerous by the mid-eighteenth century, and this use of waterways interfered with water flow and also fish migration. Carolina legislators sought to compel dam builders to provide passageways for migrating fish as well. Yet, enforcement of such acts was lax, and timber production took precedence over fish conservation.[85]

After the close of the colonial period or during the period Meinig refers to as "fixation," newly formed states began to enact legislation that encapsulated prevailing notions of water rights. Fundamental to those emerging acts was public access to navigable streams across the Southeast. In addition to acts delineating navigability, states commonly prohibited the creation of obstructions to watercourses.[86] Land owners were not allowed to impede a river's flow or to divert it onto another's property, underscoring the traditional common-law principle of natural flow.[87] South Carolina's legislature forwarded a colonial policy prohibiting the obstruction of navigable streams with felled trees.[88] As minders of the public waterways, legislatures could authorize individuals to erect dams for mills, but they could also require that the mill operator maintain the navigability of the river.[89] Mills in North Carolina were considered public operations since they tapped the power of public waterways even though operated by individuals.[90] After authorizing an individual in Georgia to build a dam and operate a mill, the legislature revoked his privileges when he failed to maintain an open channel for navigation.[91]

Colonial notions of water, as codified by early statutes, emphasized the public access to water as both a route way and as a resource for power and fisheries. Water meant access to markets, power to process agricultural produce and natural resources, and a source of foodstuffs. Water was essential to support developing economies in the new world. These European concepts figured prominently in transformations of the Southeast's biophysical environment. Dams disrupted fish migrations and led to declines in aquatic life. Mills encouraged exploitation of forest resources and also planting of grains for export. Thus, when colonial bodies drew on European concepts of water rights to maintain navigability and to authorize mill construction, they fostered timber removal and expansion of large-scale agriculture. While colonial and early federal laws recognized the ability of humans to diminish quantity and quality of water flow, legislators apparently gave scant attention to the possibility of irregular flow. Abundance was assumed unless infringed upon by other riparians.

Conclusions

During the course of what Meinig referred to as the prelude phase and within Sluyter's colonial triangle, the dominant flow of geographic concepts moved from indigenous peoples and the landscape to the European newcomers. As fixation proceeded, the dominant conceptual flow emanated from old-world peoples. Their impacts on the biophysical environment also increased as their numbers swelled and native peoples succumbed to disease and displacement. This chapter reinforces the utility of Sluyter's colonial triangle and adds another regional assessment where there were multiple colonial players who acted upon a humid and fluid biophysical setting. Even though water is mobile and through the hydrologic cycle can rejuvenate itself, unchecked social impacts can be long-lasting.

Water's fluidity rendered it a different type of material and biophysical object in both indigenous and colonial appraisals. Native cosmology considered rivers as extended spirits that coursed through their territory. In economic, political, and social geographic conceptualization, streams represented a unifying feature rather than a boundary. Moving water, flowing from highlands to lowlands, provided a means for connecting interior and coastal groups and permitting exchange of trade goods unavailable in either locale. Water was a self-renewing substance that could wash away both threats of ill-health and also past misdeeds.

During the initial stages of contact between Europeans and Native Americans, indigenous names for waterways (and even wetlands) provided the essential geographic nomenclature. The preexisting toponymy provided a shared orientation, a network of named features that guided travel through an otherwise ambiguous and poorly understood territory. Although the rivers existed independent of the initial occupants of the American Southeast, these regional inhabitants assigned names and value to the rivers that directly shaped European concepts and guided their dealings with the biophysical environment.

Europeans and indigenous peoples recognized value in waterways for transportation and as resources for food and other commodities. Native Americans relied on aquatic species as important foodstuffs. Early Spanish and English settlers, apparently unable to catch fish as effectively, faced food shortages. English colonists from a more humid homeland eventually exploited inland waterways to the point of depleting fish stocks. While natives undertook modest manipulations of water courses to enhance their catch of fish, European transformations ultimately led to demise of some natural resources. Overlapping demands placed on the rivers—food and power sources—contributed to the depletion of herring and sturgeon. Thus, as Europeans found multiple meanings in the same stream course, conflicting practices typically diminished the value of one.

Old-world diseases contributed to a major alteration in water appraisal. Wetlands, viewed by Europeans as a source of miasmatic diseases, were dreaded landscapes. Both Europeans and Africans brought technologies for modifying the wetlands and transforming them into viable agricultural lands. Well-watered, swamps and marshes were undesirable, but once drained they could become productive places.

As Europeans expanded their demands on waterways, they overlaid traditional concepts of resource management. Common law regarded waterways as public resources. This was distinct from the exclusive concept of property applied to *terra firma*. As a public commons, rivers were free for all to use for navigation, fishing, and even early mills tapping water power were considered public, not private. Use was a fundamental right available to all. Nonetheless, use could not infringe on the rights or fixed property of others. Use that altered the biophysical feature sufficiently to flood an upstream neighbor's land or to deprive a downstream user of sufficient water constituted a nuisance and opened the door to legal action to secure damage payments. Indigenous technologies presented little likelihood for such damages. It was the combination of expectations and capabilities to alter the waterway that overlaid thoroughly European legal concepts on the waters of the Southeast. Despite a more complex common law and attempts to reverse negative impacts on water, Europeans were unable to restore fish populations once these were destroyed.

By the end of the colonial period, elements of the indigenous geography continued, even with native populations largely absent. However, European concepts of and impacts on water resources predominated. Material impacts, such as depletion of fish stocks, introduction of old-world diseases, and the damming of waterways, brought on additional conceptual changes under the rubrics of public health and common law. While there have been additional impacts on how society views water resources that have been shaped by changing technologies and law since the late 1700s, the meaning of water continues to include most of the fundamental notions shared by native and exotic people at the time of contact set within a context of assumed abundance. Legal conceptualization did not include climatic vagaries, and this overlooked factor continues to shape how society deals with water in the region.

Part I

EXCESS

.

2

Saturated Landscapes

Introduction

No landscape captures more completely the essence of the South's water wealth than its wetlands. From the Dismal Swamp in Virginia, to the Florida Everglades, to Louisiana's Atchafalaya Basin, vast tracts of saturated marsh and swamp are emblematic of the region's environment. They represent both the historical perception that soggy settings hinder regional development and the more recent notion that they harbor ecological riches. From either perspective, the abundance of water was a defining quality that became firmly fixed in popular understanding of the South. According to recent accountings, wetlands historically constituted an exceptionally high percentage of the total land area of several southern states.[1] Popular writers used these pervasive landscapes to symbolize danger and the evils of slavery and in doing so created literary associations between natural features and social conditions. As Congress established nineteenth-century policy to correct these undesirable qualities, southern congressmen led the way.[2] Florida, Louisiana, and Arkansas received over 37 million acres from the federal government as part of the 1849 and 1850 Swamp Lands Acts that sought to stimulate reclamation efforts.[3] This total dwarfed the acreage granted to other states, including midwestern states with extensive wet prairies, and underscored the extent of the South's saturated landscapes. In addition, the tightly intertwined southern issues of frequent river flooding, low topographic relief, the extended season for insect-borne diseases, and copious precipitation exacerbated the wetland challenge. Over considerable periods of time the perception of wetlands as evil, dangerous locations deterred exploitation.

Even if impeded, southerners were not dissuaded from taking on the region's wetlands. Colonial-era efforts to drain and cultivate the Dismal Swamp reflect the early urge to transform these settings.[4] Planters in South Carolina, with technological expertise and hard labor supplied by enslaved Africans, reworked the coastal wetlands to grow rice.[5] Systematic drainage efforts in the nineteenth century in Florida, Louisiana, and across the region reflected a national drainage compulsion and yielded profound impacts on the water-rich environments. Yet, wetlands persisted—even if highly altered.[6]

This chapter will consider southern wetlands and efforts to transform them. After all, the notion of the South as a water-rich region begins with its wetlands. As long as southern leaders saw them as impediments to regional economic success, developers directed their efforts toward expunging excess water. And the obsession with relieving the region of surplus water has prevailed. In recent years, however, as ecological science has come to appreciate the numerous benefits of wetlands, public policy, largely crafted outside the region, increasingly sought to offset the intentional de-watering of marshes and swamps. Two great wetlands stand as examples of the shifting policies and also reflect a core myth about southern wetlands: they exemplify the region's natural watery excess. The Everglades, Florida's famous "river of grass," contains a national park with policies aimed at preserving the ecology of this wetland. Many naively consider it a pristine marsh as reflected by the appellation "watery Eden."[7] Louisiana's Atchafalaya Basin has garnered a contrasting moniker. Referred to as the "designer wetland," it serves as a hydrologic safety valve for the Mississippi River and bears the reputation of a wholly humanized environment.[8] While the contrasting nomenclature suggests that one remains a largely natural system and the other operates at the whim of the Corps of Engineers, neither designation is entirely correct and herein lies the myth. Viewed as examples of excess water, in many ways neither has enough water to sustain current demands. The Everglades—as a host of popular, scholarly, and scientific accounts attest—has been subject to extensive human modification for more than a century, while natural systems continue to operate and sometimes dominate the Atchafalaya Basin. Both areas, with their contrasting public images, have been manipulated by human activities. Through extensive replumbing of these areas the limits of environmental systems have been exposed. Both these wetlands are no longer settings simply burdened with too much water and thus they offer salient examples of the region's limits to abundance. Coping with wetlands remains a considerable challenge in these two settings, and comparable water management issues figure prominently in the great wetlands across the South.

Contrasting Accounts

Congress authorized an Everglades National Park in 1934, but it took several years to realize the hopes of supporters. Formal dedication ceremonies in 1947 placed nearly half a million acres under management of the National Park Service (NPS). With policies built on a preservation ethic, the Park Service set out to protect a portion of what was already an extensively altered environmental setting. The park's creation was the culmination of decades of efforts, led by Marjory Stoneman Douglas, to deny developers unchecked access to the glades. Granted, extensive drainage had been promoted since Florida entered the union, but Douglas fundamentally recast the popular view of the Everglades. Helen Muir claims that she "transformed the country's most menacing swamp into its most cherished wetland."[9] Indeed, Douglas's stunningly succinct description of the Everglades as a "river of grass" continues to frame how the country thinks about the Everglades.[10]

Her compelling chronicle of the Everglades has become one of the most influential works among the pantheon of American environmental writing. While fully aware of human impacts on the glades, Douglas created a popular perception of an immutable and enduring wetland environment. Of the grasses, she wrote, "Nothing less than the smashing power of some hurricane can beat it down. . . . Even so, the grass is not flattened in a continuous swath, but only here and here and over there, as if the storm bounced or lifted and smashed down again in great hammering strokes or enormous cat-licks. . . . Only one force can conquer it completely and that is fire."[11] Her 1947 account promotes a view of the Everglades as robustly resilient. Although her book uses "eleventh hour" description to portray the wetlands as endangered, a core theme in it was that the Everglades would be able to bounce back even after a half-century of extensive drainage efforts. She had fought the drainage interests and was far from naive about the complexities of the region's ecology and its susceptibility to degradation. Nonetheless, she rekindled the notion of the Everglades as an untamed wilderness. A 1960s nationally broadcast television program, "The Everglades," portrayed it in much the same way as early accounts— a wild and dangerous territory beyond civilization. When ValueJet flight 592 tragically crashed in the Everglades in 1996, its near-total disintegration upon impact suggested to some that the wetlands were a natural force more powerful than modern technology. And in 1997, the NPS set aside 1.3 million acres of the park as a federal wilderness, which receives even greater protection than the park territory.[12] This act finally preserved a tiny portion of what had been an enormous wetland for millennia and also perpetuates the view of the Everglades as an untrammeled wilderness, although it is only a small portion of the much grander Everglades ecosystem that is on a engineered life-support system of enormous scale.

The Atchafalaya Basin in Louisiana never had such a compelling spokes-person. With a tongue-twisting name, it evaded national attention long after Douglas showcased the Everglades. It was not without spokespeople, however. Yet the Acadians who came to populate it attracted more atten-tion than the environment and this contributed to the notion of the Atcha-falaya as an inhabited, if remote territory. Henry Wadsworth Longfellow's Evangeline enters the basin via Bayou Plaquemine, which he describes as "a maze of sluggish and devious waters" with "towering and tenebrous boughs of the cypress" waving like banners in an ancient cathedral and embracing the travelers in a "deathlike silence."[13] The basin was certainly a foreboding place. Nearly half a century later, a romantic writer, George Coulon, ventured into the Atchafalaya seeking to encounter "virgin na-ture . . . and "to visit those endless overflowed cypress forests or swamps."[14] He encountered wildlife, most notably mosquitoes, but also reported on the extensive cypress timber extraction that was transforming the basin into a zone of exploitation. Robert J. Flaherty's 1948 film *Louisiana Story*, while not set explicitly in the Atchafalaya Basin, introduced a national au-dience to the secluded Acadians, who earned a meager living fishing and trapping, but who readily accommodated the oil industry's arrival to their wetland refuge. Malcolm Comeaux's geographical account presents the Atchafalaya as a working wetland. He makes the case that the basin was a sanctuary for the Acadians that Longfellow immortalized and that its re-moteness enabled them to develop a regionally distinctive economy while retaining their traditional culture.[15] Yet, their presence made it an inhab-ited place and not a wilderness, a place where nature guided the annual cycle of resource collection that sustained the Acadians but was nonethe-less subservient to human activity.

A decade passed after Comeaux's sympathetic treatment of a distinctive culture group before a more environmentally attuned publication brought attention to the Atchafalaya. Photographer C. C. Lockwood helped the country visualize this wetland as an environment worthy of protection with his 1982 collection of color photographs.[16] He shared intimate por-traits of wildlife and seldom-seen landscapes with a national audience. Yet, all the while he acknowledged that this was a working swamp—home to fishermen who made a living off nature's abundance. And, the wetland was bordered by the guide levees erected by the Corps of Engineers as one of the two outlets installed to control floods on the Mississippi River. John McPhee's harrowing account of the near failure of the Old River Control Structure during the flood of 1973 solidified the view of the Atchafalaya as a humanly manipulated setting but one not entirely removed from the power of nature.[17] The floods of 2011 prompted a second use of the spillway which diverted huge volumes of floodwaters through the basin. This action echoed the limits of technology to control the flow of the Mississippi, but at the same time it conveyed the image of the Atchafalaya as conduit in the Corps's flood control system.[18]

"Watery Eden"

The Everglades, this so-called river of grass, is a portion of a larger hydrologic and biotic system. The officially designated South Florida Ecosystem encompasses over twenty-six thousand square miles and stretches from near Orlando to the Florida Keys. It includes the Kissimmee River, which drains central Florida and flows through a relatively low area, hemmed in by slightly higher ground toward either coast (fig. 2.1). The river empties into Lake Okeechobee—a large freshwater body that covers over seven hundred square miles. Before human intervention, the lake drained southward toward the Gulf of Mexico through a marsh that became known as the Everglades. This wetland, also bordered on the east and west by higher ground, covers an area roughly twenty miles wide and extends nearly one hundred miles to the south of the lake (an area of over thirteen thousand square miles). Marsh grasses visually dominate the expansive territory, although open water and some wetland forests are present (fig. 2.2).[19] The seemingly endless marsh is the unchallenged image of the territory and has been from the earliest official accounts.

In a reconnaissance assignment for the U.S. Treasury Department in 1848, Buckingham Smith described the Everglades as a vast freshwater lake extending "beyond the reach of human vision." Interrupted by occasional islands with shrubs, palmetto, and pines, "the surrounding waters, except in places that seem at first like channel ways (but which are not) are covered with the tall saw grass, shooting up its straight and slender stem from the shallow bottom of the lake to the height of often 10 feet above the surface and covering all but a few rods around from your view."[20] Such an account was not wholly dissimilar to the wet prairies farmers were draining in Indiana and Illinois and planting in corn. Encouraged by relict features shown on colonial-era maps that stood as testimony to previous drainage efforts, Smith reported "that the draining of the Everglades of 4 or 5 feet of waters will reclaim, for the profitable cultivation of coffee, sugar, tropical fruits, and other productions of tropical climates, large

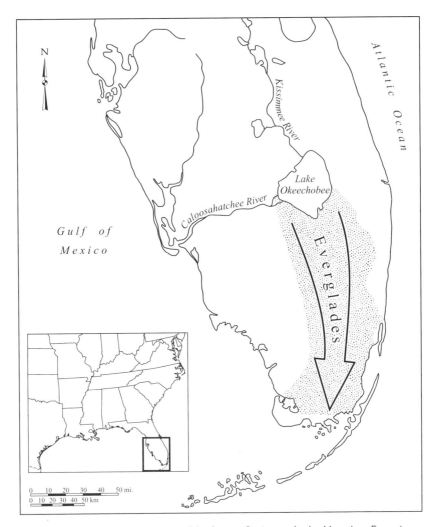

FIG. 2.1. Florida Everglades Natural Drainage. Cartography by Mary Lee Eggart.

tracts of the present subaqueous soil of the basin and the lowlands of the Atseenahoofa and the Halpatiokee Swamps."[21] While Smith was not the first to envision a tropical agricultural region within the United States, his account provided impetus for those who followed and advanced the notion that nature should be replaced with a farmer's paradise.

Conversion of the Everglades to productive agricultural lands remained the core obsession of nineteenth- and early twentieth-century development

FIG. 2.2. Everglades marshlands, 1960s. Courtesy: State Archives of Florida, Florida Memory, http://floridamemory.com/items/show/2789.

proponents. As early as 1855 after the Swamp Lands Acts transferred the area to Florida, a party sent to survey the Everglades encountered extensive dry areas which impeded their waterborne travel, and residents pointed out that portions of the wetland were filling in.[22] These observations suggested nature was already at work lowering the water level—implying humans only needed to lend a hand to complete the task. To hasten the process, the state granted railroads and canal companies substantial land concessions in exchange for promises to install transportation infrastructure. These companies envisioned productive farms paying freight charges that would reimburse their investments. But they had limited success with advancing the agricultural frontier. Despite initial frustrations and hoping to press the drainage effort forward, the state contracted with a private drainage company in the 1880s to reclaim a massive area of "overflowed lands" in exchange for 2 million acres.[23] Once again, private developers made only minimal progress toward their grand designs. The Atlantic and Gulf Coast Canal and Okeechobee Land Company suspended its efforts with the financial crash of 1893. Its initial drainage efforts had focused around Lake Okeechobee, but also included some canals south of the lake.[24] Nonetheless, the installation of canals and a reported natural filling of the Everglades encouraged state authorities. They concluded that technology, in alliance with nature, was slowly transforming the region. State legislators toured portions of the Everglades in the early twentieth century and viewed fruit orchards and successful vegetable farms.[25] They came away with an image of an agricultural Eden which emboldened them to advocate for continued drainage.

At the request of Florida officials in the early years of the twentieth century, the U.S. Department of Agriculture dispatched a team of engineers to "ascertain the practicability of draining the Everglades and making them profitable for agriculture."[26] J. O. Wright, of the U.S. Department of Agriculture, headed this investigation in 1909, and he brought the authority of engineering to the task. Ultimately, his conclusion that control of water in Lake Okeechobee and the adjacent wetlands was feasible proved to be exceptionally compelling to the development community and already optimistic progressive legislators. Several serious flaws in his assessment undermined its legitimacy, but that did not stop the state of Florida from circulating the report in hopes of fueling development.[27]

Indeed even before drainage work had made any substantial headway, real estate developers latched onto Wright's prediction, and a boom in land sales ensued in 1910. The Florida Fruit Lands Company sold more than ten thousand ten-acre plots, much of it to buyers who had never seen the wetlands they were paying for. According to historian David McCally, "It was the dream of the prosperous truck farm that drove these sales." Subsequent discovery of inaccuracies in the Wright report and also the revelation to purchasers that they owned marsh and not terra firma eventually derailed the early twentieth-century reclamation quest.[28]

Drainage and flood control that had commenced in 1906 contributed to development for several years. A series of canals, locks, and a levee around the southern shore of Lake Okeechobee reclaimed some of the wetlands. These modifications perpetuated the vision of tropical agriculture. Following state-directed drainage projects, settlement on the shores of Lake Okeechobee moved forward, aided by the completion of a rail line to urban markets in 1915. Small farmers began breaking the muck soils, but they encountered a host of environmental challenges. Soil moisture—too much or too little—low soil fertility, marsh fires, frosts, and flooding all presented considerable obstacles to profitable farming. Even with these considerable challenges, pioneering agriculturalists placed about ninety-six thousand acres under cultivation between 1906 and 1928.[29]

Devastating floods in 1926 and again in 1928 overwhelmed the drainage canals and flood-control structures and inflicted extensive damage on the agricultural settlements. The latter flood, caused by a failure of the flimsy dike along Lake Okeechobee, killed approximately two thousand farm laborers.[30] The notion that the land had been "reclaimed" and placed in cultivation had created the illusion of security, but rows of crops could not fend off high water, and in fact the damages to crops increased the total value of flood losses. The traumatic floods prompted the state to seek the assistance of the Army Corps of Engineers, and the state's timing could not have been better. In the wake of devastating floods along the Mississippi River in 1927, Congress had expanded federal flood protection responsibilities there and continued to move in that direction in Florida. It appropriated funds in 1930 for a much stronger defense, and the Corps built over eighty miles of thirty-feet-high levees, known as the Hoover Dike, around much of Lake Okeechobee between 1932 and 1938 with the intent to "tame" the Everglades.[31] This effort acknowledged that far from eradicating nature, settlement in the region exposed the persistence of natural systems, and development proponents took a step back and began a more modest agenda of managing nature.

Several years later, after the most recent management efforts were completed, a geographer described the agricultural region below the Hoover Dike. He noted it had become one of the leading winter-truck farming areas in the eastern United States, with some twenty-five thousand acres in intensive cultivation. By the 1940s, costs of developing farms heavily favored big operations, and the small farmsteads promoted two decades previously were largely forgotten.[32]

The levee holding back Lake Okeechobee held during another major flood in 1947, but when authorities discharged excess runoff though the undersized drainage canals the overflow inundated thousands of acres of agricultural lands. The 1947 hurricane-driven flooding and the deliberate discharge of overflow inflicted tremendous damage on the coastal cities and fundamentally altered the equation on managing the Everglades. In addition, the diversion of huge amounts of sediment-laden fresh water to the Atlantic disrupted commercial and sport fisheries and enlarged the group of commercial interests. The Corps reported that the flood damages in 1947 totaled in excess of $41 million dollars, and it estimated the average annual cost of flooding in the area at nearly $4 million. Ultimately, public outcries and the cost of flood damages drove additional federal action. The Corps concluded, based on public hearings, that local interests desired "a comprehensive plan of flood control and water management" that demanded a "coordinated improvement plan for the area as a whole." Managing nature remained the principal mantra.[33]

With a distinctly seasonal precipitation regime, south Florida deals with alternating water abundance and shortage—exacerbated by occasional persistent drought. In its 1948 report on comprehensive water management in south Florida, the Corps grappled with the contrasting problems of drought and flooding, of drainage and water conservation for growing urban demands, and the need to stem saltwater intrusion into the freshwater systems. Its engineers recognized the scale and scope of the problem, but this just prompted even more complex and costly designs. The water management plan conceptualized by the Corps bore the name of the Central and South Florida Project, and its estimated budget rose to $208 million in 1948 dollars. The plan called for a levee inland from the coastal cities, a levee-protected agricultural area south of Lake Okeechobee, plus a water conservation area to retain water to offset saltwater intrusion, prevent muck fires, and sustain groundwater supplies for urban uses. The ambitious plan sought to do far more than the earlier designs dedicated to establishing tropical agriculture. In some respects it sought to mimic nature in order to restore the Everglades, but with the obvious objective to manage nature, it fragmented the natural system into various administrative units. The Everglades Agricultural Area (fig. 2.3)—the zone south of Lake Okeechobee—was to receive a major plumbing overhaul for some seven hundred thousand acres that came to be dominated by sugar cane cultivation.[34]

As federal investment in water management flowed into south Florida, the region boomed during the post–World War II years. Population soared from nearly 1.9 million in 1940 to 4.9 million in 1960. This growth accelerated demand on the region's water supplies and put more people and property at risk from flooding—mostly in coastal cities. Most of the newcomers were unfamiliar with the floods of the 1920s and the 1940s. These new residents saw lovely beaches on the eastern seaboard seemingly disconnected from the interior wetlands, productive farmlands on the interior, and managed marshlands in the conservation district and national park.

Work on the water management plan moved forward slowly due to a combination of protracted design work by the Corps and inadequate appropriations from Congress. As it inched forward, the project attracted an abundance of rancor among the various water users. The Flood Control District became the target of complaints that its actions favored agricultural

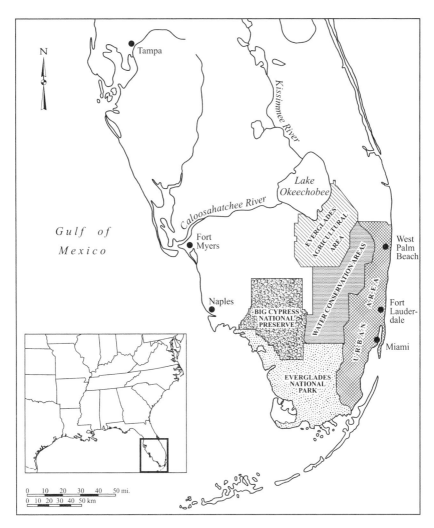

FIG. 2.3. Everglades Management Areas, ca. 2007. After U.S. Government Accountability Office, *South Florida Ecosystem: Restoration Is Moving Forward but Is Facing Significant Delays, Implementation Challenges, and Rising Costs* (Washington, DC: Government Accountability Office, GA-07–520, 2007). Cartography by Mary Lee Eggart.

interests over sportsmen and passed construction costs to urban dwellers, who received few benefits. Fragmented management spawned additional conflict and pitted disparate stakeholders against each other. Flood control, agriculture, water conservation, wildlife conservation, and national park preservation goals were not always in accord. For example, construction of three shallow impoundments known as the Water Conservation Areas, south of the Everglades Agricultural District (fig. 2.3), retained water as part of the flood-control project, to help recharge local aquifers, and to supply urban water systems. By the 1960s, the diversion of water toward the coastal cities, the construction of two cross-state highways that impeded southward flow, and an extended drought sparked shrill debate over adequate flow into the national park.[35]

The Everglades park, as a threatened wild space, became a key issue. A search for an interim solution to restore adequate water supplies to the park brought in national conservation groups and media sympathetic to the survival of the last vestige of a wild Everglades. The lengthy 1960s drought caused Florida officials to fear water shortages for the million-plus urban residents in south Florida, and they threatened to undercut a temporary plan to send more water to the park. A year of abundant rainfall in 1969 averted the impending crisis but did not solve the long-term problem. Preservation of the untamed wetland now faced its most pressing challenge from coastal cities—even though agriculture was firmly implanted in the northern portion of the region.[36]

Drainage for agriculture had irreversibly altered the land within the Everglades Agricultural District. Oxidation of the muck soils and subsidence lowered the territory well below its previous elevation. As discussions for restoring flow through this area to help repair wetlands to the south came to the fore, it became obvious that natural flow was impossible and that more expensive hydrological engineering would be necessary.

The environmental impulse of the 1960s coincided with the water shortage crisis in the Everglades and prompted a host of related responses that elevated the environmental dimension of water management in south Florida. The outcry over the threatened destruction of the national park's wetlands, plus federal laws that demanded environmental impact statements for federal projects and court decisions that expanded government oversight over wetlands, shifted the approach taken toward the Everglades from simple management for development toward protecting the environment itself. With much of the south Florida wetlands under the administration of water management districts, protection took a decidedly urban turn. During the 1970s, Florida water planners worked with projections that indicated massive urban population growth. With this increase in mind, they viewed their mandate as preventing pollution of water supplies, facilitating recharge of over-used aquifers, and extending the supply well into the future.[37]

Preservation of the wetlands themselves also emerged as a competing issue. A knockdown, drag-out political battle over the development of a giant airport in the Big Cypress Swamp, northwest of the Everglades, further galvanized public interest in preserving what was left of the wilder side of the south Florida in the early 1970s. This struggle ended in eventual defeat of the planned airport and came to characterize the changing dynamics and the emerging emphasis on wetland protection by denying any additional encroachments on the valued environmental setting.[38]

By the 1990s, after decades of administrative fragmentation, the environmental protection ethos evolved into one that aimed to restore the Everglades. A first step was to re-unify the Everglades as a single geographic territory. Drawing on larger designations of regional-scale ecosystems, one step toward envisioning a unified hydrologic and biologic system was adopting the South Florida Ecosystem label. Additionally, planners reconfigured their maps to depict the three water conservation impoundments and the national park territories as the Everglades Protection Area (fig. 2.3). This cartographic reconfiguration reflected a fundamental shift in management objectives. Plans were revamped to address the larger ecological units, rejecting the practices that had balkanized the region's management. With the establishment of an Ecosystem Restoration Task Force in 1993, the federal government took a lead role in seeking to appropriate water to restore and preserve natural habitats and to foster compatible natural and human systems. This effort emphasized the restoration of natural systems as much as possible. A key goal of the Comprehensive Everglades Restoration Plan, quite different in intent from the 1940s comprehensive flood-control plan, was restoring the region's water flow—not just providing flood protection or water quality protection. This new design involved hundreds of separate water management projects. A number of these projects explicitly sought to "restore a more natural flow to the Everglades National Park and improve water quality in the ecosystem." Thus, for many observers restoration meant reestablishing water systems to enable the damaged park and associated undeveloped territory to heal. Cost increases and delays caused by many technical and economic issues have impeded the overall restoration effort, and the sequencing of the many smaller projects reveals the water managers' inability to deal with the entire ecosystem territory. Yet restoration remains at the forefront of the public view of Everglades management.[39]

Despite the noble goal of restoring the South Florida Ecosystem, decades of manipulation have pirated most natural elements of the region's hydrology, and restoration efforts depend on many more complex and interrelated technical fixes. Water storage systems for urban consumers, canals and pumps to move water to desired locations on schedule, impoundments to enhance pollution treatment, and canals for flood control reflect the huge diversity of engineering works within the overarching program. Periodic drought exposes the inadequate supply to meet the many demands. Even the state's purchase in 2008 of a vast portion of the Everglades Agricultural Area for restoration cannot raise the lands that have subsided for decades. The extent of human alteration has even had an impact on microclimates. With less standing water, the fruit orchards are now exposed to more frequent frosts. Additionally, efforts to eradicate invasive animal and plant species and restore habitat in the region reflect the human impacts. One of the more pressing issues has been the arrival and proliferation of Burmese pythons, which are threatening existing wildlife in the wetlands. So although not native, the pythons, in one sense, make the Everglades a wilder, less managed place. Yet, they complicate the efforts to restore the larger ecosystem. Still, massive federal and state funds flow into restoration projects. As geographer Christopher Meindl expresses it, "As more of south Florida becomes filled with development and choked with traffic, citizens are likely to cling even tighter to the idea of a rehabilitated Everglades." Just as with the early twentieth-century vision of an expansive agricultural paradise, the dream of a watery wilderness or "Florida's Liquid Heart," however fantastic, continues to shape attitudes about the Everglades and drives vast appropriations which cannot produce sufficient water to meet the many demands.[40]

"Designer Wetland"

Traveling from Florida westward along the Gulf of Mexico coast, there are hundreds of miles of sandy beaches fronting the many barrier islands. As one nears the mouth of the Mississippi River, the waters of the Gulf grade from clear blue to murky, heavily laden with sediments transported from Great Plains and Midwest farms by the mighty river's many tributaries. Since the last ice age the Mississippi has deposited soil from the continental interior to create the relatively new geologic feature known as the bird's-foot delta and several older relict deltas. Running roughly parallel to the Mississippi across this recent deltaic landscape is its largest distributary, the Atchafalaya River. With a length of only 137 miles it is a relatively short stream, but has served a vitally important function in the lower Mississippi River basin (fig. 2.4). It was formerly a natural relief valve that accommodated a portion of the Mississippi's flow, particularly during spring floods. Today, several massive structures constructed by the Corps of Engineers maintain a flow of 30 percent of the Mississippi's discharge through the Atchafalaya. Bordered on the west by a terrace and the Mississippi River's natural levee on the east, the Atchafalaya's basin is roughly twenty miles wide. Alongside the river is an extensive wetland, mostly cypress swamp on the river's upper section, and grading into marsh toward the coast. During high water, the area becomes a forested lake, but in the fall and winter it is a series of bayous, sloughs, lakes, and forested tracts. Described as the nation's largest river swamp, it contains about 1 million acres from its headwaters to the Gulf of Mexico. In reference to Marjory Douglas's label for the Everglades, the U.S. Geological Survey has called the Atchafalaya the "river of trees" (fig. 2.5).[41]

This basin is the home of the once reclusive Acadians and the scene of

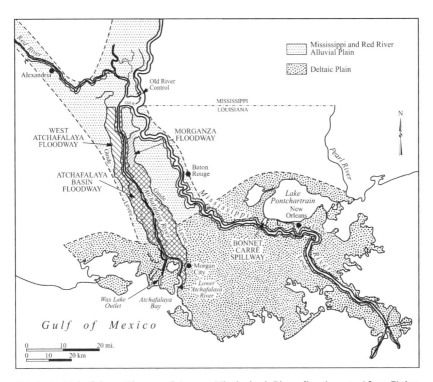

FIG. 2.4. Atchafalaya River and Lower Mississippi River floodways. After Elaine Yodis and Craig Colten, *Louisiana Geography* (New York: McGraw-Hill Primis Custom Publishing, 2012). Cartography by Mary Lee Eggart.

FIG. 2.5. Cypress forest in St. Martin Parish, Atchafalaya Basin, 1934. Photographer W. K. Winters, Works Progress Administration of Louisiana. Used with permission of the Louisiana State Library.

their historically thriving resource collection activities, including Spanish moss gathering, fishing, crawfishing, and of course cypress harvesting. The dense forest has been the hallmark of the Atchafalaya Basin, not grassy wetlands. Although there have been limited efforts to drain the swamp for agriculture, the compulsion to cultivate has never been the driving force for development. Resource extraction guided initial management, and more recently flood control on the Mississippi River has dominated decision making.

Historically, observers found the Louisiana swamps foreboding and mysterious. Writing in the 1870s, an unnamed contributor to William Cullen Bryant's *Picturesque America* stated the "scenery of the undisturbed forests of the Lower Mississippi is of a mysterious interest."[42] In a nineteenth-century compilation of the state's geography from about the same time, Samuel Lockett observed, "The swamps are of little value to the state at present. Considerable quantities of cypress are felled in them and floated out in rafts for use of the sawmills along the Mississippi. No doubt a great deal of the swamp lands are reclaimable; but the question whether they are or not possess but little interest for Louisiana, when so much of her best lands is untilled."[43] The timber and fisheries offered sufficient economic return and dissuaded extensive reclamation, particularly given the abundance of prime floodplain land along other rivers. The principal value of the Atchafalaya in recent decades has been its use to reduce flood risks to the more intensively developed and densely inhabited Mississippi River floodplain. From initial French settlement in the early 1700s to the Louisiana Purchase in 1803, planters sought to work the rich alluvial soils along the Mississippi to harvest fortunes from indigo, rice, and later sugar cane. They built levees to protect their investments from regular, seasonal inundation. Several bayous that diverged from the main channel provided outlets to the sea and carried off excess flow during the spring floods. As early as 1817, William Darby noted the potential value of the Atchafalaya as an artificial sluice to divert floods from the wealthy plantation lands. But he also commented explicitly on the fact that it would make the basin a sacrifice zone: "It would be ruining one part of the community to benefit another."[44]

Through the Civil War, the Atchafalaya Basin remained a backwater—both environmentally and economically. Commercial fisheries expanded linkages to external markets in the 1870s and began a slow economic transformation. Initially, fish brokers towed live fish in semi-submerged live boxes and by the late nineteenth century packed their catch on ice for shipment to the important New Orleans market.[45] The late nineteenth-century expansion of commercial cypress operations further emphasized the Atchafalaya as a resource extraction zone and not a territory for agricultural development. Louisiana secured title to over 10 million acres from the Swamp Land Acts of 1849 and 1850—much of that in the Atchafalaya Basin. Few buyers sought to acquire the inaccessible swamps in the Atchafalaya before the Civil War.[46] Indeed, it was not until the 1880s that timber companies acquired sizable holdings and launched commercial operations. With the deployment of "swampers" in floating dormitories and the use of steam winches on pull boats to drag felled cypress to collection points, the systematic removal of millions of board feet of cypress progressed through the basin. Morgan City, near the mouth of the Atchafalaya, became the center for the basin's commercial fish distribution and cypress milling. The timber industry boomed during the early years of the twentieth century, but with no conservation practices to accompany the tree removal, aggressive exploitation soon exhausted the once-abundant cypress stands. By 1930, commercial operators had removed most virgin trees, and the last of the cypress timber mills closed in the 1950s.[47]

Despite the near depletion of the first-growth cypress forests, the annual flooding and the persistence of a wetland forest discouraged agricultural plans in Louisiana's Atchafalaya comparable to those in Florida's Everglades. To manage high water, local interests constructed levees along the Atchafalaya during the late nineteenth century, but they were not entirely effective. And by forcing the river to flow through its channel, rather than debouching across the floodplain, it enlarged its flow by capturing more and more water from the Red and the Mississippi.[48]

With the disastrous Mississippi River flood of 1927, the Corps of Engineers rethought its "levees only" policy along the lower Mississippi and shifted to a "levees and outlets" management strategy (see chap. 3). This new approach called for a pair of "outlets" or floodways to mimic the traditional function of the numerous distributary bayous that had served as safety valves for the Mississippi. Indeed, the Atchafalaya Basin served this function and endured considerable flooding in 1927 as the Mississippi overwhelmed the lower river basin. With numerous smaller distributaries closed by levees since the nineteenth century, outlets became central to the post-1927 flood-control plans. The larger of the two proposed outlets was to be the Atchafalaya Basin Floodway System.[49]

The post-1927 plan called for the diversion of excess Mississippi discharge during high flood stages that would be funneled to the Gulf of Mexico between two parallel guide levees set about twenty miles apart.[50] Engineers had focused on flood control and gave little thought to other environmental concerns such as maintaining wildlife habitat, which remained an important economic interest in the basin. Their actions fundamentally shifted environmental management in the Atchafalaya from resource extraction to flood management—although the basin remained a working wetland. Also as part of the effort to manage floods, the Corps began a dredging program on the Atchafalaya in the late 1930s to enlarge the capacity of the now-hemmed-in river. One impact of the levees and dredging was to increase significantly the flow of water through the Atchafalaya from 7 percent of the Mississippi's flow to 25 percent in 1950. This situation raised fears that the shorter Atchafalaya channel with a steeper gradient might capture the flow of the Mississippi and cause havoc to commerce on the larger waterway. A second impact was sedimentation of lower river lakes and wetlands. Material dredged from the upper channel settled out when the water entered the relatively still waters of Grand and Six Mile lakes close to Morgan City. Filling these water bodies reduced habitat for aquatic life, which was a prime object of commercial exploitation in the region. As the Atchafalaya Basin floodway neared completion in the 1950s, the Corps began a frantic effort to control the portion of the flow passing down the Atchafalaya. Seeking to sustain the 25 percent diversion, the Corps added a structure at the juncture of the Mississippi and Old River—the Old River Control Structure that was completed in 1963. The overall impact of the Corps's narrowly focused flood-control work was disruptive to the working ecology of the basin, and by the 1960s Louisiana officials began to push for water management that would sustain fishing and oil extraction activities. Some local leaders even proposed the creation of a national park or at least steps to protect portions of the basin.[51]

In 1963, local outdoors writer Grits Gresham authored a booklet for the state Wild Life and Fisheries Commission titled the *Atchafalaya Basin Crisis.* He argued that the Corps's management of water levels, with the completion of the Old River Control Structure, would disrupt the normal spring inundation followed by regular summer and fall drying of the basin that sustained aquatic life. By denying the basin its normal cycle it would destroy the last "semi-wilderness" of its kind. He noted the rapid expansion of sport fishing since the 1940s and the continuation of commercial fishing, which harvested 9 million pounds of fish from the basin in 1962. His report acknowledged the importance of oil extraction and assumed that it would continue. He argued that closure of the basin would increase the damage of oil brine releases from producing wells that no longer would be diluted by Mississippi River water. Gresham's forecast crisis was not the destruction of nature, but the disruption of a working, thoroughly humanized ecology. The basin was not a wilderness, but a semi-wilderness and one that provided income and recreation for area fishermen. The Corps's activities challenged that functional ecosystem.[52]

Over the ensuing decades, amid controversy and rancor, state agencies, the Corps, and the Fish and Wildlife Service worked toward a management system that would retain the key flood management functions of the basin while preserving most landowner interests and protecting areas for wildlife and recreation. Although initially resistant to post-1970 environmental legislation that challenged existing flood-control plans, eventually the Corps dropped a plan to dredge a deeper main channel that locals opposed. As national interest in preserving wetlands grew during the 1970s, the U.S. Environmental Protection Agency pushed for water management in the basin that took wildlife into account and not just flood control. In the late 1970s, the U.S. Fish and Wildlife Service launched an attempt to acquire property in the basin for wildlife habitat. Locals saw this effort as a land grab by the federal government that would deny landowners

basic rights. Eventually, a compromise enabled federal authorities to acquire flowage easements to permit flooding when the Corps diverted water
through the floodway and created several modestly sized state and federal wildlife areas.[53] The U.S. Fish and Wildlife Service (FWS) and Louisiana Department of Wildlife and Fisheries share a conservation mission,
rather than a preservation mandate. Consequently, their goals do not include plans to set aside wilderness areas.[54] Existing development has continued, as wildlife management blended interests of sportsmen with concerns over endangered species such as the black bear. Restoration was part
of the management strategy, but there were no projects to set aside remaining pristine territory. Indeed, the FWS review of its holdings found
no area that met its qualifications for a wilderness designation.[55] The refuges serve sport fishermen, even though commercial fishing has largely
given way to farm-raised crawfish and catfish. Oil interests still search
the basin for extractible minerals, and the Corps still controls the flow of
water through the basin.

In recent years, Louisiana politicians persuaded federal authorities to
create one of its newer park units, a national heritage area, in the basin.
This designation does not require the conflicts seen with federal purchase
of land for wildlife areas. It is a "soft" type of park unit, a cartographic depiction that infuses NPS expertise into the shaping of regional interpretive
programs and knits together various existing historic sites for visitors to
tour. It does not impinge on existing mineral extraction or commercial activities in the basin and thus does not impose the NPS preservation land-
management practices on the area.[56] With no wilderness or national park
property in the Atchafalaya, conservation and flood-control practices take
priority and the basin remains a working wetland.

During high water on the Mississippi River in 1973, the Corps of Engineers called on the basin to do its job. Their flood-control efforts relative
to the Atchafalaya hinged on the Old River Control Structure that had
sparked controversy a decade before. Waters began rising in the Mississippi River basin in late 1972 and recurrent heavy rains during the early
spring led to flood stages for most of the lower basin by early April. The
combined discharge from the eastern and western basins produced a record period of eighty-eight days above flood stage at Vicksburg.[57] During
peak discharge, exceptionally high river stages and powerful currents
scoured supporting sediment from beneath the Old River Control Structure's concrete foundation and nearly caused its collapse. To reduce the
threat of flooding downstream, the Corps opened one of the passages to

the Atchafalaya Floodway, the Morganza Spillway, for nearly two months in 1973, which caused extensive flooding in the Atchafalaya and proved devastating to wildlife unable to escape to high ground. It threatened communities in the Atchafalaya Basin, particularly Morgan City near the river's mouth. Commenting on the causes of the high stages and the role of flood-control works, one hydrologist concluded, "Navigation works and levees make big floods out of moderate ones."[58] Nonetheless, after the waters receded, the Corps substantially reinforced the control structure and embarked on levee improvements in the lower basin. The engineers' devotion to flood control exemplified their priorities and the overarching management strategy for the Atchafalaya Basin.

Subsequent high water continued to reveal the presence of nature in the basin and the pervasiveness of environmental management shaped by flood concerns. During the 1997 flood, although the Corps did not open the Morganza Spillway, the 30 percent flow through the Atchafalaya River remained in flood for four months.[59] A near repeat of the 1973 scenario unfolded during the winter of 2011. A considerable snowpack across the Midwest, followed by a series of persistently heavy rain events swelled the upper Mississippi drainage basin waterways for extended periods. As the floodwaters rose in the Mississippi and slowly coursed toward the Old River Control Structure, hydrologists estimated a peak discharge of 1.8 million cubic feet per second—well above the highest measured volume since the Corps commenced its post-1927 flood-control project and above the trigger point to open the Morganza Spillway. The Corps began making plans for a slow release to minimize impact on wildlife in the basin.[60] When they partially opened the Morganza Spillway for only the second time in early May, the diverted waters flooded about forty-six hundred square miles of swampland. Water depths were lower than expected in the Atchafalaya wetlands, due in part to a prevailing drought in Louisiana which allowed the unsaturated soils in the basin to rapidly absorb much of the overflow. Massive preparations such as temporary levees and evacuations turned out to be overly cautious. Economic disruption was much more pervasive on the Mississippi where limits on navigation interrupted commerce and industrial activities, although there were no serious levee breaches. Nonetheless, the flood of 2011 reawakened basin residents to the urgency of flooding after decades of complacency. The Atchafalaya Floodway was there for use as an outlet when needed, and residents needed to remember that fact. The designer wetland was designed to serve this purpose when nature unleashed an exceptional flood. The massive structures of the Corps of Engineers had not eliminated the risk of flooding, and the threat of high water prevails. Nature continues to punctuate water management efforts on a somewhat irregular schedule.

And there remains the concern of the possible capture of the Mississippi by the Atchafalaya if the Old River Control Structure were to fail. Diversion of the majority of the system's flow through the distributary channel would wreak havoc on southern Louisiana and the Atchafalaya Basin. Increased stages would destroy bridges built over the Atchafalaya and pipelines laid beneath it. Spring floods would disrupt existing agriculture, community life, and oil extraction in the basin. Meanwhile, greatly reduced flow in the main stem of the Mississippi would render it incapable of supporting current navigation activity and also allow salt water to reach the New Orleans water intakes, making its public water supply undrinkable.[61] In the unlikely event that this scenario plays out, there would not be enough water to sustain the various demands on the lower Mississippi River, to say nothing of emerging plans to use sediment in the river's overflow to help restore the disappearing coastal wetlands.

Conclusion

Wetlands rose to a *cause célèbre* in the 1980s. They became the endangered species of physical landscapes. Increased federal attention to the definition and protection of wetlands expanded the Corps of Engineers' authority over the threatened environments, created opportunities for wetland banking, and fostered conflict over the cost of preserving these saturated territories.[62] This national attention greatly enhanced the visibility of both the Everglades and the Atchafalaya and strengthened efforts to preserve what was left of them. Despite heroic struggles to preserve the Everglades, a century of engineering has repeatedly discovered a shortage of water to accomplish the many tasks required of this wetland. Adequately providing for agriculture, urban water consumers, and preservation of natural systems has proven a challenge that becomes more complex, and water managers attempt to sequence projects into operation. With the arrival of periodic drought, the shortages become all too evident. The relatively small portions of the Everglades protected within the National Park or wilderness areas are inadequate to truly restore the wetland ecology of south Florida. And in some respects, the existence of these protected areas serves as a salve for the national conscience while complete restoration remains a dream.

In the Atchafalaya, intentional diversion of the 70 percent of the Mississippi's flow through its main channel, along with deepening of the Atchafalaya's channel, deprives this wetland of seasonal floods. Should the engineering works that control the flow fail, there would be too much water coursing through the Atchafalaya, but not enough down the Mississippi. Contrived shortages imperil the Atchafalaya wetland even though portions have been set aside as wildlife preserves. The absence of a compelling spokesperson for the Atchafalaya Basin, plus its history as a working environment, has hindered efforts to launch restoration on a grand scale. Even when rebranded as "America's Wetland" to overcome the tongue-twisting name, there has been no national embrace of the Atchafalaya as has been the case with the Everglades. But despite their disparate national images, the Atchafalaya and the Everglades are emblematic of the limits to abundance and the imposition of federal authority over the watery environs of the South.

3

Overflowing Waters

Introduction

Floods represent the most compelling example of abundant, more precisely overabundant, water in the American South. Coping with this plentitude has demanded a mixture of technical expertise coupled with political influence. Extending federal engineering capabilities and fiscal resources to managing floods in the South followed vigorous nineteenth-century debates in the American Congress about the role of the federal government in building public works in the frontier states.[1] Regional concerns drove demands for public roadways and clearing waterways. Only as public works programs rose from regional to national priorities could they find adequate legislative support to secure funding and implementation.

In the twentieth century, requests for regional public works arose around excess waters. Following federal investments in navigation improvements, apprehension over the disastrous consequences of flooding, both riparian and hurricane, compelled Congress to contend with high-water hazards. While the American South has no monopoly on floods, it has a dense network of waterways, and its states have some of the highest percentages of total land area in floodplains.[2] As a consequence of this topographic reality, major calamities along the region's rivers and coasts provided the impetus for expansive federal actions. The devastating flood along the lower Mississippi River in 1927 inspired a major overhaul of flood protection policies; hurricanes that dumped copious precipitation along the eastern seaboard in the 1950s motivated national hurricane planning, and a landmark hurricane strike on the gulf coast in 1965 pushed Congress to implement a flood insurance program. Each policy adjustment followed dramatic and deadly events that elevated a regional concern to the national level.[3]

This process is significant as we consider how a society prepares for and responds to hazardous events linked to excess water. A central question is how can a region that bears the brunt of national- and international-scale physical systems manage the costs of coping with floods? Hazards are not uniformly spread across the landscape, and some locations are more vulnerable than others to events that flow from physical systems spawned at an entirely different geographic scale. River floods at New Orleans, for example, result from drainage of the huge Mississippi River basin. For a society to implement appropriately scaled protective policies and to spread the costs equitably, it is imperative for decision makers to respond at the scale of the hazard, not just at the local level. Flood protection on the Rhine required international cooperation, and water supplies in the arid southwestern United States demanded engineered systems at an interstate scale.[4] This chapter will consider the transition from locally oriented hazards management to national protection policies and the role of the South in the federal commitment to flood protection.

John Barry has argued that the flood of 1927 changed the American approach to contending with excess water along the Mississippi River.[5] While this event was critical in revamping the engineering approach to floods, the political approach to disaster responses was already moving inexorably toward a more extensive federal role. Disaster relief, in particular, had become a fundamental component of what legal historian Michele Dauber refers to as the "sympathetic state." During the nineteenth century Congress readily set aside constitutional questions when disaster relief measures came to the floor and supported distribution of funds to those who suffered from circumstances beyond their control. And the 1927 flood provided ample justification for subsequent legislation that expanded the federal role in both flood protection and disaster relief.[6] Flooding in other regions comparable to southern inundations, particularly the 1937 Ohio and Mississippi rivers floods, eventually inspired national sympathies, and the South gained allies who voiced arguments honed by southern lawmakers when similar tragedies befell their regions. New Deal advocates also pressed for direct federal funding for disaster relief.[7] Ultimately, the blending of regional demands into a single national chorus drove the passage of federal hazards management and disaster response policies. Calamities provided the visibility to these issues and revealed a national posture that assumed it was reasonable to spread the cost of hazard mitigation and recovery to diminish the impacts of overflowing waters on the American economy. Coping with excess waters relied on deflecting floods and responding to devastation.

The 1927 Flood and Flood Protection

The great Mississippi River flood of 1927 captured the attention of the nation as surging waters tore through levees and inundated twenty-six thousand square miles of floodplain, forced more than seven hundred thousand individuals to flee their homes, and left over three hundred people dead.[8] This event tested a flood protection system more than two centuries in the making and demonstrated convincingly it was not up to the task (figs. 3.1 and 3.2). During the long history of fortifying river fronts, responsibility initially lay with landowners or local governments. It was not a national obligation. In Louisiana, colonial French policy mandated that individual riparian planters had to erect levees on their properties that would, in time, constitute a unified barrier. By the time of statehood, parish governments had assumed the expensive burden. Assistance through the auspices of the Swamp Lands Acts of 1849 and 1850 allowed states to sell wetlands transferred from the federal government and to apply the proceeds to flood protection works. Even then, there was no direct federal involvement in the design and construction of the levees.[9]

As floods continued to torment the planters and cities along the lower river following the Civil War, southern politicians began honing arguments that their home districts could not bear the cost of protecting their citizens against a river that drained nearly half the nation—that is, the scale of the hazard far exceeded local abilities to control the impacts. This

FIG. 3.1. Flooded business district in Melville, Louisiana, 1927. Used with the permission of the Louisiana State Library.

argument had particular poignancy during Reconstruction when riparian landowners, economically devastated by the war, had few resources to repair levees neglected during the conflict.[10] Only following Reconstruction, as the U.S. Army Corps of Engineers took on river improvements across the country, were southern politicians able to align themselves with navigation interests to secure support for levees along the lower river.[11] They succeeded, with the unwitting expertise of engineers who argued levees would enhance navigation and thereby serve national economic interests.[12] When Congress established the Mississippi River Commission (MRC) in 1879, its assignment was to build a well-engineered and consistent levee system to ensure navigability of the Mississippi River.[13]

The creation of the Mississippi River Commission was a major step forward in the shift of flood control from local to federal coffers, albeit couched in terms of navigation improvements. Indeed, a core argument for flood control along the lower river was that the flood problem was national in scope. A river that drains roughly 41 percent of the national territory guided floodwaters by only a handful of lower river states, especially

FIG. 3.2. Repairing levees during flood of 1927. Louisiana Digital Library. Used with the permission of the Louisiana State Library.

Louisiana and Mississippi, which had to cope with gargantuan volumes of water. Lower river flood-control proponents also pointed out that deforestation and cultivation across the Midwest and Great Plains added to the flood risk. Furthermore they argued that the expense of a viable protection system would be recouped by the nation's treasury through prosperity built on river-related commerce.[14] This economic argument elevated benefits to the national level as it attempted to defer the direct costs of hazard protection.

As the MRC advanced the construction of levees along the lower Mississippi River and contended with repeat floods, it ultimately came to argue for levees with the specific intent to provide flood protection. Floods in other regions also highlighted the risks that high water posed to development along major waterways. Flooding along the Sacramento River in 1903 and 1904, on the Ohio in 1913, and reinforced by flooding on the Mississippi in 1912, 1913, and again in 1916, impelled Congress to pass the Flood Control Act of 1917. This legislation, for the first time, contained funding explicitly dedicated to flood control—along the Mississippi and Sacramento rivers. With its new mandate to provide flood protection, the MRC had to design levees based on the local flood history, not with the intent to enhance navigation. By 1926, the MRC expressed confidence that the levees finally offered protection against the flood potential of the Mississippi River. The record flood that occurred during the spring of 1927 overwhelmed the flood barriers, caused monumental human and financial losses, and undermined the commission's and the Corps of Engineers' credibility. In the wake of this calamity, Congress once again sought a plan that would strengthen protection along the lower Mississippi River.[15]

By November 1927, Congress was conducting hearings to consider a revised approach to flood protection. The massive destruction unleashed by the spring floods called into question the viability of the long-accepted "levees only" approach. While there had been periodic promotion of outlets to supplement levees, Louisiana flood-control proponents generally found reasons to steer the discussions back to levees only, and the Army Engineers' ideas about hydrology supported this position. But after the 1927 flood, the "levees and outlets" approach rapidly gained favor, particularly as upper river congressmen pushed for a national flood protection plan. While southerners might not have been at the vanguard of this legislative effort, the core argument that flooding was a national issue was advanced by northern congressmen who sought protection from hazards in their own districts.[16]

Mayor A. J. O'Keefe of New Orleans appealed to Congress to provide relief for the flood-weary residents of the lower valley. He argued that "we have built levees until it hurt. We have taken care of the waters from 31 States of this Union. We are trying to do what we can for one another, and I say it behooves the National Government to take charge of this flood problem and solve it." He also claimed that the artificial crevasse created at Caernarvon in 1927 "saved the city of New Orleans."[17] Shreveport, Louisiana, mayor Lee Thomas reminded congressmen that some twelve to thirteen states were carved from the Louisiana Purchase, underscoring the historical connections between the upper and lower river portions of the basin. He further testified that recent events such as World War I had unified the nation and equated a national solution with patriotic duty. Finally, he summed up his appeal to a broader constituency by stating that "the problem is not a local one."[18] At the core of their pleas was that the problem was national in scale and required federal action that included outlets to supplement the failed levee system.

From the upper reaches of the basin, Illinois politicians joined the chorus. Chicago mayor William Thompson recalled a frightening steamboat trip taken by five hundred Chicago businessmen down the Mississippi River during the flood. Planned as a celebration of federal legislation authorizing creation of a nine-foot channel on the Illinois River, it turned into a harrowing opportunity to witness the flood's devastation. It also alerted the Chicago delegation to the basin-wide scope of the flood problem on the Mississippi River.[19] The governor of Illinois argued that flooding was a national concern because "the flood areas are too large, the flood damages too great, and the flood sources too remote for effective local or even State administration."[20] He discussed recent flood damage suffered in his state along both the Mississippi and its tributary the Illinois River and noted that levee construction and channel constriction had caused flood stages to rise. His appeal to Congress was for federal assistance in controlling the flood situation in general—including in his own state. Illinois representative W. E. Hull echoed the governor's comments, claiming that damage along the Illinois River was ten times more costly per acre than in the "sunny South." In closing, he noted that Illinoisans wanted to help residents of the South, along with those living along the other tributaries of the Mississippi. But he insisted that the Illinois River be included in the flood protection legislation.[21]

Proponents from across the country weighed in on the flood-control issue. And at the core of the arguments were the intertwined notions that flood control was not limited to the lower Mississippi River and that it was a problem of national proportion. Few congressmen were willing to have their districts excluded from the potential benefits of flood protection. Political scientist Karen O'Neill rightly makes that case that northern representatives propelled the 1928 act through Congress.[22] But at the center of their arguments were positions long staked out by lower river flood protection advocates. And the shift from levees only to levees and outlets reflects the incorporation of ideas touted by southerners for decades. These concerns were included with the passage of the 1928 Flood Control Act, which assigned the duty of levee design and construction along the lower Mississippi and the Sacramento rivers to the Corps of Engineers. While not fully national in its reach, the political collaboration reflected Congress's acceptance of an economic benefit argument.

An earlier development, however, had expanded the Corps of Engineers' attention to the national scope of flood protection. In 1920, Congress passed the Water Power Act that authorized the Corps to conduct a nationwide survey of navigable river basins for navigation, water power, and flood-control projects. When Congress finally authorized funds to begin these so-called "308" surveys following the 1927 flood, the engineers began assembling systematic reports that specifically addressed flood control.[23] These surveys bolstered the Corps's position when Congress finally deliberated a national flood-control policy in 1936. Testifying before Congress, the chief of the Army Engineers remarked on the true priority of flood control and its national character:

> The first mental approach of the establishment of a Federal interest and expenditure appears to me to involve this consideration, broadly throughout the United States there is water pouring from one State into another state. The first State is not being hurt, and thus, has no interest whatever, in constructing anything that relates to flood control, the second State is vastly hurt and is not able, because of State boundaries and legal limitations, to do anything about it. There is no one who can do anything about it except the Federal Government.[24]

Although the Corps dutifully prepared reports for basins across the country, the greatest flood risk remained along the Mississippi and its tributaries. Nonetheless, a series of floods in 1935 and 1936 underscored the limitations of the 1928 act and galvanized legislative support from a broader approach—and the Corps's 308 reports offered detailed insight into the scope of the flood problem.

Among the many 308 reports the Corps of Engineers produced was one for the Potomac River and its tributaries. This waterway is exceptionally important since it flows by Washington, DC, the seat of federal authority, and over the years it has served as a barometer for national water policy. It drains a mountainous portion of western Virginia and Maryland, along with small portions of neighboring Pennsylvania. Although largely a southern river, it straddles the traditional Mason-Dixon Line. The Corps characterized floods along the Potomac as "sudden and violent." Despite a sizable number of observed floods, the report's authors observed that these inundations had caused relatively little damage because there had been modest floodplain development. Two exceptions were Cumberland, Maryland, and Washington, DC.[25]

The Corps recommended a combined diversion and levee construction for the upland city of Cumberland. Engineers plotted a straightened channel through an older section of town. By shortening the river, they could increase the discharge and lower flood stages. In addition, this construction would require the removal of many of the most flood-prone structures. Levees would supplement the diversion for other low-lying sections of the small city. The report also recommended a special assessment on those properties that would directly benefit from the flood protection.[26]

For Washington, DC, where the Potomac cascades over the last rapids before emptying into a large, tidally influenced stretch that meanders to the sea, the Corps offered a different approach. The authors noted that there had been irregular floods caused by a combination of snow melt and spring rainfall, and that they had not inflicted serious damage in recent years. High water, however, could inundate low-lying sections of Georgetown, the park area near the waterfront, sections of downtown Washington, and airfields and military installations downriver from the city proper.[27] Ultimately, the engineers recommended no protection for Georgetown, but incorporated a system of levees as part of waterfront park development to protect the city center and government structures near the mall. The critical role of the military facilities and airfields led the authors to conclude that benefits of levee protection would exceed the costs, and they recommended levees to protect these vital installations as well.[28] The engineers also evaluated flood-control reservoirs, but deemed them uneconomical.

A report on the Tennessee River and its tributaries took on a much larger and more complex basin in the upper South. Draining the western slopes of the rain-drenched Appalachian Mountains, the Tennessee system offered tremendous potential for hydroelectric power and presented a modest flood threat. The report acknowledged that the 1926 flood caused serious damage, but projected that a flood of that magnitude could be expected no more frequently than once in five hundred years. Furthermore, it pointed out that the only locality that endured concentrated damage was Chattanooga, Tennessee, and that local structures could reduce flood risk there. When weighing the benefits of a string of reservoirs dedicated to mitigate flooding on the Mississippi, the Corps concluded that they would have negligible impact and such structures would undermine efficient tapping of hydroelectric potential and also inhibit navigation improvements.[29] Consequently, the overall thrust of the 308 report emphasized the benefits of power and navigation, with flood control receiving secondary consideration.

The plan for flood control on the lower Mississippi River contained a major adjustment from the pre-1927 "levees only" policy. In 1931 the Corps summarized the flood-control plan adopted after the 1927 flood. It noted that reliance on levees was too expensive, and the cost of damages in the event of a levee failure would spiral in proportion to the expense of raising the barriers. Furthermore, it was not cost effective to build "permanent" levees since channel changes required the relocation of some sections and the low-cost earthen barriers were more affordable temporary structures.[30] Nonetheless, the plan called for raising levees approximately three feet to contend with a maximum probable flood, or "superflood."[31] The principal adjustment from the 1927 flood-control policy was the explicit adoption of "outlets" or structures to guide the "escape of excess water from the main stem." The Corps was in the process of developing two major diversions—one that would be capable of redirecting some 900,000 cubic feet per second (cfs) of water to the Gulf of Mexico through the Atchafalaya River basin and a second to send 250,000 cfs into Lake Pontchartrain (see fig. 2.4, chap. 2). These outlets would reduce the threat to agriculture and communities below the Red River. The Corps rejected a third component of flood control, reservoirs, as too costly given the scale of the basin and the required storage capacity.[32]

Coping with floods was an obvious concern for the many streams along the eastern seaboard and the gulf coast between the Potomac and the Mississippi. A massive federal effort to expand rational resource planning during the 1930s reported on developing rivers across the South's coastal plain. In brief, it noted that flooding was largely a local issue and seldom caused loss of life. Recommendations offered were to include some flood-control capacity in reservoirs built for navigation and power production and also to encourage localities to erect levees where necessary. Plans for river development depict only one flood-control dam across the region, while projecting many navigation and hydropower structures. Hurricane-spawned flooding in Florida in the 1920s prompted Congress to assign flood protection in the Lake Okeechobee vicinity to the Corps (see chap. 2). Despite an expanded view of federal responsibility for flood control, the official extension to all localities had not occurred.[33]

Given the underlying mandate for the 308 reports and the Depression-era planning efforts, it should be no surprise that flood control did not receive the emphasis given to power or navigation potential. Yet the floods of 1935 and 1936 swiftly shifted flood protection's position on the priority list. A series of fronts moved across the northern Blue Ridge and southern New England in March 1936. The rapid succession of heavy rain and a sizable snow pack unleashed floods along the upper Ohio River on the western side of the Appalachians and even more rapid river rises in the Potomac basin and across New England.[34] As Congress deliberated the 1936 flood-control act, water rose toward the Capitol, covered the district's riverfront parks, inundated a riverfront airport, and threatened the Red Cross headquarters—making the impact of floods become all too obvious to Congress. Cities as far-flung as Pittsburgh, Pennsylvania, and Hartford, Connecticut, suffered along with Washington. The timing of the high water with a vigorous debate on flood control ensured unprecedented eastern support for flood-control measures.[35] What had been a remote southern, and to a lesser extent western issue, was now national in scope, and opponents silenced their challengers to the 1936 act.

Congressmen from New England testified that the floods of 1936 were unprecedented and acknowledged the interstate nature of flooding. Connecticut, for example, suffered from floods that originated in New Hampshire, Vermont, and Massachusetts.[36] Likewise, Senator Guffey from Pennsylvania, a state which suffered extensive damage from the 1936 floods, argued that high water on the Ohio was the shared concern of "12 or 14 states." Ultimately, he claimed flooding and the cost of flood control was a national concern.[37] Thus, after an expanded federal role along the lower Mississippi River in 1928, the preparation of 308 reports that provided plans for flood protection nationally, and the serious flooding along the Ohio and in New England, the core argument made by southern lawmakers and flood-control proponents became the central justification for a truly national program for coping with watery excesses.

Significantly, the South derived exceptional benefits from flood protection programs over the next several decades (fig. 3.3). The relative territory susceptible to riverine flooding is a contributing factor. Studies point out that significant areas of the South, particularly the lower Mississippi River basin and the South Atlantic-Gulf coastal plain, are subject to stream overflow flooding. Approximately, 56 percent of the total 146,601 square miles of floodplain nationally is in southern states.[38] The concentration of federal expenditures to protect these lands is impressive. Corps of Engineers' levees provide nearly six thousand miles of protection in the South, or 42 percent of its total levee mileage.[39] And the reported benefits are stunning. The Corps claims that the country has invested close to $14 billion in flood control on the lower Mississippi and prevented over $478 billion in damages.[40] These self-promoting tallies of damages prevented deserve scrutiny; nonetheless they reflect the huge federal investment in

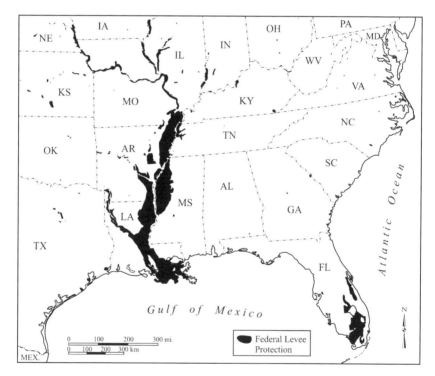

FIG. 3.3. Areas protected by federal levees, 2012. After Corps of Engineers, National Levee Data Base [http://nld.usace.army.mil/egis/f?p=471:32:8415374752022 01::NO], 2012. Cartography by Mary Lee Eggart.

flood protection in the South. And in many respects levees and related structures provide a massive federal subsidy for agriculture, industry, and urban development that face a lower flood risk across the region.

Hurricanes Surges, 1950s

Hurricanes are tropical weather systems that can deliver powerful winds and torrential rains which can inundate coastal areas with storm surge and high waves, but also riparian floodplains as runoff from interior uplands flows back toward the sea. While the impacts of such storms in the United States are most pronounced along the Atlantic shore south of Virginia and the gulf coast states, there have been wayward hurricanes that have blown over the more northerly seaboard states and unleashed coastal and inland flooding with startling consequences, including Hurricane Sandy in 2012. Before 1950, the southern coasts visited most frequently by hurricanes were not highly urbanized and the irregular arrival of powerful storms produced modestly scaled calamities. Without question the 1900 hurricane in Galveston, which killed over six thousand and the 1928 south Florida storm that killed over eighteen hundred were horrendous, but they did not strike major population centers like New York or Boston. Additionally, historian Ted Steinberg makes the case that our collective memory of some of the more dramatic hurricanes is diminished since many of the victims were poor blacks.[41] Between the fact that the South had fewer large cities and many victims were marginalized residents, there was little national impetus for planning and structures to cope with hurricane-driven floods.

Locally, however, communities erected limited structural protections against storm-blown waves and surge. In Charleston, South Carolina, a stone embankment dating back to the nineteenth century provided structural protection against storms, but it was primarily a military fortification. Perhaps the best-known example of structural protection is the seawall in Galveston. Following the massive destruction of the 1900 storm, Galveston residents approved a plan to erect a concrete wall along its beachfront (fig. 3.4). The city bore most of the costs for the initial segment, which was about three miles long. Federal authorities added nearly another mile to protect a military installation adjacent to the city. To supplement the barrier, the city undertook an even grander endeavor to pump sand in behind the seawall and raise the level of much of the city as much as ten feet. This involved elevating more than two thousand houses and businesses before delivering the sand. By 1911, the city was completely re-worked with over five hundred blocks of the city protected from future storms by its seawall and raised urban territory. Local funding paid for the bulk of this substantial effort.[42]

FIG. 3.4. Two men standing on riprap at the base of the Galveston seawall, 1904. Courtesy of Rosenberg Library, Galveston, Texas.

A powerful storm that pummeled the Mississippi and Louisiana coastal areas in 1915 prompted similar structural protection projects. Between 1915 and 1928, the small town of Bay St. Louis, Mississippi, erected a con-crete seawall to protect its business district. Soon thereafter, the county added another ten miles of stepped seawall. In adjacent Harrison County, local interests paid for the construction of twenty-five miles of eight-feet-high seawall to protect Biloxi, Pass Christian, and other communities.[43] Likewise in New Orleans, local officials responded to the 1915 storm. For nearly twenty years, the Orleans Levee Board guided a project to erect a seawall along the city's lakefront, its most vulnerable waterfront. Its engi-neers relied on years of experience with riverfront levees and constructed a stepped seawall that rose 9.5 feet and stretched for about six miles along the lakefront, designed to fend off a storm equal to the 1915 hurricane. As in Galveston, land raising behind the new barrier created an elevated tract of property which developers intended to market to home builders.[44]

The calamitous 1926 hurricane that struck Miami prompted local officials to undertake steps to reduce future damage there. They revised building codes to encourage flood-proof structures, and they constructed an eight-feet-high seawall along much of Biscayne Bay and the city's oceanfront.[45]

Perhaps more commonly, small coastal communities retreated when overwhelmed by storms. Summer visitors abandoned the resort at Last Isle in Louisiana after the storm of 1856. An 1899 hurricane drove residents from North Carolina's Outer Banks community of Diamond City, while Indianola, Texas, residents retreated inland after a pair of storms demolished the community in 1875 and 1886. Other small communities in the Louisiana coastal wetlands, such as Chenier Caminada and Manila Village, also retreated after hurricanes.[46]

Requests for federal assistance with hurricane protection followed World War II. When a destructive storm hit New Orleans in 1947, the lakefront barrier failed to prevent damage to neighborhoods in the city proper. In addition, newly erected postwar suburbs and the city's principal airport in adjacent Jefferson Parish endured extended inundation and costly damages in the absence of hurricane protection levees. Political leaders called on the U.S. Army Corps of Engineers to construct levees to protect the emerging suburban districts. The Corps secured funding from Congress and set to work raising ten miles of earthen levee across Jefferson Parish that complemented the concrete seawall in neighboring Orleans Parish.[47] This action opened the door for more direct federal involvement in hurricane protection, which included shifting the principal financial burden to the federal treasury.

A series of hurricanes in the 1950s that delivered costly consequences beyond the typical hurricane coasts motivated a major federal hurricane research project. Three storms in 1954 spread flooding across large sections of the Northeast. Hurricane Carol charged up the eastern seaboard in late August and merely grazed the Carolina Outer Banks with winds of modest hurricane intensity, but it continued northward and its more powerful eastern side battered Long Island and unleashed winds exceeding 120 miles per hour in Rhode Island. Damages in New England topped $460 million and the storm left sixty dead in that region. Barely a week passed before Hurricane Edna followed a similar path off the eastern shore. While smaller and weaker than its predecessor, Edna caused much more loss of life and damage in New England than it did in North Carolina. Hurricane Hazel moved onshore in mid-October, tracking northward near Wilmington, North Carolina; it passed over the western suburbs of Washington,

DC, and continued across the Appalachians into Pennsylvania and southern Canada. While it pummeled the coasts of the Carolinas with winds reaching 130 miles per hour and caused extensive damage to coastal infrastructure, it dumped up to ten inches of rain across the Appalachians, which resulted in extensive flooding and seventy-eight fatalities—far more than the lives lost in the coastal areas it impacted.[48] The devastating consequences of these storms on the more heavily populated states from Maryland to Pennsylvania and New England compelled Congress to take action.

Congress passed Public Law 71 in early 1955; it called for the Corps of Engineers to prepare a series of interim hurricane surveys that would provide information essential to reducing loss of life and property damage due to hurricanes. A series of reports on coastal areas tabulated historical hurricane information, inventoried existing hurricane protection, and prepared recommendations for additional federal protection systems. As the Corps was conducting its investigations, Congress also increased funding to the Weather Bureau, which launched the National Hurricane Research Project. As part of this endeavor, the Weather Bureau embarked on a series of studies of the physics and climatology of hurricanes, the bureau's forecasting capabilities, and the physical impacts of hurricanes.[49]

Before any substantial progress was made on these dual efforts, a second set of hurricanes overwhelmed the eastern seaboard in 1955 with heavy rains.[50] Hurricane Connie dumped huge amounts of rain across North Carolina in August and continued to release copious volumes of precipitation as it moved across Chesapeake Bay and into southern New York state. The Weather Bureau characterized it as one of the "most disastrous and costly floods of record in the northeastern states." Days later, Hurricane Diane reached the North Carolina coast where it caused modest damage near Wilmington. The most severe damage occurred across inland river basins as the storm moved ashore and proceeded across New England (fig. 3.5). Observers characterized Diane as the first "billion dollar hurricane" and its two hundred fatalities starkly underscore its impact.[51] Diane's arrival near the nation's capital coincided with deliberations for supplemental funding for the National Hurricane Research Project and likely insured passage of those appropriations.[52] With extensive damage beyond the southern coastlines, these storms reinforced the newfound impetus to develop a national hurricane protection program.

The Corps's interim hurricane studies were the coastal equivalent to its 308 reports assessing riparian flood risks. They reveal an expansive region that, due to urban and industrial expansion in the preceding decades,

FIG. 3.5A (*top*). Flooding produced by Hurricane Diane in Naugatuck, Connecticut, August 19, 1955 (55flood19). And **FIG. 3.5B** (*bottom*), Flood damage in Naugatuck, Connecticut, August 1955 (55flood23). Used with permission of the Connecticut State Library.

was increasingly at risk. Yet, almost universally the Corps recommended against federal involvement in hurricane protection. Structural protection was often too costly and too disruptive to existing coastal and port activities. For example, despite extensive damages from cyclones in 1945 and 1950 in Miami and the observation that the city was susceptible to another devastating storm, the Corps recommended against protection structures to augment existing local efforts. Similarly, for Charleston, South Carolina, and coastal Georgia, the Corps could not justify recommending federal expenditures on raising the barrier along the waterfront.[53]

Moving into the Gulf of Mexico, limited coastal urbanization undermined any economic justification for federal projects as well. As part of its inventory of hurricane strikes and damages in northwest Florida, a coastal area visited frequently by tropical cyclones, the Corps noted that the barrier islands of the Florida panhandle were undergoing extensive recreational development, placing more people and real estate at risk. Additionally, cities like Pensacola and Panama City were growing rapidly. Despite the increased risks, the Corps unequivocally recommended against structural protections. Instead, it encouraged local officials to evaluate their own situations and identified building codes, zoning regulations, and emergency preparedness as the most effective techniques to minimize risk. For Alabama's coastal zone, the Corps noted a similar rush to develop recreational beaches, but it recommended against structural protection for both the beach zones and the urban and industrial core of Mobile. In its investigation of the Mississippi shore, the Corps noted that property losses were on the increase due to increasing beachfront development. Nonetheless, the Corps once again advocated against fortifying or improving locally built seawalls. Instead, it called on local authorities to strengthen building codes, zoning, and emergency preparedness.[54]

Louisiana and Texas stand out as distinct departures from the nonstructural recommendations made by the Corps. Corps investigators observed that rapid urbanization of Galveston, due in part to wartime housing demands, had extended the city well beyond the existing seawall. It recommended adding about three more miles of protective barrier. With a cost of some $8 million and protected property valued at $57 million, this project would yield benefits far exceeding costs according to the Corps's calculations.[55] In March 1964, the Corps of Engineers submitted its report on the New Orleans area to Congress. It recommended a considerable expansion of the existing structural protections, largely erected along the Lake Pontchartrain shore across the northern suburbs of New Orleans and adjacent Jefferson Parish. At the time, the protection system was a hybrid of federally and locally built levees. The Corps proposed an extension of the seawalls around the less-developed eastern New Orleans wetlands, raising levees to a consistent grade where they existed, creating a barrier across the eastern end of Lake Pontchartrain to prevent storm surge from entering the lake, and adding protective barriers around quickly developing St. Bernard Parish on the city's southeastern flank. At the time, the Corps estimated the project would require expenditures exceeding $64 million but averred that the benefits would far exceed costs.[56]

The timing of this proposal was remarkable. It was under consideration by Congress when Hurricane Betsy made landfall in September 1965 and became the template for the plan that received appropriations in the immediate wake of that devastating storm.[57] Betsy inflicted massive damage to New Orleans and coastal Louisiana. Nearly half the city was inundated, along with extensive areas of coastal marshes. Only four years later the even more intense Hurricane Camille (1969) inflicted even more horrendous damage as it tore across the Mississippi shore. Once again large areas of Louisiana wetlands suffered inundation, but this storm obliterated vast sections of beachfront development in Mississippi. These two storms inspired sufficient national sympathy to prompt Congress to approve funding for the massive barrier project for coastal Louisiana and New Orleans.[58] While there has been no comparable structural projects across either the South or into more populated regions, a southern tragedy sparked a national response. The structural approach prevailed in the search for relief from hurricane floods in Louisiana and was feasible only with federal funds.

Hurricane Betsy and Flood Insurances, 1960s

The most prominent national response to Hurricane Betsy was the passage and eventual implementation of the National Flood Insurance Program in 1968 (PL 90–448). With so little support for structural protection against hurricanes, and an emerging reluctance to rely primarily on disaster relief funds, plus the absence of commercial flood insurance coverage, Congress responded with a program seeking to distribute costs among likely victims.

Flood insurance discussions began before the mid-1960s. Gilbert White's seminal analysis exposed the rising costs of flood damages even as flood-control expenditures spiraled upward. His work dramatically exposed the ineffectiveness of relying solely on structural protection and opened the door to the discussion of spreading the costs through insurance.[59] Congress deliberated a much broader disaster insurance program after the serious hurricane-induced floods in 1954 and 1955, and it even passed a flood-control act in 1956 (PL 84–1016). This represented a pared-down agenda from a more comprehensive but less politically palatable disaster insurance option. Nonetheless, it was the vigorous 1954–55 storms that inspired a search for insurance that would provide coverage beyond the normal hurricane belt and for other types of floods. Indeed, a 1956 tabulation of twentieth-century flood damage in the United States revealed that the most recent hurricanes had pushed the northeastern states ahead of the South—$1.1 billion in damage compared to $1.0 billion.[60] Of course this reflects as much the extent of development in floodplains and the value of property susceptible to damage as the frequency of flood events. Given this economic reality, it is no surprise that six of the seven locations where hearings took place were outside the South, and consequently witnesses from the northeastern states dominated the proceedings.[61] Yet their arguments, though perhaps not directly adopted from the script of southern politicians, bore a striking similarity. Connecticut's delegation made the case that while hurricanes had been rare in New England, recent events suggested they now shared that risk with Florida.[62] Representative Dodd of Connecticut, while taking an accommodating position toward his state's insurance industry, argued that the federal government was "obligated to promote the general welfare of its people" and that subsidizing insurance was one way to do that.[63] The general message was that the problem was national in scale and localities should not be expected to bear the full financial burden. The 1956 act reflected widespread geographical support, but the insurance program remained unfunded and not operational.

In the wake of Hurricane Betsy in 1965 and with images of its massive flood damages in the public eye, Congress held an emergency hearing to consider disaster relief and flood insurance. This action resumed the federal discussion of an issue dear to southern lawmakers. Hale Boggs of Louisiana reiterated the notion that disasters of the magnitude of a Betsy exceeded the capacity of existing laws. He claimed the storm caused over a billion dollars in damage in Louisiana alone. And looking toward the future he advocated revisiting the flood insurance program. He pointed out that while hurricane flood risks were limited in geographic extent, in order to build a sufficient risk pool a national flood insurance program was necessary. He added that a federal subsidy would be necessary. Ultimately, he argued that it might be more costly not to have an insurance program and to rely on disaster relief appropriations.[64] Contained in the disaster relief bill was funding for a study of the flood insurance issue.

The 1966 flood insurance report offered several key findings. It acknowledged the work by Gilbert White and others that had pointed out the rising costs of flood damage, despite rising expenditures on flood protection structures.[65] With ongoing intensive floodplain and coastal development, damage costs were likely to continue rising. These observations called into question a devotion to the structural approach embraced by earlier riparian flood-control programs. The report also noted the escalating costs of disaster relief and also two recent actions where an increased share of relief recovery loans was forgiven. The authors observed that property owners, knowing the government would be likely to offer relief, would be prone to gamble and build in flood hazard zones. By reducing the risk of financial loss, disaster relief was indirectly promoting development in hazardous locations. The Department of Housing and Urban Development report recommended a national system of flood insurance in order to pool the risks and minimize costs and distribute burden equitably. It also called for an accurate delineation of flood hazard zones and development of local land-use programs to reduce future construction in hazard zones.[66] Thus, the proposed program would include risk assessment, insurance coverage, and land-use provisions.

When Congress convened hearings on flood insurance in 1967, a central concern among lawmakers was how to equitably distribute the costs of flood recovery. Proponents of insurance noted that the Red Cross took care of the most needy, even helping rebuild and refurnish their houses. Big businesses, with operations in multiple locations, spread their risks internally and thereby could overcome flood losses in one impacted location. Small, local businesses faced the biggest threat. Too big to take advantage of Red Cross aid and too little to absorb losses within a multi-site enterprise, small business owners had few options. And an emerging tendency to forgive a portion of disaster relief loans was increasing the burden on taxpayers. Congressmen took this concern a step farther, pointing out that citizens were already paying the cost of recovery in two ways. Taxes funded the spiraling disaster relief load. And meanwhile, the Red Cross had spent over $17 million in the wake of the 1950s hurricane-induced floods in New England. Its funds came from taxpayers through donations to the not-for-profit relief organization.[67] Insurance would offer a way out of this situation. Louisiana Congressman Hale Boggs made the case that insurance would reduce the demands on the federal treasury for disaster relief payments.[68] This argument was supplemented by Florida congressman Claude Pepper, who reiterated the familiar theme that disasters were national in scope, while emphasizing the fairness of asking at-risk property owners to bear a share of the cost through insurance premiums.[69]

While hardly a piece of southern legislation, the 1968 National Flood Insurance Act arose from deliberations in the wake of hurricane strikes in the mid-1950s. Typically associated with the coastal South, cyclones that struck the urbanized Northeast in rapid succession elevated flood insurance to a national level. But it took the massive impact of Hurricane Betsy along the gulf coast in 1965 to propel the legislation through Congress. The flood-damaged South provided the image necessary to prompt action. Yet, while New Orleans, Miami, and Houston were sizable cities at the time, there was no region in the South that compared to Megalopolis in terms of population density and urban land-use intensity. In all likelihood, the South had more territory exposed to both hurricane and riparian flooding, but not the population or real property found in the Northeast or Midwest. Through 1956, the South had also tabulated more frequent flood impacts— when both river and tropical storms are considered. Thus the South stood to benefit much more than other regions.

Lasting Impacts

Viewing the American South from the perspective of the early twenty-first century reveals a complex flood protection apparatus. River flooding in the region with high susceptibility is no longer the threat it once was. This suggests some benefits from the federal investments in flood protection, supplemented by river modifications for power and navigation. Hurricane damage, however, has increased, largely due to increased coastal development. Meanwhile, flood insurance is available in most areas of the South, but the system is in financial trouble because of huge losses between 2004 and 2012 due to tropical cyclones.

River Floods. Before 1950, the American South had sustained some of the highest flood damage totals, most notably along the lower Mississippi River. Despite lower population density and less urban development than the Midwest or the Northeast, the region was notable for its exposure to episodic inundation. After midcentury this changed. Between 1955 and 1978, only Texas and Virginia were among the ten states with the highest flood damages. Pennsylvania, California, and New York dominated the tally. Between 1983 and 1999, only Louisiana and Texas were among the southern states that sustained the highest damage totals.[70] Notably, a potentially catastrophic flood on the lower Mississippi River in 1973 did not overwhelm the considerable levee fortifications that protected farms, refineries, and cities along the waterway. That said, the engineered diversion of water flooded over twelve hundred square miles of land and caused $37 million in damages.[71] Indeed, the 1973 flood provided the first test of the full outlet system developed after the 1927 high water event. Diversion of water through both the Bonnet Carré and Morganza spillways controlled the crest and spared floodplain developments downriver from serious and costly flooding. Including fortifications along the Mississippi, there are over fifty-nine hundred miles of federal levees protecting over 100 million acres of southern floodplains. Put another way, 42 percent of federal levees are in the South and they guard 87 percent of the area protected by these barriers.[72] Also since 1927, hydroelectric dams built along the Tennessee and its tributaries have reduced flood risk within its basin, as have dams along countless other rivers that drain the eastern Appalachian chain from the Potomac to the Alabama River. Similarly, reservoirs and levees along the numerous Texas rivers have restrained riparian flooding there.

In one study the "Southeast" had the highest regional average precipitation in the United States in the late twentieth century, but the area had among the lowest regional damages. Total damages for the larger "South," which included Louisiana and Texas, however were the highest.[73] Flood risk remains a reality across the South, but structures have reduced its threat along many waterways. Nonetheless, when high water exceeds the design limits of the dams and levees, catastrophic losses can result. The Mississippi River tested the Corps's structural protection again in 2011 and prompted only the second simultaneous opening of the two Louisiana diversion structures. The system held, but even the 2011 event did not equal the "superflood" projected by the Corps when it built the protective system. As the crest rose in 2011, evacuations from the floodways and along the river and the erection of temporary structures to fortify the existing levees revealed how society has refused to retreat from the floodplain or embrace nonstructural approaches while exposing the limits of structural protection. Emergency operations cost the state of Louisiana over $53 million and total public assistance topped $64 million, but these expenditures helped keep actual damages to a minimum.[74] Nonetheless, Corps historian Charles Camillo noted that the long lapse between the use of diversions and the very existence of structural protection lulled residents of the Atchafalaya Basin "into complacency."[75] This is exactly the social response forecast by Gilbert White half a century earlier. Although structures now protect much of the South's floodplains, few complementary land-use restrictions followed at the local level. Risk has not been eliminated, merely deferred, and this takes on greater prominence when climate change is factored in. Authorities project more intense precipitation events which will strain the existing local flood-control works. In the low-lying states of Florida and Louisiana, sea level rise will exacerbate riparian floods.[76]

Hurricanes. In 1992 Hurricane Andrew ripped through suburbs near Miami with winds exceeding 160 miles per hour. Contrary to common experiences, wind, rather than surge, proved to be the major destructive force as it destroyed or damaged over 125,000 houses. In the aftermath of the storm's passage, investigators discovered that poor construction techniques, outdated building codes, and ineffective inspections all contributed to the fact that a sizable portion of newly built homes were not designed to withstand hurricane-force winds. Some 25 percent of insured losses resulted from building code violations.[77] Despite 1960s advice from the Corps of Engineers to strengthen building codes, Florida had not demanded that contractors erect structures that would ensure residents basic protection. Florida, along with other hurricane-prone states, has since ramped up wind-resistant roofing requirements. In 1995 Florida adopted much more stringent building codes to minimize wind damage and further upgraded them in 2004. Vigorous 2004 and 2005 hurricane seasons tested the new codes, and researchers found measurable differences in wind damage sustained by homes built under newer codes and the older ones. Following the Florida lead, Louisiana required an upgrade of building codes across the state after a pair of devastating hurricanes in 2005, although the state was slow to staff the programs and begin enforcement. Additionally, an industry trade journal reports that the neighboring states of Alabama and Mississippi failed to follow suit.[78] Establishing codes and enforcing them have contributed to only modest and geographically uneven adjustments along the gulf coast.

Likewise land-use restrictions have suffered in hurricane-prone states. After the horrific devastation to the Mississippi shore caused by Hurricane Camille in 1969, local governments gradually dismantled poststorm efforts to restrict land uses in exposed locations. By the 1990s, looking for quick revenue from new gambling casinos, the state actually required construction over the water and thereby in the most dangerous sites. Similarly, sections of New Orleans inundated by Hurricane Betsy in 1965 became the zones of most active residential and commercial development in subsequent years. The obvious lack of local development restrictions in flood-susceptible locations allowed some of the most devastating consequences when Hurricane Katrina made landfall in 2005.[79] An extensive review of hurricane damages between 1925 and 1995 concluded that social changes, not environmental differences, were the prime cause of increased hurricane damages. Inflation, coastal population increases, and the greater concentration of wealth in hurricane-susceptible areas constitute the key factors leading to spiraling losses.[80] This conclusion echoes the absence of effective land-use restrictions in locations exposed to tropical cyclone wind and surge.

Hurricanes Rita (2005) and Ike (2008) delivered substantial storm surge and wave damages to Louisiana and Texas. Studies after these storms again revealed inadequate construction, although elevation rather than roofing practices was the key issue. Federal Emergency Management Agency (FEMA) recommendations following these events called for improvements in the design of coastal structures to account for high water and also to protect against scour and erosion. The federal agency also encouraged Texas and Louisiana officials to steer development inland and to prohibit reconstruction of damaged properties.[81] These recommendations point toward a lingering resistance on the part of local governments to call for safety over economic development. Redevelopment of beachfront areas from Pensacola to Galveston since 2004 demonstrates an unwillingness to retreat from storm-susceptible locations. Impending sea level rise and more intense storms produced by climate change will aggravate the situation.[82]

Flood Insurance. The National Flood Insurance Act of 1968 sought to prompt adjustments in how communities allowed development in the most flood-prone areas, while offering federally underwritten insurance. Yet the program was very slow to reach most potential victims due to the absence of the essential floodplain maps. To address this, the National Flood Insurance Program spent $1 billion over two decades mapping the "100-year floodplains," which was the first step toward enabling local floodplain management. Yet flood insurance subscribership remained dismally low. In order to enlarge the pool of insured property owners, Congress ratcheted up pressure on homeowners after massive eastern seaboard flooding caused by Hurricane Agnes in 1972. It mandated that borrowers obtaining federally regulated loans for properties in special flood hazard zones had to purchase flood insurance. This accelerated both the number of communities participating and the number of policies written. By 1987 the program had achieved a self-supporting financial status and participation continued to grow. In 1990, 18,200 communities were enrolled in the program, and by 2012 the number rose to 22,000. Nonetheless, large numbers of claims that accompanied vigorous hurricane seasons regularly produced deficits in the fund.[83]

As flood insurance became more commonplace, rapid growth of "sunbelt" cities during the years placed more residences in areas of possible inundation. When Hurricane Hugo slammed ashore near Charleston, South Carolina, in 1989, wind, wave, and surge in Charleston, plus inland flooding across the Carolina Piedmont, produced $6.4 billion in losses in South Carolina alone. Initial estimates of insured losses were less than half of the total $2.9 billion in damages caused by wind and water.[84] Poststorm analyses revealed that structures with the recommended flood proofing of National Flood Insurance Protection (NFIP) fared better than structures without protective designs, but of the nearly $3 billion in residential losses, the federal flood insurance program covered only about $365 million. The lack of hurricane-proof building standards in South Carolina during the years leading up to Hugo allowed the construction of many unsafe structures.[85] Some of the worst damage was to beachfront areas with recent development, and this situation exposed shortcomings in the federal flood insurance program. Staff at FEMA noted in particular that inadequate erosion-resistant building codes for coastal areas reduced the effectiveness of the NFIP.[86] Thus more than twenty years after the federal program began, many deficiencies remained and they were amplified in the hurricane-prone southern coasts. When hurricanes Dennis and Floyd struck North Carolina's coast in 1999, they left over $6 billion in damages, and, emphasizing the program's inadequacies, most properties had no flood insurance.[87] Coastal development relentlessly occupied barrier islands, and owners failed to purchase protection.

This situation reoccurred with regularity as storms battered the gulf coast in later years. Hurricane Ivan lashed ashore near Pensacola and Mobile in 2004 and caused extensive damage to beachfront developments. Serious erosion toppled many beachfront properties, highlighting the ongoing encroachment along the shore.[88] The powerful hurricanes Charley, Frances, and Jeanne battered Florida that year and again exposed the increased risk that accompanied coastal development. By the time hurricanes Katrina and Rita made landfall in 2005, the national flood insurance program was strained. The unprecedented number of storms that year and the extraordinary expenses of Katrina and Rita plunged the program into a deficit situation. Hurricane Wilma struck Florida late in the 2005 season and added to the burden faced by the federal program. With NFIP payments totaling nearly $16 billion for Katrina and Rita alone, there were inadequate reserves on hand and the program had to borrow from the treasury. As a region, the gulf coast states had seen extraordinary NFIP losses between 1978 and 2008 and far exceeded other regions in the country in total payments under the program.[89] In the metropolitan Northeast, only the two rare hurricane strikes in 2011 and 2012 rank among the most costly NFIP payouts.[90] Thus impacts of tropical cyclones had drained the national program's reserves as the southern states saw the funds flow into restoration efforts. Subsequent reviews of the NFIP concluded that rates charged to policy holders did not accurately reflect risk, and analysts called for substantial revisions to FEMA's out-of-date rate-setting procedures to avoid a repeat of that situation.[91] Nonetheless, Katrina largely forced a rethinking of the flood insurance program and other disaster relief programs. At the center of the argument is whether or not local costs should be borne by federal programs that do not equally benefit all regions.[92] As hurricanes have come to dominate the NFIP payments, the Southeast will continue to receive a disproportionate share.

Conclusions

Southern states have long advocated the use of federal funds to underwrite public works and for controlling water. Road building and navigation improvements were the primary infrastructures sought in the nineteenth century. By the twentieth century, southern leaders pushed for flood protection and eventually they won allies from other regions, usually when their states also suffered disastrous floods. The 1927 Mississippi River flood set the standard by which other floods were measured, but heavy floods in the Midwest and Northeast in 1936 and 1937 eventually galvanized broad support for a federally funded structural flood protection program. This adjustment redirected the costs to a national scale and enabled the highly flood-prone South to benefit disproportionately.

While southern urban development along its coasts lagged behind that of the Northeast, regular hurricane strikes inspired little national compassion. Even the horrible storms in Galveston and Miami failed to spark discussions about hurricane protection, and structural protection remained largely local before World War II. New Orleans and Galveston area leaders were able to secure limited federal assistance for hurricane protection structures by midcentury. A series of hurricanes that caused massive damages in New England and the urbanized Northeast prompted a major reconsideration of hurricane protection and disaster insurance. Congress mandated a series of hurricane studies that advocated against structural protection, with two exceptions—New Orleans and Galveston. Chief among the recommendations for reducing damages were improved building codes, zoning regulations, and emergency preparedness.

When Congress considered and ultimately passed a national flood insurance program, a series of hurricanes during the 1950s and finally Betsy in 1965 provided compelling evidence that the country needed some form of protection other than disaster relief. The southern states figured prominently in making the case for flood insurance, although as with riparian flood control, floods in the Northeast galvanized a broad base of support. What had languished as a regional problem gained national impetus as storms raked Megalopolis.

Maps that depict the areas enclosed by levees and the investments in hurricane protection clearly delimit disproportionate flood protection expenditures in the American South. Coping with excess water remains a critical concern in the South, and more intense storms along with rising sea level in the future may strain existing structural systems with their designs based on historical floods and not on climate-change predictions.

4

Excess and Illness

Introduction

Historians for decades have debated the characteristics that make the American South distinctive: its climate and diseases figure prominently among other social and demographic traits.[1] Climate, while central to these deliberations, is often discussed selectively, with an emphasis only on temperature and how it provides a suitable setting for the persistence of tropical diseases. Yet the South's abundant precipitation also contributes to its disease-rich ecology. Copious precipitation characterizes much of the region and it has produced a high density of streams and expansive wetlands. Settlement along waterways has concentrated population on or near floodplains where topography allows water to accumulate in sloughs, swales, ponds, and other depressions. These locations harbor the highest risk for either waterborne disease or mosquito-borne maladies. Beginning in the colonial era, accelerating in the nineteenth century, and climaxing in the twentieth century, southern efforts to control disease risk were largely directed toward managing water. Miasmatic theory drove the compulsion to eliminate standing water before the acceptance of the germ theory of disease. With identification of mosquitoes as carriers of bacteria for both yellow fever and malaria, a principal objective of insect control was draining standing water and thereby destroying prime habitat. Combating cholera, typhus, and other waterborne disease in cities and in the countryside relied on protecting water's purity.[2]

Conevery Bolton Valencius argues persuasively that for nineteenth-century settlers on the Missouri frontier, water defined a place. These pioneers, and their counterparts downriver, considered waters as beneficial when used for drinking and transportation. But waters could also pose a threat through floods or miasmatic illness. At a very fundamental level, wet places were risky.[3] Managing risk meant managing water, and this chapter considers the ongoing efforts in the South to minimize environmental risks by controlling water. By no means is water the region's only source of hazards, nor did the South face water-related risks on its own. Yet, by the nineteenth century, yellow fever and malaria, plus such waterborne diseases as typhoid, proved doggedly persistent in the southern states. A cooler climate enabled the northeastern and midwestern states to shake the yellow fever and malaria threat well before the South. Aridity in the western states alleviated the risk of mosquito-borne maladies there. Following the Civil War, southern cities figured prominently in the discussion about how best to control yellow fever while rural areas became the target for malaria-eradication programs. The 1878 yellow fever epidemic drove discussions of a national health policy, which strengthened the U.S. Public Health Service.[4] It subsequently guided much of the battle against malaria and also sanitation improvements to reduce typhoid and dysentery.

Regional politics more so than risk control frequently drove nineteenth-century debates. A key issue was the geographic nature of the problem. Proper sanitation was beyond the financial grasp of most southern cities, and urban filth contributed to miasmatic conditions. Quarantine, a fundamentally geographic approach to arresting disease spread, was the solution favored by some inland southern cities, but this was disparaged by the commercial interests in leading ports. Ultimately, both a shift in medical understanding of yellow fever and malaria etiology and a willingness to accept federal financial aid for sanitation and mosquito control prompted a shift in the southern position. Political alliances, forged in the wake of extreme epidemics, provided public support for policies to address these concerns that would benefit the American South.

Water and Yellow Fever

Colonists along the southern Atlantic seaboard realized in the seventeenth century that safe water was essential to their precarious settlements. Geographer Carville Earle makes a powerful case that after struggling with high mortality due to the waterborne disease of typhoid, Jamestown's leaders demanded seasonal shifts to inland sites where safe spring water was available. As a second wave of leaders neglected this acquired wisdom, they saw mortality rise dramatically. Only after a second adoption of scattered inland settlements was the colony able to succeed.[5] In South Carolina, colonists introduced malaria to the region and outbreaks followed low-country settlement. Residents soon came to associate the swamps with mosquitoes and death. The belief that coastal wetlands were insalubrious was prominent in the nineteenth-century European medical community and applied particularly well to the colonial experiences on the margins of the estuaries and swamps near the Atlantic and Gulf seaboards. Two centuries of coastal settlement and agricultural development did little to eliminate the waterlogged, miasmatic environs around ports and near plantations and farms.[6]

There were fundamental shifts in medical understanding of the etiology of water-related diseases during the nineteenth century and also in society's approach to managing them. Margaret Humphries argues that the rise of the U.S. Public Health Service was "strongly dependent on defending the nation against yellow fever" during the last quarter of the nineteenth century. At that time, the disease ravaged southern cities more than any other region. Thus, a largely southern affliction motivated the expansion of a federal program to protect the public from a horrible killer.[7] The disease's tight connection with the South had not always been the case. During the colonial period, yellow fever tormented urban residents in both the North and the South. In particular, it made deadly but erratic appearances in ports that traded with the Caribbean. By the early nineteenth century, epidemics erupted mainly in seaboard cities along the southern Atlantic and gulf coasts.[8] Medical opinion about the cause and control of yellow fever was far from a consensus, and public health practices reflected the prevailing medical view in a given locality and also how those practices might impact the local economy.

New Orleans experienced frequent outbreaks, and medical authorities there staunchly defended the miasmatic theory as the cause for its high incidence. Surrounded by expansive swamps and marshes, subject to regular inundation despite its growing levee system, built on nearly flat terrain that allowed sewage and refuse to collect in the streets, with large open canals with virtually no current that accumulated urban filth, and active urban growth that disturbed ground, the city offered exceptionally conducive conditions for both the presumed causes and the propagation of the mosquitoes that carried the killer. Following the particularly severe 1853 epidemic, which killed approximately eight thousand people, the local Sanitary Commission concluded that "no *epidemic* has occurred that has not been preceded and accompanied by a great disturbance of the original soil of the country (in digging and clearing out canals, basins, &c.)."[9] Local physician Edward Barton, principal author of an expansive report on the outbreak, mapped the numerous local "nuisances" that contributed to yellow fever (fig. 4.1). These nuisance sites included disturbed ground, cemeteries, tenements, slaughterhouses, empty lots, and undrained swamps or places of filth and moisture where mosquitoes could breed. He argued that no location required more sanitary reform than New Orleans. Barton bluntly proclaimed "New Orleans is one of the dirtiest . . . and is consequently the sickliest city in the Union."[10] Despite the prevalence of nuisances throughout the city, the Sanitary Commission report also revealed a degree of optimism by asserting that the causes of the city's insalubrity were "ascribable to local conditions which are mainly removable."[11] In the eyes of local authorities, installation of economically related infrastructure such as canals and railroads disturbed the floodplain soils, as did urban expansion into the surrounding wetland, and these activities enhanced the disease-rich environment. They remained hopeful, however, that remedial steps could control these undesirable conditions. Temporary alleviation of nuisances followed the Union army's occupation of the city during the Civil War, but New Orleans was unable to sustain sanitary improvements following the conflict and regular yellow fever outbreaks resumed between 1867 and 1876.[12]

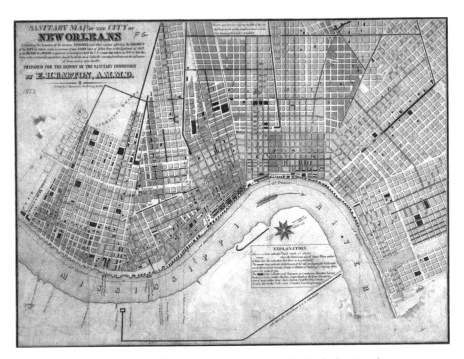

FIG. 4.1. Sanitation Map of New Orleans, 1854. Dark blocks indicate nuisance conditions associated with the environmental generation of yellow fever. From Edward Barton, "Report on the Sanitary Condition of New Orleans, in City Council of New Orleans," in *Report of the Sanitary Commission of New Orleans on the Yellow Fever Epidemic of 1853* (New Orleans: Picayune, 1954), see 397. Courtesy of the Collections of the Louisiana State Museum.

Elsewhere around the South by midcentury, physicians were making arguments that the disease did not arise *de nova,* but could be transported from one location to another. Ohio physician Daniel Drake noted that transmission was a likely cause of the frequent outbreaks in New Orleans.[13] Medical authorities based their conclusions on the absence of the disease inland from the coast during years when major ports like New Orleans had no outbreaks. The diffusion of the particularly deadly epidemic of 1853 up the Mississippi River from New Orleans reinforced the transmission theory. With broad-based acceptance of transmission as the agent for the disease's spread, inland cities called for quarantines to impede introduction of the disease into ports and thereby eliminate its spread to interior locations. But cities like New Orleans chaffed at inland cities' pleas, fearing quarantines would inhibit commerce. A distinct geography of medical theory was emerging that reflected political and commercial aims as much as public health knowledge.[14]

By the 1870s germ theory was taking hold in the medical community and provided a new explanation for how individuals contracted the disease. Yet the mechanism for its dispersal remained undetermined and left the matter of control equally uncertain. New Orleans officials remained intent on improving drainage and sewage, albeit their ineffective projects were designed primarily to restore confidence in the city's commercial capabilities.[15] Likewise across the South, public health officials believed that sanitation could contribute to reducing disease outbreaks but they found little financial support from legislatures.[16] The New Orleans public health community eventually accepted that yellow fever was a pathogen transported through the air and that fumigation of infected ships would enable officials to isolate and purify a potential threat on specific ships, while not blockading all trade.

The massive outbreak in the lower Mississippi valley in 1878 proved transformative in terms of public health and mosquito-borne disease in the South. Despite efforts to quarantine the fever, the epidemic swiftly spread from New Orleans, up the Mississippi River, into Mississippi, Tennessee, and Kentucky. By the time fall frosts curtailed mosquito activity, medical authorities had witnessed one of the worst medical calamities in the country's history. They estimated 120,000 cases and as many as twenty thousand fatalities that year throughout the Mississippi River basin. Memphis officials reported that of the twenty thousand who did not flee the city, an astounding seventeen thousand contracted the disease, and five thousand died. In New Orleans, another four thousand succumbed to the awful affliction.[17] Quarantines arrested commerce more than the spread of the disease and the emerging southern rail lines suffered tremendous losses. Likewise New Orleans and Memphis, along with other smaller cities, endured massive economic disruptions.

Following the 1878 epidemic, Memphis sought a sanitary solution and embarked on a major reworking of its municipal infrastructure. It garnered state funding for its public works initiative. With much acclaim, the city, under the supervision of Colonel George Waring, installed a drainage, sewerage, and water system to eliminate the filth and standing water that were associated with yellow fever generation. Despite inadequacies and delays, the system perhaps did more to rehabilitate the image of Memphis as a safe setting for commerce than to improve its sanitary condition. And basing its actions on the notion that filth generated the disease, it did not eliminate mosquito habitat.[18] Other southern cities also attacked poor sanitary conditions, but most lagged behind Memphis. Baltimore, on the fringes of the yellow fever zone, had a reputation for inadequate sewage and drainage until the twentieth century.[19] Atlanta made improvements following the 1878 epidemic, but still had large numbers of urban blacks living in alleys with no sewage and poor drainage at the turn of the century.[20] And leaders in Houston in 1889 acknowledged inadequate drainage and sewerage service when they called for infrastructure improvement to augment urban growth.[21]

At the epicenter of the yellow fever debate, New Orleans citizens sought to improve sanitary conditions, but with modest success. A citizen's committee sought to flush the street gutters using the city's municipal water system. With a limited number of hydrants and a water system that served only a portion of the city, this initiative was wholly inadequate. Financial challenges and the absence of public support thwarted attempts to install a municipal sewerage system. Initiatives to deal with garbage likewise foundered, and urban sanitation remained a prime issue in public health.[22] Although outbreaks were not as common in the last two decades of the century, effective drainage and efficient sewage removal were far from adequate by 1900.

In the eyes of some authorities, quarantines offered a more manageable approach than sanitation, one that required much less public investment in infrastructure. An additional advantage was that this approach received federal backing. Following the 1878 outbreak, debates over a national health board arose and revealed deeply entrenched regional interests. Memphis authorities saw federal intervention as a way to protect its citizens from the dreaded downriver source of disease, but Louisiana officials feared interference by a national organization.[23] Congressmen battled over the formation of a federal health organization. A National Board of Health finally emerged from the congressional wrangling in 1879, and it played a role in strengthening quarantines. Public attitudes toward the board took on an obvious geographic pattern—inland communities favored federal quarantines, while coastal cities opposed a nationally mandated program. Eventually, alliances among major ports in both southern and northern states led to the board's demise,[24] although the Marine Hospital Service maintained a series of quarantine hospitals to sequester infected crew members from ships headed to U.S. ports. These stations provided a sense of security since the few outbreaks between 1885 and the turn of the century were traced to vessels that entered ports illegally. Also, Louisiana developed its own quarantine and fumigation program that would restrict only ships that its officials deemed a threat. Nonetheless, the federal quarantine system produced great anxieties among southern business leaders when public health authorities held ships during several outbreaks during the 1880s.[25]

Yellow fever persisted in the South's coastal cities set amidst wetlands in the late nineteenth century, but changes to this situation came around the turn of the century and fundamentally altered disease prevention practices. Discovery of the mosquito's role in yellow fever and malaria and also the implementation of effective insect-control measures in Havana and along the Panama Canal construction zone opened new perspectives on eliminating these two persistent infirmities. To control this largely urban disease, preventive techniques focused on controlling the *Aedes aegypti* mosquito in the numerous small impoundments where mosquitoes could breed within cities. In Havana in 1898, U.S. military authorities attacked urban breeding grounds such as cisterns, puddles and roof gutters, and pools of water on the urban fringes. Regular inspection and relentless draining of potential breeding sites, supplemented with a quarantine, lifted the threat of yellow fever in Cuba.[26] Meanwhile, mosquito control in Panama used drainage, oiling, larvicides, and killing adult mosquitoes— and in the case of malaria, screening worker housing and treating workers with quinine to combat threat. The success of mosquito control indicated that coordinated attacks could suppress vector populations and prevent epidemic outbreaks even in the most susceptible and waterlogged locations.

In the context of the gulf coast, the U.S. Public Health Service (USPHS) brought similar methods to south Texas and Louisiana. Public Health Service personnel received credit for restraining a yellow fever outbreak in Laredo, Texas, in 1903 by using mosquito-control techniques.[27] In 1905 they arrived in New Orleans to assist an underfunded state battle with yellow fever. Immediately following the identification of the outbreak, New Orleans authorities required residents to empty all water receptacles, to screen cisterns, and to place oil on the contents of privies. When this did not break the disease's spread, local officials called on the Public Health Service for assistance. The USPHS launched an even more aggressive attack on mosquitoes and the water where they bred. They launched a systematic campaign to prevent breeding in cisterns and standing water in the streets and house gutters, to fumigate and screen homes, and to isolate infected patients.[28] Well before the first frosts that fall, the epidemic had been contained and the outcome offered compelling proof of the role of mosquitoes in yellow fever spread and the value of sanitation in controlling an epidemic. It also added weight to the authority of the USPHS. To augment the mosquito-control program, Congress authorized the Public Health Service to establish several quarantine stations in the South and "called for federal hegemony over southern quarantine." As part of this act, the USPHS acquired Louisiana's quarantine station and in doing so usurped the state's quarantine authority.[29] With these combined tools, public health bodies did not have to fight any more major yellow fever outbreaks in the South, and state boards of health turned to other diseases—malaria among them.

Controlling yellow fever gradually advanced federal influence into the South and instituted a national culture of public health, albeit one still shaped by racism and poverty in the South. The growing influence of the U.S. Public Health Service provided access to federal dollars to supplement the underfunded state programs in the South and to disseminate a more consistent medical approach to environmentally based diseases. As mosquitoes spread a largely urban disease, mosquito control was highly focused on small breeding areas such as puddles, gutters, containers, and cisterns. Programs to drain these small receptacles did not lead to major hydrological transformations of cities and towns. Eventually, Progressive Era sanitation programs improved urban drainage and contributed more to the reduction of waterborne diseases such as typhoid and dysentery than to a reworking of the region's urban hydrology.

Watery Environs and Malaria

Malaria, in contrast to yellow fever, did not inspire urban terror and massive evacuations. It arrived to the American South with Europeans colonists and became a chronic and debilitating affliction largely of rural dwellers. In the mid-nineteenth century, physician Daniel Drake characterized it as "the great cause of mortality" in the lower Mississippi River valley.[30] In his analysis of conditions that give rise to "autumnal fever," Drake noted the disease could occur outside the South but it was more prevalent in warmer latitudes, and he also pointed out other conditions that favored its occurrence such as soils rich in decaying organic matter, agricultural settlement and its attendant clearing of forests, warm temperatures, and abundant surface water. Indeed, he concluded that "water is a necessary element, in all the hypotheses which have been framed to account for autumnal fever."[31] Its nineteenth-century association with water was well accepted. By the 1860s, malaria had retreated from most of the northern states following extensive hydrological alterations in the form of clearing, drainage, and cultivation; and the disease acquired a southern geography tied to wet and swampy lands. In the ensuing years, drainage of areas with excess water and decaying vegetation became a central strategy for eliminating the miasmas considered responsible for the disease.[32]

In the early twentieth century medical science identified the mosquito as the vector for malaria, and the U.S. Public Health Service responded to a spike in malaria cases in 1913 with a major effort to gauge its persistence, reporting that the disease was still endemic across the entire southeastern section of the country and that its studies made clear the disease's relationship to water.[33] Acknowledging many weaknesses in its survey methods, agency personnel attempted to collect postcards each month from physicians reporting on cases under their supervision. With frustratingly meager, modest response rates, the USPHS published a series of reports that revealed seasonal and geographic patterns. A cartographic depiction of its national distribution clearly indicates it as a southern disease (fig. 4.2).[34]

A consistent theme in the state-level reports was that the disease peaked in the late summer. This season is typically both the warmest and rainiest, and the reports thus tied the disease to regional climatic conditions. Maps in the reports portrayed very distinct concentrations within states. In the Carolinas, for example, the western mountains had very low rates of incidence. And, as might be expected, the coastal plains, with lower topographic relief, numerous rivers, and wetlands, reported higher rates. But there was great variation even in the coastal regions. South Carolina's central river basins and North Carolina's northeastern counties stood out as having more malaria.[35] The U.S. surgeon general observed in 1919 that the rate in North Carolina was lower than it had been in the 1880s. He

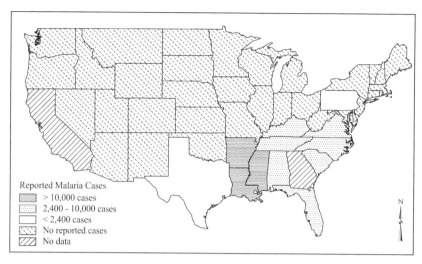

FIG. 4.2. Reported cases of malaria, 1915. Most states did not even report on malaria (N.R.), but the U.S. Public Health Service tabulated sizable concentrations across the South. After R. H. Van Ezdof, "Malaria in the United States: Its Prevalence and Geographic Distribution," *Public Health Reports* 30, no. 22 (1915): 1603–24. Cartography by Mary Lee Eggart.

attributed this to the rise in cotton prices that brought greater prosperity, better drainage of agricultural lands, and more purchases of quinine.[36]

The Public Health Service declared in 1924, "Malaria is an exotic in the United States . . . and does not flourish . . . except under abnormal drainage and subnormal living conditions."[37] After nearly two decades of close observation, the USPHS reported a decline in malaria in the South in 1929, but observed high concentrations persisted along the major rivers.[38] In the midst of the Great Depression follow-up studies indicated a retreat but pointed out malaria remained prevalent along the Mississippi River and in Florida.[39] A federal review of river basins also indicated the prevalence of malaria along rivers across the South.[40] Thus specialists consistently identified a linkage of the disease to water bodies where mosquitoes bred, and drainage remained a central *Anopheles*-control strategy—albeit in distinction from the prior century, having as it did the objective of destroying habitat rather than eliminating miasmas. Authorities also recognized substandard living conditions and poverty as contributing factors. Despite identification of the casual factors, efforts to control malaria were beyond the resources of poorly funded state public health programs; the South relied on federal programs and, to a lesser extent, on private businesses to control the environments that sustained the disease.[41]

The relationship between cultivation and malaria incidence is very important but underappreciated. Geographers have debated the environmental consequences of cotton agriculture for years without considering the relationship of erosion and sedimentation to malaria ecology.[42] While historians have discussed the relationship of poverty to incidence and various aspects of malaria's ecology, they have not examined the role of soil movement from uplands to lowlands and the creation of wetlands that could host malaria mosquitos.[43] The surgeon general's observations in 1919 suggest prosperity reduced the incidence, and this has been a standard argument in historical scholarship. It should also be noted however, that the surgeon general declared that "I count drainage, especially tile drainage, the key to the rural malaria problem."[44] And in his conceptualization, prosperity enabled farmers to invest in effective drainage. Tile drainage was very common in the Midwest, but southern planters, dealing with different soil conditions, never installed the massive mileage of underground tiles that midwestern corn farmers did.[45]

Erosion and conspicuous sediment damage were most prominent in the southern Piedmont. While accounts of stream sedimentation date back to the early nineteenth century, the problem was becoming more pronounced by the later part of the century and drew national attention by the early twentieth century.[46] Soil conservation champion Hugh Hammond Bennett estimated that 50 percent of the southern Piedmont's formerly cultivated alluvial area had been covered by erosional debris by 1931. As a result, it had been rendered useless for row crops and reclassified as meadow.[47] An analysis of sediments by USDA soil scientists in Mississippi indicates a peak of erosion before World War I, with improvements in soil management by the 1920s that greatly reduced sedimentation.[48] The movement of sediment from uplands to lowlands would have enlarged mosquito habitat.

Sedimentation transformed what had been prime agricultural lands in Piedmont Georgia, an inadvertent conversion to swamp. Following intensive antebellum cultivation, the Alcovy River bottomlands experienced an expansion of swamps by the end of the Civil War. During the early twentieth century sedimentation produced even more expansive wetlands. Farmers responded and tried to reclaim these newly formed swamps between 1917 and 1935 by forming drainage districts and dredging ditches. By the 1930s, what had gradually progressed from tillable land to moist pasture had become marsh or swamp.[49]

Geographer Stanley Trimble reports on regional variation in "erosive land use" in the Southeast, but he documents a marked increase in land clearing and cotton cultivation in a belt traversing the Piedmont in north-east Georgia and western South Carolina. This resulted from the expansion of cultivation into formerly forested slopes. Increased erosion, floods, and downstream sedimentation expanded the region's wetlands.[50] Thus on consideration of the expansion of cotton into erosion-susceptible areas, it appears that the downstream consequences produced mosquito habitat.

Ditching and other drainage practices in North Carolina also contributed to erosion by lowering the water table and enabling greater movement of sediment through the artificial channels. Ultimately these sediments collected downstream in reservoirs, on floodplains, or in wetlands adjacent to waterways. Even drainage improvements could contribute to an expanding mosquito habitat.[51]

As noted by the surgeon general, planters vigorously increased cotton acreage in the late nineteenth century. This expansion contributed to increased erosion and the related downstream sedimentation, particularly with the movement of cultivation into the Piedmont between 1870 and 1910. Furthermore, the 1912 spike in malaria is likely a partial consequence of agricultural success.[52]

When launching its inquiry into increased malaria across the South, the USPHS looked closely at Alabama and linked increased incidence to heavy precipitation. Its report states that average monthly precipitation was well above average in 1912, when there was also a spike in malaria cases. The Public Health Service commented as well, "It was also a year when rivers and streams were high, overflowing many lands during the early spring so that upon receding of the waters many mosquito breeding places were probably created."[53] Mortality was highest in a pair of counties in the Tennessee River valley in the north and in the central "black belt" region, which is traversed by several rivers. While offering no explicit guidance on how to cope with extreme precipitation, the report emphasizes the linkage between moisture and mosquitoes. In a series of comparable reports prepared in the 1910s, the USPHS tabulated malaria incidence across the South. Comparing malaria incidence and U.S. Weather Service historical rainfall, there seems to be no clear relationship between precipitation and malaria. Northern Alabama was the USPHS's prime example (table 4.1). Eastern Arkansas had a high incidence without major rainfall, but did see malaria drop during the following dry summer. However, several locations experienced dry weather and high malaria—North Carolina in 1915 and Tennessee in 1916. North Carolina had ideal wet conditions in 1916, but low incidence. Such confusing relationships obscured any specific conditions leading to epidemics, although controlling water remained a cornerstone of public- and private-control programs. Furthermore the involvement of the USPHS in these malaria studies did much to expose the extent of this rural affliction and directed federal personnel into the field to help eradicate a disease the South could not conquer on its own.[54]

Public Health Service assistance went beyond inventorying the prevalence and distribution of the disease as the agency participated in mosquito-control efforts in the South. Working with Arkansas officials and

TABLE 4.1 Precipitation and Malaria

Location	Year	Precipitation	Malaria
Northern Alabama	1912	Wet year with flooding	High incidence
Eastern Arkansas	1915	Modest spring and summer rain	High incidence
	1916	Dry spring and summer	Lower incidence
Northwestern Florida	1915	Dry winter and near average summer	High incidence in September
	1916	Dry winter, wet summer	Lower incidence
Northeastern Louisiana	1915	Wet winter, near average for rest of year	Steady malaria
	1916	Very wet summer	Steady malaria
Central South Carolina	1915	Dry winter, near average summer	Modest malaria
Northeastern North Carolina	1915	Dry summer	September spike in incidence
	1916	Dry winter, very wet summer	Low incidence
Western Tennessee	1915	Dry spring, near average summer	Low incidence
	1916	Low spring, very dry summer	High incidence
Eastern Texas	1915	Near average	High incidence
	1916	Wet winter, dry summer	Lower incidence (partial record)

Sources: USPHS state reports on malaria, 1914–16; see n. 54 and NOAA Precipitation Site, [http://www7.ncdc.noaa.gov/CDO/CDODivisionalSelect.jsp#].

private-sector physicians, the USPHS initiated a mosquito-control effort in the lumber mill company town of Crossett. It was a small community with about two thousand residents, an abundance of industrial ponds and borrow pits that could serve as breeding sites, plus open storm drains and an incomplete sewerage system—sewage for the white neighborhood and privies for the African American area. The principal control efforts focused on clearing ditches so that they would not hold water, "training" streams to reduce still water, installing ditches to drain impoundments and borrow pits, and removing vegetation from fish ponds to eliminate ideal breeding conditions. USPHS officials also instituted a maintenance program to sustain the drainage improvements. Oiling water bodies and local educational programs completed the control measures. Between 1915 and 1916, the incidence of malaria cases reported by physicians dropped from 2,500 to 741, and the USPHS concluded that its program contributed to this marked decline.[55]

Since malaria was seen as a rural disease, the USPHS sought to conduct a comparative study alongside the Crossett project. It approached the mosquito issue differently in a nearby rural settlement. About four hundred people lived on several plantations along the banks of Lake Chicot in southern Arkansas. Situated on the Mississippi River floodplain, this area had a low-lying topography and ample sites for standing water and mosquito breeding habitat. Residential housing varied greatly from solid homes with screens for plantation owners and white managers to dilapidated shacks for black tenants. Since there were much greater efficiencies with drainage in urban areas, the primary approach for controlling mosquitoes in rural areas was to prevent human exposure by installing screens and also "immunizing" residents with quinine. The USPHS reported that malaria incidence declined in areas where these control measures were put in place compared to the surrounding countryside.[56]

There were also efforts by corporate managers to arrest malaria, which they saw as a drain on the productivity of their laborers. Railroads and timber companies across the South were modifying local hydrology and had workers doing their jobs in prime mosquito habitat. Traversing wetland tracts, railroad employees became targets for the *Anopheles* as they labored during the day and as they slept in rolling dormitories. Lumber mill towns, such as Crossett, Arkansas, often had mill ponds and poor drainage, and laborers in the forest faced insects under the shade of pine and cypress trees. Companies were most concerned with loss of productivity and justified investments in mosquito control in achieving greater efficiencies, and the U.S. Public Health Service supported this view. R. C. Derivaux, who authored the report on drainage in Crossett, Arkansas, argued that "railroad construction operations have long been notorious for their incidental contributions to malaria hazards by creating conditions favoring the development of Anopheles mosquitoes." He pointed out that borrow pits, poorly cut ditches, and ineffective drainage systems along right-of-ways created habitat, and that remedial drainage could solve that problem. He emphasized the serious loss of productivity when malaria prevailed and touted successful mosquito-control campaigns in both Italy and the United States that had saved companies substantial sums by improving worker health and thereby improving their productivity.[57]

In addition to the USPHS demonstration project in Crossett, the St. Louis Southwestern Railway Line malaria-control effort is the prime example of a corporate antimosquito mobilization. Citing the influence of USPHS projects, the company's sanitary engineer argued "by far the greatest cost of malaria to a railroad is from the large number of men who continue to work while infected, sometimes for years, and who return but feeble effort for their salary and wages."[58] In a less pragmatic and more benevolent assertion, he reported that the disease not only impacted employees and their families but also handicapped communities and industries along rail lines and rendered farmland unprofitable. While the company expressed concern for communities along its route, its bottom line suffered if industry and agriculture were not profitable.[59] Acting on this concept, the company's founder created a trust fund to underwrite mosquito-control actions. Focusing initially on the timber mill towns of Tyler and Lufkin, Texas, along its route, the company launched drainage and oiling operations in 1917. In 1918 and 1919 drainage efforts expanded to other towns where the railroad company convinced communities to share in the cost of local drainage efforts. The program augmented the attack on *Anopheles* habitat with public education, screening, and quinine distribution. Throughout the multiyear program, the USPHS assisted with tracking malaria incidence. The company proudly touted bringing upward of 70 percent of its employees under "mosquito control" by 1920, and since much of its efforts was in towns, nonemployee residents also benefited. As a measure of its success, the report claimed a 58 percent reduction in malaria cases handled in its hospitals in the years following the mosquito-control program.[60] In an indirect and supportive way the USPHS penetrated the southern landscape with drainage works as the private sector and local communities collaborated on mosquito-control efforts.

Due to a combination of factors, malaria declined across the South during the 1910s and 1920s, and during that time, restoration of traditional erosion-control methods produced the indirect effect of decreasing sedimentation, which reversed the growth of mosquito habitat.[61] According to historian John Duffy, southern states were too impoverished to attack malaria effectively, although state public health departments across the region drew on their limited resources to address the problem, often with federal or nonprofit assistance. Southern states campaigned to drain areas that had become ideal mosquito habitat in the preceding decades. Alabama continued efforts to improve urban drainage and targeted rural swamps for drainage during the 1920s. The state's malaria-control effort included a survey of several swamps encompassing over thirty thousand acres in western Alabama. While conceding that "due to economical conditions, none of the major swamps were drained," state officials, with USPHS assistance, worked with Montgomery County officials to drain an urban wetland.[62] The state provided technical assistance to communities to guide drainage efforts and worked to convince farmers to stock ponds with minnows to eat mosquito larvae.[63] Despite low budgets, the Alabama Board of Health reduced prime habitat by convincing municipalities or private landowners to bear the cost.

By far, Alabama's greatest investment came in trying to cope with the new habitats created by reservoirs built by power utilities.[64] After the completion of the Lock 12 reservoir on the Coosa River in 1912, neighbors suffered a terrifying increase in malaria cases. In 1914 the number of affected individuals spiked at six hundred after only twenty-five cases the preceding year.[65] This outbreak reportedly cost the power company $100,000 in lawsuits and labor inefficiencies. Following the Lock 12 epidemic, the USPHS began conducting surveys of the conditions on reservoirs that contributed to malaria. It found that "floatage," or floating debris near the shore, provided protected habitat where larvae could thrive. Acting on this information, Alabama enacted regulations in 1923 mandating that reservoir builders follow mosquito-control practices. The key element of these regulations was the requirement that the land area be cleared within twenty-five feet of the planned high-water mark to eliminate debris accumulation near the shore.[66] Yet, in 1923 the River Falls Power Company began filling its reservoir near the town of Gantt without properly clearing vegetation. Despite legal intervention by the state, the company continued filling the reservoir in 1924. That summer, there was a "violent" malaria outbreak, with 238 cases in a village of 742 residents. In November, the state settled its standing case against the power company after corporate officials agreed to draw down the reservoir and properly clear the high-water zone. Follow-up studies revealed substantial reductions in malaria during the years after corrective action by the power company.[67]

Permitting of hydroelectric power reservoirs also fell under the jurisdiction of the Federal Power Commission. In 1922 it began requiring power companies to follow antimalaria regulations developed in consultation with the USPHS in order to secure a federal license. Historian Margaret Humphries reports that power companies experienced too many suits and eventually determined it was less expensive to follow regulations than to fight legal battles.[68] Alabama was not alone in enacting regulations and deploying inspectors to monitor reservoir construction. Even if these states could not fund adequate drainage, they did not want new malaria challenges emerging in association with economic development projects. Relying in part on the federal permitting system and supplementing it with regulations, states were able to divert the major costs of controlling new mosquito breeding areas to the private sector and thereby stretched their modest public health budgets.

One area that regulations did not directly cover was sedimentation in new reservoirs. Alabama reported that siltation following heavy rains produced conditions favoring *Anopheles* propagation.[69] State officials did not document how widespread this problem was, but each major reservoir had multiple streams feeding it. Often situated in places with considerable slope, reservoirs were subject to accumulation of eroded soil as streams created small deltas where they entered the standing water. In locations where there was little erosion control, local sediment transport continued to augment risk unaddressed by regulations. Although some wetlands were inundated, other new ones formed where streams emptied into reservoirs.

State public health departments demonstrated their opportunism in controlling malaria following unrelated calamities. In the wake of the disastrous 1927 Mississippi River flood, Tennessee received assistance from the Red Cross to launch a major drainage effort in the areas that had been inundated. Its public health department used oil to destroy breeding sites, applied larvicides to standing water in the river bottoms, and stocked ponds with mosquito-eating minnows. It also promoted drainage in towns to eliminate breeding areas.[70] Consultants from the USPHS assisted with expanding mosquito eradication programs in western Tennessee in ensuing years.[71] These efforts focused on drainage, oiling, larvicides, and screening and continued into the 1930s.[72] Opportunism did not translate into long-term fixes, and these efforts ground to a halt with the Great Depression in the 1930s. Tennessee reported several years of successful screen installations, but in 1932, house screening virtually ceased.[73] State-supported drainage proceeded only in Shelby County—home to Memphis, the state's largest city. Thus, active efforts to eradicate mosquitoes or to prevent human exposure greatly diminished during the national economic crisis, and drainage was largely an urban program.

Across the South, the Great Depression produced a sizable surge in malaria cases as funds to control this problem dried up. Federal programs had been reduced in the late 1920s and nonprofits saw their funds for malaria disappear in the stock market crash, leaving state agencies unprepared for the renewed outbreak. Delayed somewhat by drought in 1930 and 1931, the malaria rate soared in most southern states from 1933 through 1935. Two very distinct clusters existed: (1) counties along the Mississippi River from northern Arkansas and Tennessee, across the Mississippi Delta into northeast Louisiana, and (2) counties from the panhandle of Florida, across southeast Alabama, the Piedmont of Georgia, and into southeast South Carolina (fig. 4.3).[74] This pattern makes obvious that several of the most extensive wetlands in the country—the Everglades and the Atchafalaya Basin—did not exhibit high rates of malaria. Instead, areas of intense agriculture, high percentages of African Americans, and poverty constituted the malaria belt.

The 1930s malaria outbreak was the result of several related circumstances, and Margaret Humphries argues persuasively that poverty was one important element.[75] The reduction in external funding also contributed, as did budget tightening that restricted what the individual states could do to control the watery settings where mosquitoes thrived. The battle to combat the disease was fought on several fronts and most notably funded with federal and nonprofit-organization dollars. An infusion of outside support was hugely important in reversing the rate of malaria incidence and driving it to near eradication by 1940. It is important to note that the fight was not just a public health program, although that was central to the federal response. Nonetheless, indirect benefits came from other federal programs such as the TVA and the Soil Conservation Service.

The more widely discussed external aid came through the USPHS and charitable organizations. While many of the clinically oriented programs emphasized inventorying the extent of malaria and offering treatments to

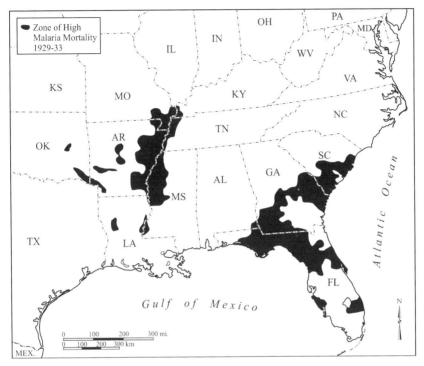

FIG. 4.3. Malaria mortality in the southeastern United States, 1934. After C. C. Dauer and Ernest C. Faust, "Malaria Mortality in the Southern United States for 1934 with Supplementary Data for Previous Years," *Southern Medical Journal* 29, no. 7 (1936): 757–64. Cartography by Mary Lee Eggart.

victims, drainage remained a component to eradication. During much of the 1920s, the Florida Anti-Malaria Association held annual meetings to generate interest in the state's plight and to propel actions toward controlling mosquitoes. This organization had limited success before additional assistance arrived with the outbreak during the Great Depression. In 1931, the Rockefeller Foundation established a malaria research station at Tallahassee that collaborated with the Florida Board of Health and federal agencies such as the USPHS, the Department of Agriculture, the military, and eventually the various relief agencies. By 1941, the relief programs, carried out in consultation with USPHS engineers, had dug over fifteen hundred miles of drainage ditches.[76] The Florida Department of Health reported that its research to find treatments and medical solutions had helped reduce the disease's impacts.[77] The state department, in association with the Rockefeller Foundation, also set up a demonstration project in Escambia County that filled in an extensive area of mosquito breeding wetlands and provided drainage in Pensacola.[78] After the country's entry into World War II, the state participated in targeted DDT spraying to arrest an outbreak in 1944 and shortly after the war, malaria-control efforts appeared to have driven rates to all-time lows.[79] Without this coordinated attack, which included drainage, paid for largely with external funds, Florida's successes might have been later in coming.

New Deal programs delivered funds and labor to carry out aggressive water-control projects to support mosquito eradication, and most southern states had launched drainage programs by 1935. Federally funded labor crews dug ditches to drain potential mosquito breeding areas. While states reported hundreds of miles of ditches and tens of thousands of acres of water eliminated (table 4.2), the quality of the initial work and subsequent maintenance was questionable.[80] The Public Health Service itemized initial accomplishments in 1935 with great pride: 6,000 miles of ditches dug, 100,000 acres of ponds and 200,000 acres of swamp drained, and the threat to an estimated 8 million people relieved.[81] A year later, an even more stunning report appeared. It proclaimed that 3 million acres of mosquito breeding ground had been drained by about one hundred thousand miles of ditches. Inadequate planning of the hurried projects, unskilled labor without trained supervisors, and poor engineering undermined their long-term effectiveness. Nonetheless, health officials claimed these efforts were effective tools in battling the outbreaks of 1934 and 1935.[82] A survey of the benefits of improved drainage and filling of wetlands in Mississippi noted a decline in malaria incidence in the mid-1930s. Improved agricultural drainage plus a commitment by the state highway department to drain borrow pits augmented the drainage paid for with federal relief dollars.[83]

TABLE 4.2 Drainage with Federal Assistance, 1935

State	Miles of Ditch	Acres of Water Drained
Alabama	342	28,863
Mississippi	212	13,587
North Carolina	648	3,642
Tennessee	614	3,128

Source: Mark Boyd, "A Review of Malaria Control Activities in Southern States during 1934," *Southern Medical Journal* 28, no. 8 (1935): 764.

Overall, the relief funds helped raise the expectations and delivered expertise that could be applied to drainage projects targeting mosquito habitat. Even if inexpertly executed and only temporary, the miles of ditches and acres drained produced some benefits. The American Society for Civil Engineering (ASCE) boasted that refinements in engineering approaches helped address the issue. The ASCE's national association declared that drainage was "the most effective permanent method of reducing or controlling malaria" and that engineers brought expertise to the task. In particular, engineers noted that there were fundamentally different objectives between agricultural drainage and malaria control. Farmers sought removal of both surface and subsurface water, but mosquito control aimed to move only surface water. While agricultural drainage could benefit public health objectives, poorly designed field drainage systems could create new mosquito breeding areas. The ASCE encouraged engineers to consider the relationship of the two distinct practices and also admonished its members to address drainage in association with rail and highway construction.[84]

The Tennessee Valley Authority, in addition to its primary missions of navigation, flood control, and hydroelectric power, took on a sizable mosquito-control role as well. As it began constructing hydroelectric dams in Tennessee and Alabama, it drew on the experience of the War Department, the Public Health Service, and private companies and addressed the potential for creating breeding sites for *Anopheles*. It instituted a careful series of studies to minimize floatage, to avoid ponding along shorelines, to eliminate any mosquito populations that emerged, and also to regulate the lake levels to minimize breeding.[85] Crews cleared wide swaths of land prior to filling the reservoirs to reduce vegetation emerging above the pool elevation and creating still water where mosquito larvae could survive. Tennessee Valley Authority managers planned to lower water at the start of the breeding season to pull the water level below any shoreline vegetation and expose a bare shore to waves and fish that preyed on larvae. To ensure adequate amounts of water to regulate levels, dam designers built in a "malaria surcharge," or added one foot to dam heights. During the breeding season, deliberate fluctuations of the surface level by draining and then refilling the "surcharge" impeded mosquito propagation.[86] Extensive testing of supplemental control methods such as larvicides, aerial spraying, drainage of adjacent wetlands, and also quinine distribution enabled the TVA to fend off any serious outbreaks.[87]

Malaria abatement projects created tensions within the TVA. In particular the "malaria surcharge" conflicted with spring flood control. Storing extra water in winter and early spring that could be released as the insect's breeding season began in late spring conflicted with the need to keep pools low for flood storage during the late winter and spring.[88] Additionally, conservationists charged that mosquito-control water-level fluctuations along with larvicides damaged fish populations.[89] And finally, those responsible for producing power claimed the cyclic drawdowns cost up to $60,000 in lost power and could interfere with national defense.[90] With a solid federal budget to support basic research on these questions and a grand scheme to put in place, the TVA antimalaria program found arguments to rebut challengers. It claimed that aquatic life suffered no harm from the seasonal drawdowns and that the reduced cost of malaria outbreaks more than offset any losses of hydropower potential.[91] Indeed, TVA officials claimed that reservoirs improved overall public health conditions in the malaria-prone sections of the Tennessee Valley. The inundation of Wheeler Reservoir in north Alabama in 1937 submerged former wetlands and ponds that had previously served as breeding habitat. A drop in malaria after this reservoir was filled prompted the TVA to report: "impoundage of water in situations where malaria existed prior to the impounding may actually result in an alleviation of the problem."[92] While the TVA relied on a multi-pronged malaria-control approach, it ultimately argued that its impoundments were in and of themselves beneficial. In terms of areal extent, this program expanded during the 1930s and into the 1940s. With each new federal reservoir there was adherence to mosquito abatement techniques and also the flooding of riparian wetlands that had previously supported malaria's persistence. Federal dams and reservoirs reach well beyond the TVA territory (see fig. 5.2), and whether for navigation, flood control, or hydroelectric power, these structures have contributed to mosquito control.

The less-recognized component of disease control was indirect, namely soil erosion control. The establishment of the Soil Conservation Service in 1935 launched an additional federal influence on southern waters that had the capability to reduce the growth of unwanted breeding areas. The massive erosion of the late nineteenth century was followed by reduced soil losses as commodity prices fell after World War I and farmers took erodible land out of cultivation as prices remained low during the 1920s. The great erosion gullies of the Piedmont, used by Hugh Hammond Bennett as examples of reckless stewardship in his writing during the 1920s, had been formed by the 1890s and were not the result of reckless cultivation during the preceding decade.[93] While the damage was in place before the onset of the Great Depression, which did not inspire renewed tillage of marginal lands, the new federal agency provided assistance to arrest any lingering erosion. The Soil Conservation Service (SCS) assisted farmers in reshaping fields with terraces and planting erosion-prone slopes with trees, kudzu, and pasture, along with a range of additional techniques. In doing so, it too expanded the reach of a federal authority over water in the South.[94]

The new agency made gradual progress, moving from conducting surveys of erosion problems to implementing a set of demonstration projects and initiating larger endeavors. One fundamental building block involved the formation of local conservation districts across the country. These districts, authorized by state legislatures, established legal entities that could request aid from state and federal authorities and provided a mechanism to apply those funds to particular local problems. Federal assistance, in large measure, came through the assignment of Civilian Conservation Corps workers to construct flood-control structures in watersheds, install erosion-impeding devices in gullies, and assist with terracing, drainage, and forest planting. By 1940, there were over 100 million acres in the South legally enrolled in conservation districts (table 4.3). A more direct measure of its outreach is the acreage encompassed by watershed, land use, and forest programs. In South Carolina, the SCS and its CCC crews attacked gullies on the Piedmont near Switzer. They installed temporary check dams and planted vegetation in the eroded channels to promote sedimentation and reduce future erosion.[95] The SCS claimed to have more than 12 million acres across the South within its watershed, land use, and forest programs by 1940 (table 4.3).

Depressed markets may have contributed as much as active conservation measures to reducing erosion, but in the long run the SCS provided vital federal support to reduce conditions that exacerbated formation of new mosquito habitat. Emergency CCC assistance disappeared as the United States entered World War II, but conservation programs encouraged erosion-resistant cultivation, planting forests and pastures on slopes, and watershed management to reduce floods and sedimentation. Erosion control proceeded both on private property and on federal lands— including national forests and the submarginal lands acquired by the federal government during the Great Depression. Erosion control and vegetation cover restoration were key components of the management of these

TABLE 4.3 Soil Conservation Service Projects, 1940

State	Conservation Districts (acres)	Watershed Projects (acres)	Land Use Projects (acres)	Forestry Projects (acres)
Alabama	17,084,160	202,879	202,404	No data
Arkansas	7,928,070	326,245	1,167,675	64,000
Florida	250,000	37,940	830,147	627,200
Georgia	20,739,536	253,333	1,036,664	217,600
Kentucky	No data	83,880	206,103	No data
Louisiana	10,856,465	226,941	32,550	64,000
Mississippi	9,288,349	327,396	461,286	1,223,139
North Carolina	11,423,040	492,258	444,768	No data
South Carolina	9,265,360	282,795	169,426	704,000
Tennessee	No data	64,829	108,280	379,115
Texas	6,800,895	248,170	305,786	No data
Virginia	7,236,513	291,800	97,520	1,000,000
TOTALS	100,872,388	2,838,466	5,062,609	4,279,054

Source: USDA, Soil Conservation Service, *Report of the Chief of the Soil Conservation Service, 1940* (Washington, DC: 1940), tables 1, 6–7.

properties.[96] Thus the reach of federal authority extended to both private and public lands and in doing so reduced some of the pockets of surplus water that had sheltered disease-carrying vectors.

Conclusions

The shift in medical thinking from miasmatic disease origin to mosquito-borne bacteria was transformational for physicians and their approach to major epidemics that plagued the South, but much less so in terms of attempts to manage southern hydrology. When Edward Barton identified the various nuisances in New Orleans as causes for yellow fever after the 1853 epidemic, the public health response was to fill wetlands and improve the city's drainage. While ineffective in the short term, these remedies remained part of the basic strategy through the next major outbreak in 1878. Managing water offered what medical authorities and municipal officials considered a viable mechanism to reduce the disease threat. Even after turn-of-the-century acceptance of insect-borne vector theories and practical experiences with mosquito control, drainage of standing water, along with application of larvicides to cisterns and other water receptacles, sustained the focus on water. Eliminating mosquito habitat, rather than sources of miasmas, became the dominant principle and provided a solid justification for efforts to improve urban sanitation and drainage. The U.S. Public Health Service was central to disseminating proven mosquito-eradication programs and thereby assisted southern states in finally conquering the long-dreaded yellow fever by the early twentieth century.

Across the rural South, malaria persisted in the new century, and a spike in the 1910s prompted action by the U.S. Public Health Service. Its investigators helped map the zones where it was prevalent and raise awareness among state public health agencies, communities, and private companies. Even when state agencies were unable to muster adequate funds to combat it, they worked with communities to improve drainage and destroy mosquito habitat. After a decline in cases during the 1920s, an eruption in the early years of the Great Depression instigated a federal response on several fronts. The USPHS, the TVA, the Soil Conservation Service, and the War Department, along with charitable organizations, attacked the problem through loosely coordinated programs. Improved drainage, de-watering wetlands, and managing water levels in new reservoirs were central to these efforts. Ultimately, a resculpting of the rural southern hydrology—combined with a chemical attack on the vectors, the extension of medical services, and public health education—finally reduced the malaria threat. There is more standing water in the South now than in 1900, but it no longer poses the same risk due in large measure to the arrival of federal programs that supported local efforts to combat water-related diseases. Undesirable surpluses were drained, and massive reservoirs added to the landscape to create a new form of managed abundance.

Part II

SHORTAGE

5

Navigating Emerging Conflicts

Introduction

Navigating along the Atlantic-Gulf coastal plain from the Potomac to the Pearl, European settlers encountered an abundance of waterways that offered routes to the interior and the resources found there. Draining the eastern and southern flanks of the Appalachian Mountains, these streams provided the arteries for an emerging transportation network and also power for incipient backwoods manufacturing. These modest water routes were interrupted by the mighty Mississippi and with its exceptional capacity for watercraft, but lesser waterways resumed across western Louisiana and along the broad arc of Texas's coastline (fig 5.1). Canoes, bateaux, pirogues, and flatboats carried furs and agricultural produce from the interior, and gravity-driven currents propelled timber toward coastal ports. When waterways proved insufficient to fulfill all demands and conflicts among users erupted, the colonial legal systems sought to resolve disputes among shippers, millers, and fisherfolk. Riparian principles applied to legal issues in the English colonies and sustained a fundamental public right to navigation. This historic precedent continues to shape public policy toward navigable waterways.

Navigation opportunities in the South differed from other eastern seaboard regions. In New England and most of the Middle Atlantic region, numerous small rivers tumbled over rapids and waterfalls a short distance inland from the coast. Both the size of rivers and inland geologic barriers there greatly restricted commercial inland navigation—with the Connecticut River serving as the principal exception in New England, the Hudson in New York, and the Susquehanna and Delaware in Pennsylvania as obvious routes to the interior. Nonetheless, the streams of New England and those across the Middle Atlantic states provided excellent waterpower sites for industrial development. South of Baltimore, the geologic barrier, or fall zone, veered inland from the coast and this increased unimproved navigation opportunities as one traveled southward. In Virginia ships could navigate a few dozen miles inland, while in Georgia and Alabama rivers could carry cargo over a hundred miles inland before encountering the

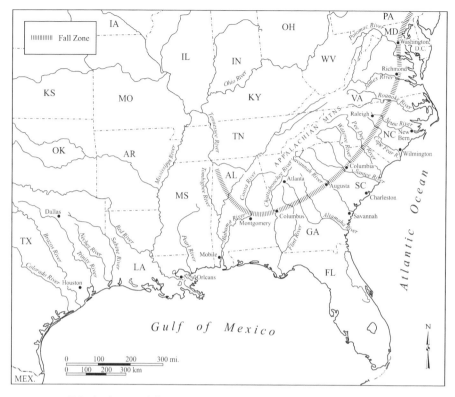

FIG. 5.1. Principal coastal rivers and fall zone. Cartography by Mary Lee Eggart.

fall zone (fig. 5.1). Texas rivers also permitted seasonal movement of agricultural staples from some distance inland. Despite the impediment presented by the fall zone, southern planters and entrepreneurs dreamed of riparian transformations that would allow waterborne penetration across the Piedmont and beyond. Indeed, influential founding fathers such as George Washington and Thomas Jefferson both recognized the potential for river transport. Washington actively promoted water links between the Tidewater and the Ohio River valley before the Revolution.[1] Jefferson comments on the navigation potential on the James River, noting that ocean-going ships could sail upstream to Richmond, and above the fall zone canoes and bateaux could navigate to within ten miles of the Blue Ridge.[2] Colonial and state legislative bodies took matters a step further. They defined navigable waterways, and by their actions overlaid a legal framework on waterways that reflected their ambitions as much as a river's physical realities. By defining a stream as navigable, governments codified public access and diminished the rights of private concerns to obstruct a watercourse. This classification imposed an entirely different meaning to a river. As a public highway, a navigable stream became a common resource. In many cases, for a river to live up to that designation, channel clearing or even locks and dams were necessary—and the designation implicitly authorized such environmental alterations, or "improvements" as they were known at the time.

Colonial- and early national-era navigation laws and policies tended to assume a continuation of hydrologic abundance in the humid East. Court decisions, state statutes, and development of transportation and hydropower infrastructure did not factor in diminishing supplies—whether a decrease in the actual volume of water due to drought or water availability to all riparian users as a consequence of overlapping demands. Yet, even in the eighteenth century, competing interests were already straining the sustainable use of river resources. Navigation, hydropower, and fishing were not entirely compatible. And new technologies and increasing demands on rivers amplified the obvious limits of rivers' utility. Courts and legislatures coped with limits to abundance when navigators sued mill owners for obstructing their movement on rivers. Similarly, they sought to resolve disputes between mill owners and fisherfolk when fish populations declined. In recent years, federal involvement in the construction of navigation systems and permitting hydroelectric installations have compounded the legal questions, as have explicitly environmental laws that limit the use of rivers as sewage sinks or protect certain habitats to sustain threatened aquatic species. While there are core environmental concerns in these legal issues, they often remain framed by questions of public access and economic rights wrapped up in the question of navigability.

This chapter considers the concept of "navigable waters" as defined by state legislatures as a means to initiate hydrologic manipulations, as well as how judicial decisions and state and federal policies over time contributed to the reordering of the South's fluvial geography. The legal approach provides two complementary insights. First, it reveals the most fundamental assignment of authority over fluvial resources and establishes one of the origins of environmental management. An examination of state legislation that guided the establishments of mills and navigation companies and of appellate court decisions on the question of navigability reveals a transformative impulse among southerners. This impetus permitted the overhaul of fluvial systems. The resulting structural projects have had environmental impacts—some more enduring than others. Litigation over navigation works exposes conflicts over common access versus private use, particularly when a waterway proves inadequate to satisfy the many demands imposed by society. Second, the legal approach exposes regional differences in the management of riverine environments through the application of the law. Given regional differences in water resources and economic activities, application and practice of the law also has taken on regional distinctions. An expanding federal role in water management during the late nineteenth and twentieth century lessened state influences and eventually reshaped the landscapes of southern waters. Federal expenditures on navigation and subsequent litigation permitted a national influence on water management and delivered long-lasting environmental changes. Despite strong states' rights posturing, southerners eagerly sought federal navigation projects, and in doing so, they unwittingly relinquished local power over defining navigable waters and thereby lessened state authority. Environmental laws enacted in the late twentieth century furthered the federal government's influence.

Historical Narratives

Historians in the United States have explored several key themes about inland navigation in their country: (1) the evolution of legal conflicts over competing uses of navigable waterways, (2) the technological progress of navigational systems, (3) the political contest over the use of federal funds to "improve" rivers, and (4) the transformation of the southern backcountry economy. Each of these complementary narratives provides valuable insights, but none truly focuses on the riparian environment or the impacts of human actions on fluvial systems. This chapter will examine the legal context, in particular the litigation history, that pertains to efforts to define and reshape waterways in the American Southeast. Law, politics, economics, and technology all factor in, and I will draw on the findings of prior scholarship. At the same time, I will expand on these discussions by foregrounding the environment, while acknowledging that legal decisions, public policy, economic agendas, and most technological innovations well into the twentieth century were not oriented toward environmental concerns. Nonetheless, they produced impacts, many with long-lasting consequences. And it is the persistence of these historical actions that is critical to our examination of river systems today and in managing them for the future.

The first of these narratives focuses on the emerging conflicts between traditional uses of waterways and industries. As they industrialized the region, New England mill owners battled with riparians over the right to build dams, inundate fields, and disrupt fish migrations. Jurists supported their efforts and rolled back traditional riparian rights while expanding the rights of mill owners.[3] There were indirect environmental consequences from the expansion of industry and its use of waterways for power and waste removal. A second line of inquiry has examined technological development of river transportation.[4] These accounts trace the interrelated economic development of the southern interior with advances in steamboat technology and advances in river modification capabilities. Clearing riparian forests for fuel and promoting agricultural expansion, and consequent soil erosion, are among the environmental consequences of this dimension of river history. The third theme examines the contentious debate that surrounded federally funded navigation improvements on the nation's western rivers. Supporters gradually secured authorization for federal expenditures to aid waterborne commerce, mainly on the larger western rivers.[5] Historian Paul Paskoff makes the case that funding for river safety was one of the earliest insertions of federal influence into the nation's commerce, and as a process that modified rivers, it was also an early extension of federal authority into environmental management. A fourth set of narratives centers on capitalist development of the southern backcountry. Framed as a transition in power, the focus is less on rivers per se than on the shifting demands placed on rivers shaped by an emerging political (and economic) force.[6] Political decisions that supported particular economic practices contributed to the removal of forests and the expansion of cultivated land in the backcountry. While vital to our understanding of how the country's economic priorities shaped the use and management of waterways, none of these broad discussions examine the more fundamental matters of how society defined fluvial environments and what that means in terms of managing hydrological resources or how legal definitions contributed to the environmental transformation of the country's rivers.

There has been an emerging, if as yet less cohesive, set of histories dealing with southern rivers as functioning parts of social-environmental systems. These provide insight into an emerging environmental conflict over the Tennessee-Tombigbee Waterway, interstate pollution conflicts on the Pigeon River, the intersection of state and federal interests in the Atchafalaya Basin, and the tensions created by the desires to transform the

Mississippi River floodplain into a setting for farming, cities, and industry.[7] What they amply illustrate is that public policy and legal decisions impacted not just the economy and society, but the environment as well. Regardless of legislative or judicial leanings on economic development, the implementation of policies that could alter the environment—in name or in fact—underlaid all subsequent economic influences. This chapter will step back from the ensuing economic consequences and consider how laws that defined navigation constituted one of the early forms of environmental management on the southeastern Piedmont and coastal plain. Opportunities for navigation were extremely limited on New England's waterways, and damming the massive inland rivers was not feasible in the early nineteenth century. Thus, legislatures and courts in the American South, economic and social differences aside, faced distinct issues in dealing with navigable waters—and they consistently proceeded on the assumption of continued abundance of water.

Legal Background

English common law, which provided the legal framework for most states in the American Southeast, prioritized navigation over other uses of public waterways.[8] Colonial and early state laws incorporated this concept into their nascent statutes.[9] In New England, however, navigation was virtually absent in the riparian litigation that pitted farmers against mill owners. On the main branches of the Mississippi River, where much of the early debate over public funding for internal improvements played out, navigability was assumed and dams that blocked navigation were absent during the nineteenth century. Navigation improvements on major western rivers like the Mississippi and Ohio consisted mainly of snag removal, small wing dams to direct flow, and channel straightening. Across the coastal plain of the American Southeast, however, the question of navigation proved to be a central issue in managing a basic environmental resource and extending the reach of engineered waterways. Thus, designating a stream as navigable opened the door for modifications and potential conflicts. Defining, transforming, impacting, and managing the environment were precursors to the eventual settlement landscape and regional economic development.

The English notion that navigable rivers that were subject to tidal influence proved inadequate in an American territory with massive internal rivers that saw no rise or fall caused by tides. American courts took a pragmatic turn and determined that streams that could actually float commercial traffic a fair portion of the year were navigable.[10] Among the original thirteen states, Virginia and North Carolina legislatures decided which streams were navigable and specified that status through legislation.[11] Virginia enacted state laws in the early nineteenth century that required mill owners to secure permission from the local courts before erecting dams in navigable waterways. In addition, the state act required dam builders to enable passage of watercraft and fish. North Carolina enacted similar legislation that prohibited individuals from impeding the free passage of boats and authorizing local courts to approve mill dams on public waterways. Dams had to be built such that they would enable the passage of boats and fish.[12]

Expectations for navigational protections did not end with colonial or state legislatures. Requests for federal assistance to improve navigation emanated from seaboard states in the early national period. Local leaders in Richmond, Virginia, petitioned to have the army engineers survey the James River during the 1830s in hopes that they would remove obstacles and permit ships to reach the state capital. The survey overseen by a Lieutenant Abert concluded that ocean-going ships could not navigate to Richmond due to shoals that obstructed the river, and as a consequence the "trade of Richmond is . . . burdened with heavy charges for lighterage and transshipment," which reduced profits for local merchants. While offering an estimate for dredging the shoals and proposing jetties to keep the channel open, the engineer was pessimistic that improvements would be enduring. He opined that sediments would continue to accumulate and numerous, costly jetties would be required to sustain a navigable channel.[13] Southward along the eastern seaboard, residents of North Carolina also appealed to Congress for river improvements. Inhabitants of Wilmington reported that obstructions on the Cape Fear River impeded their ability to export lumber and naval stores at competitive prices. The primary obstructions in the Cape Fear River were sailing vessels intentionally scuttled during the Revolutionary War to prevent British naval ships from reaching the city. These wrecks blocked passage and also contributed to the formation of shoals. In addition, the natural configuration of the river that carried upland sediments produced shoals near Wilmington.[14] After work began on improvements, Congress interrupted funding and the work ceased by 1836. As a consequence, petitions for additional interventions ensued.[15] The multiple requests expose a dynamic environmental situation and also rising expectations for adequate channel depth. Inland forest removal and expanding cultivation increased the sediment borne by the

Cape Fear, and natural processes continued to cause sedimentation and shoal growth. Larger maritime vessels prompted requests for even deeper passages. Economic motivations, and not simply an urge to modify the river, provided the impetus for these improvements. Thus, the interrelated natural processes and human activity propelled environmental transformations that attempted to sustain a legally designated navigable river in spite of a variety of forces operating in opposition to the desired condition.

The South Carolina legislature and courts also assiduously protected navigation on public waters. The colonial legislature enacted a law in 1726 that sought to preserve both navigation and fisheries. In response to felling trees that blocked waterways, the legislature imposed a fine for anyone impeding waterborne commerce. Subsequent legislation forbid flooding a neighbor's land with water impounded behind a dam.[16] An 1825 act prohibited building a mill dam across a navigable river without providing sufficient locks or other means to circumnavigate the obstruction. In later years, the state's courts regularly upheld public rights to the use of waterways that were capable of transporting goods.[17] The legal protections sought to enable floating commodities downstream, including timber and other forest products. Most of the early sawmills occupied sites on tributaries of the larger rivers that logging interests maintained for their commerce. By the mid-nineteenth century, however, conflicts between sawmill operators emerged as they competed for limited hydropower on smaller streams and lumbermen who desired open channels to float logs.[18] The main channels, however, served as public highways without significant challenge. Even though courts ruled some small tributaries were navigable, in fact, they lacked sufficient capacity to meet the multiple demands—transport, power, and fish habitat. Early conflicts centered on situations where there were clear limits to abundance.

Georgia had taken action to prevent individuals from impeding navigation as early as 1763 when the colonial legislature prohibited the dumping of trash or ballast or felling trees in navigable waters. During early statehood, the legislature passed an act to prevent the obstruction of the Savannah River that would inhibit navigation or free passage of fish.[19] Further, the legislature retained authority over granting individuals the right to erect mill dams. When the state withdrew its authorization for one mill owner on Ebenezer Mill Creek in the 1830s, it reported that citizens had complained that the dam injured navigation and lessened the value of riparian property.[20] Thus, unimpeded public use of waterways for navigation took precedence over private milling. Dams as environmental modifications were acceptable as long as they did not interfere with public travel.

Beyond the original thirteen colonies, states that joined the union after the Revolution shared a common framework for establishing navigability. Congress passed legislation in 1796 that stated "all navigable rivers, within the territory to be disposed of by virtue of this act shall be deemed to be, and remain, public highways." Subsequent acts pertaining to states admitted south of Tennessee contain the same wording.[21] That is, the federal government authorized states to define navigability. Complicating matters, however, the states south of Tennessee entered the Union during the time when mill owners in New England were challenging traditional riparian rights and common law was in a state of flux.

Alabama, when enacting legislation to prevent obstruction of navigable waterways in 1819, declared that "all water-courses reported to be navigable, or which may hereafter be reported to be navigable, by the surveyor of the United States, employed in surveying the lands in this State, shall be and remain free and open."[22] The legislature initially delegated the responsibility to a federal representative. In his survey of various inland waterways, William Barnett apparently did not "feel myself specially called on to speak."[23] Local memorialists, however, did feel called to voice their opinion about navigability. They petitioned Congress to dedicate funds from land sales in the Tennessee River valley to removing rocks and constructing sluices at Mussel Shoals to improve navigability—thus converting a navigation hazard into a commercial thoroughfare that would enhance land values in the region.[24] Barnett also refrained from commenting on the Tombigbee River. Again, Alabama residents felt compelled to petition Congress to fund improvements of this important waterway. Arguing that navigable rivers are the "Highways of National Commerce," they claimed that improvements would facilitate commerce and enhance land value.[25] Residents of the region clearly sought to overcome nature's limitations on the movement of commerce.

Barnett also reported to the Secretary of War that the Great Falls on the Coosa River were a serious impediment to navigation and any improvements would be costly. He noted, however, that the Black Warrior River offered much greater promise as a navigable waterway.[26] Unsatisfied with the surveyor's assessment of the Coosa, Alabama's legislature enacted a law in 1823 to improve the Coosa and overcome the obstruction posed by the falls.[27] Acknowledging shortcomings of the federal observer, the legislature also authorized the governor to hire a surveyor to inspect certain rivers and determine their navigability and the potential cost of improving their ability to handle commercial traffic.[28] Alabama's interest in improving navigability produced legislation that declared segments of several small streams "public highways," illustrating the state's desire to take charge of defining a river's potential for commerce and even to manipulate the waterway to make travel feasible.[29] Placing several streams and larger waterways under the rubric of "public highways" prohibited the obstruction of free navigation. It also mandated that the legislature retain the authority to grant permission for erecting mill dams. Any potential obstruction had to have state approval, and this usually entailed mill dams.

While rivers were considered public thoroughfares, milling in the early nineteenth century also was considered a public good, and this produced potential for conflict over whether navigation or milling deserved priority status under the law.[30] This emerging point of contention highlighted that the assumed abundance of eastern waterways was not up to the growing demands. Legal historians Morton Horwitz and Ted Steinberg report on a decidedly instrumental drift in New England court decisions that favored mill operators in that region. As Horwitz argues, judges during the northeastern boom in mill construction sought to eliminate the ability of riparians to obstruct new economic activities and to recognize that some damage to other landowners was an inevitable consequence of economic development.[31] In contrast, Downey claims that the South Carolina legislature and courts had to tread a fine line between preserving public access and private gain.[32] Indeed, early nineteenth-century appellate decisions across the South demonstrate a solid judicial backing of public use of waterways for transportation.[33] And southern memorialists appealed to Congress to fund the removal of obstructions to navigation and achieve "safe and perfect navigation."[34] Limitations in terms of river size or topographic hazards prompted efforts to rework waterways and thereby make them navigable. Law and policy worked to provide navigability where it was not always practicable.

Navigable Waterways and Internal Improvements

Not only were rivers themselves sometimes inadequate to serve the demands of economic development, but sometimes they were not where society wanted them. In those situations, canals, or artificial rivers, could provide strategic links and remedy nature's inadequacies. Southern states moved through two distinct periods of transforming waterways to fulfill

their designations as navigable waters. Colonial assemblies and state legislatures authorized several navigation projects to enhance commerce in the
late eighteenth and early nineteenth centuries, and territorial legislatures
solicited federal funds to build canals where there were no rivers.[35] The
canal companies, financed in part by local subscription, drew on limited
private funds that legislatures eventually supplemented. Some were grand
schemes and others more modest, but they commonly involved filling perceived inadequacies in the natural network of waterways to accommodate cargo-laden craft. To facilitate the transformation of rivers into viable
transportation corridors, state laws and court decisions backed modifications considered as serving the public good.[36] Over time, the courts cau-
tiously followed the lead of New England decisions and enlarged the rights
of other riparians, such as mill owners and urban landowners, yet the fundamental power for defining navigable waters remained with the states,
and they consistently worked to support public access on navigable waterways. A second wave of internal improvements followed the Civil War and
will be discussed in the following section.

In many respects southern states emulated, although not equaling, the
industrial development of New England during the first phase of river
transformations. The numerous navigation companies, formed mainly in
the early nineteenth century, reflected a desire both to capture power at
fall-zone sites and to expand the navigability of the streams flowing across
the Piedmont onto the coastal plain.[37] Some have argued that navigation
across the coastal plain impeded urbanization in the lowland South, although the formation of fall-zone towns defies this interpretation.[38] Certainly, the possibility for river transportation was superior across the South
to that in New England, and by the mid-1700s, there was a string of towns
established along the Virginia fall zone.[39] They served as break-in-bulk
points for grain exports and for inland movement of imported consumer
goods. Additionally, millers at the fall zone could process grain into flour
for export. These sites, endowed with usable water power, became the locations of urban and industrial development. Historian Louis Hunter, however, observes that until the arrival of the railroads, the more southerly and
inland fall-zone sites were too inaccessible for effective industrial development.[40] Despite Hunter's dismissal of industry-driven urbanization, small
cities where water-powered manufacturing activity clustered had become
established at most heads of navigation by the end of the eighteenth century—including Camden, South Carolina, and Augusta, Georgia.[41] With
available waterpower, fall-zone towns provided modest nodes for industry,

commerce, and in some cases administration. And with these functions came environmental transformations. To serve these budding commercial centers, state legislatures across the Southeast authorized navigation companies and most invested in their development. It was not uncommon, as was done in colonial Virginia and Maryland, for states to grant a private company the right to improve navigation around obstructions at the fall zone or elsewhere that natural obstructions existed.

Promoters of canals and navigation works were more common than successful. Noted southern reformer Thomas Ruffin was among the advocates who touted the importance of public waterworks in the South, and he voiced a bias against milling. He chastised mills and their ponds as sources of miasmas that threatened the health of the region and as impediments to effective drainage that would enable agricultural expansion.[42] Navigation works, in his view, would address these concerns and also serve agrarian interests seeking to export staple crops. Thus, legislation that sanctioned navigation companies also served agricultural development. Before the Civil War, numerous navigation companies, backed by local investors and also state treasuries, had launched river improvement schemes with mixed success across the coastal plain.[43] These works provided vital transportation arteries,[44] but they only temporarily reworked the regime of Piedmont and coastal plain rivers.[45] During their functional periods, the navigation works encouraged agricultural expansion. In doing so, river modifications accelerated forest removal and breaking soil for cultivation, and these changes led to the consequent erosion, flooding, and channel siltation. Maintaining viable works was a perpetual problem and a chronic expense.[46] The movement of goods on these waterways was one form of connection between the coast and the backcountry, but as sediment eroded from tilled land accumulated in canals and riverbeds, it produced an undesirable linkage between uplands and lowlands that was geomorphic and not economic. And this environmental consequence diminished the viability of waterways, or in other words, reduced the abundance of transportation capacity.

Efforts to make the Potomac River navigable derive from legislative actions in Virginia and Maryland beginning in 1784. The respective legislative bodies created the Potomac Company, which over the next thirty years struggled to assemble capital and overcome engineering challenges, climatic vagaries, and weak commercial demand. Ultimately a failure, the navigation project exemplifies both the legal framework and economic context of southern river improvement projects. With authority delegated by the federal government, the states could permit a private company to collect fees from waterway users and invest those funds in navigation improvements. The two legislatures granted the Potomac Company the exclusive right to make the river navigable with a combination of channel clearings and moving-water canals (without locks) and to collect tolls "forever" on vessels passing through its improved sections. Despite great hopes and occasional profitable years, by 1821 floods and ice had rendered the waterway impassable.[47] There were only modest enduring environmental consequences.

Another early effort was the Santee Canal in South Carolina. Incorporated in 1786, it cut a twenty-two-mile canal between the Santee and Cooper rivers to link the port of Charleston to the Santee's larger drainage basin. The purpose was to overcome the absence of a viable waterway to the state's major port city, Charleston. Even before its completion in 1800, floods would refill recently excavated sections with the unconsolidated sediments of the coastal plain, and eventually maintenance became a chronic problem. The canal offered only modest transportation benefits for planters along its course and proved to be a commercial failure.[48] Nonetheless, it stands as an example of state-supported internal improvements that attempted to fix an inadequacy in nature's hydrologic network. In addition, South Carolina followed New York's lead and launched additional canal construction in the 1810s. Reports produced by its superintendent of public works recount the efforts and frustrations of building and maintaining canals and waterways to effect an adequate transportation system.[49] Among its efforts, the state attempted to construct locks, dams, and canals to circumvent the shoals at the fall zone on the Wateree River above the fall-zone city of Camden, but the project never reached completion and ultimately produced negligible environmental and economic impacts.[50]

North Carolina also invested in an extensive set of early nineteenth-century internal improvement projects. Its legislature investigated and later authorized several river improvement projects—on the Cape Fear, Roanoke, Tar, and Neuse rivers beginning in 1816. The legislature granted exclusive right to the respective companies to improve the rivers. Companies could sell stock to private investors, and in most cases the state eventually obligated itself to purchase a portion of the shares. Authorizing legislation also allowed the navigation companies to collect tolls to finance their operation.[51] Their efforts consisted mainly of clearing the channels of their respective streams, pulling snags, and dredging bars. Such alterations had relatively brief impacts and were largely obliterated by floods and other natural processes by the late 1800s. Locks and dams on the Cape Fear and Roanoke remained in place but had fallen into disuse by 1880.[52] Poor financing, inadequate engineering, and a lack of maintenance during the Civil War led to the demise of most environmental transformations by the last quarter of the nineteenth century. As elsewhere, sedimentation and snags reduced the capacity of the waterways.

Florida residents petitioned Congress to fund the construction of a canal across the state—creating an artificial river to link the gulf coast with the Atlantic. This effort reflects the urge to complete an inadequate navigation network and avoid maritime hazards sailing around the southern tip of Florida. To enhance the prospects of their memorial, the authors proposed extending the canal to Mobile and New Orleans through the estuaries inland from the gulf coast's many barrier islands.[53] While Congress did not fund the project at the time, it highlights a vision for a more complete navigation network.

As legislatures authorized and invested in navigation works, state courts backed the navigation companies and their abilities to do business and overcome natural obstacles. In general, antebellum judicial decisions upheld legislation that gave private companies the rights to modify waterways and to collect tolls on the revamped waterways. Despite challenges that tolls ran contrary to "free" passage on public highways, the courts reasoned that by making improvements, the companies had made waterways navigable, when they were not navigable before. Thus, navigation companies were entitled to compensation in the form of tolls.[54] Through efforts that straightened channels, increased water depth with dams, or provided passage around rapids, private companies expanded the navigability of southern waters, and the courts supported this enterprise. Navigation was seldom the issue in the New England mill dam cases, and so the legal issues in the South were distinct and the decisions, while national in scope, were largely regional in their immediate impact. The efforts to enlarge navigability and the court's backing of the private-public projects, endorsed traditional agrarian-oriented navigation to an extent. As public highways, rivers were vital passageways for the export of agricultural commodities. At the same time, however, the decisions acknowledge and implicitly approve new uses of rivers and the construction of dams to make the locks around falls possible. Navigability functioned in an uneasy concert with both tradition and reform in the early national period, although navigation remained a more prominent concern than mill dams along southern seaboard rivers.[55]

Legal backing could not overcome poor engineering or construction and did not ensure the lasting success of navigation enterprises. Despite considerable investment, South Carolina's river improvements on the Wateree had fallen into disrepair in the postbellum period.[56] In an 1880 inventory of water-power sites, George Swain notes the Roanoke and Dan rivers in Virginia had been made navigable in the past but were either impassable or only carried bateaux.[57] Likewise the Cape Fear River in North Carolina had been made navigable some distance inland before the Civil War, but the project was an economic failure and the improvements fell into disuse and disrepair.[58] Although crews encountered relatively modest topographic challenges, southern canal projects were far less successful than the massive cross-state projects in New York, Pennsylvania, and Ohio. Local financing and inadequate demand for navigation diminished the prospects for these numerous projects.[59] Poor construction exacerbating the absence of maintenance during the Civil War also undermined the improvements. Water power was important in the success of fall-zone cities, but early joint state-private financing for navigation efforts produced short-lived, if any, success. As navigation companies faltered financially, natural processes such as floods largely erased their environmental imprint.

Conflict with mill owners proved fundamentally different in the South than in New England. Downey has argued that mill owners were often landowners and also shippers. Thus riparian legal conflicts were among parties with shared interests, unlike the farmers and industrialists in New England. In South Carolina, there were modest erosions in navigation rights to accommodate milling,[60] and a Virginia example highlights judicial limits imposed on navigational improvements. The Slate River Company had secured incorporation from the Virginia legislature in 1819. Legislation declared that when the company made the Slate passable for boats drawing one foot of water, it would become a navigable river. It also declared that when improvements encountered existing mill dams, the owners would be required to erect locks and canals to enable free passage of watercraft. In practice, when the navigation company completed improvements to a mill dam owned by Asbury and Thomas Crenshaw, at a point below a series of extensive rapids, it encountered resistance, not acceptance. Upon reaching the dam, the navigation company demanded that the millers construct the locks and dams required by the state's legislation. Yet the mill owners challenged the demand by arguing that the county had authorized the dam in 1765, and in 1802 a local court had ruled that the

dam would not obstruct ordinary navigation. Based on these legal deter-
minations, the mill owners claimed they were not obligated to construct
locks. In addition, they argued that the cost of construction would drive
them out of business and that the river was not navigable above their mill,
making the proposed locks useless. Neither party was willing to give up its
enterprise, and they took the issue to the courts.[61]

Initially, a lower court ruled in favor of the navigation company, declaring that the mill owners were obliged to follow the legislature's requirements. Subsequently, an appeals court overturned the initial ruling.
Among the reasons for the appellate decision was the fact that mills provided a vital public service and that interruption of this service would inconvenience the larger public. In addition, since the navigation company
had not made the river navigable above the dam, the court determined that
it had not in fact made the river navigable.[62] Until actually made navigable,
the Slate River was not subject to the act's requirement and remained in
effect a private waterway, not a public highway. Witnesses even testified
that they would prefer the mill without navigation.[63] Further, the court
determined that the estimated cost of constructing the locks would be
burdensome on the mill owners and perhaps drive them out of business.
Ultimately, the appeals court declared the law authorizing the navigation
company unconstitutional. On the surface, this decision might seem parallel to the decisions in New England that favored mill dams. But, the
question was not whether the dam caused injury to other riparians, but
whether the new economic activity—in this case expanded navigation—
deserved public accommodation or would yield a greater public benefit.
The court ruled in favor of the established economic enterprise that served
the agricultural community. Boats already could ply the river below the
mill dam, and denying the navigation company a subsidy from the dam
owners would not inhibit existing commerce. Thus, this case that favored
mill owners was the reverse of the instrumental decisions emanating from
courts in New England and reveals the perpetuation of the status quo in
terms of navigability on southern rivers.

The failure of the numerous canal and navigation companies exposes
inadequate capital and engineering capabilities. The formation of these
companies, however, denotes the shortcomings of the South's hydrologic
system to serve the region's expanding expectations, just as the legal conflicts, such as the Slate River Company suit, illustrate the inabilities of
the rivers to serve all users. Despite legal designations and technological
improvements, demands on waterways, even in this region of hydrologic
abundance, commonly exceeded their capacities.

Erosion of Local Authority

To disrupt the southern economy during the Civil War (1861–65), invading northern forces burned bridges and destroyed locks and dams while the Union navy sank ships in rivers and harbor entrances. To help restore a battered regional economy after the hostilities, the U.S. government responded to desperate appeals from southern officials to restore navigation capabilities. This initiated the second phase of navigation improvements, which shifted the financial burden from local investors to the federal treasury. Surveys and construction fell to the nation's leading hydraulic experts, the Army Corps of Engineers.[64] "Improvement" of rivers remained a central objective, and congressional authorization of individual projects enabled channel modifications. The Corps's projects wrapped the fluvial landscapes of the Southeast in a different legal mantle. With navigation works designed and built by the army to serve both military mobility and national commerce, local definitions of navigability and local riparian rights often ran aground. Waterway transformation, however, remained a fundamental component of the "navigable" designation. And with federal involvement, many improvement projects had extended longevity—especially compared to their predecessors.

Petitions from southern authorities to the Army Engineers set in motion a series of surveys and plans for postwar river modifications to restore rivers' adequacy to enable movement of goods.[65] During the 1870s the Corps assessed the navigability of rivers across the coastal plain from Virginia to Texas. With appropriations from Congress, the engineers pushed the second phase of internal improvements forward during the 1880s. Initial surveys on the Cape Fear, Roanoke, Dan, Pee Dee, Santee, Savannah, Oconee, Alabama, Coosa, and Chattahoochee/Flint rivers had been completed by 1880. Some projects were little more than efforts to clear snags and downed trees, others involved channel enlargement, ongoing maintenance, and some called for locks and dams.[66] This second phase of navigation improvements delivered much stronger financial backing and relieved localities of the burden of supporting their own economic development. It also greatly emphasized the legal priority for navigation and produced more persistent environmental transformations. No longer was navigation just a state or private business matter. Undertakings by the federal military reordered the priority of navigation improvements, as did funding from the federal treasury. Waterways became routes that served national interests—even when there was modest traffic and commerce.[67]

Prior to the arrival of federally financed improvements, court cases in the late nineteenth century began inserting subtle inflections in the definition of navigability. In 1888, an Alabama court ruled that a brief history of floating timber on a stream did not make it navigable in fact and refused to order a long-established mill owner to take down an obstruction.[68] In this case, the older mill took precedence over more recent navigation activities. A Kentucky court acknowledged that prior use of a river for floating logs rendered it navigable in fact, but it also determined that it was not permissible for this activity to damage property of riparian land owners.[69] Thus, the jurists offered protections to new urban riparian land uses which encroached on public passage or the river banks, and in doing so they narrowed traditional navigational rights.

Once Corps-built navigation works were in place, appellate courts tended to rule that the value of their navigation projects overshadowed traditional riparian rights. The U.S. district court in Georgia, for example, considered the impacts of a navigation project on a rice plantation. The plaintiff, a riparian planter, claimed that a new "cross-tides dam" on the Savannah River raised water levels and destroyed the earthworks he used to drain the wetland rice fields and that the federally erected dams would force him to make substantial investments to build new drainage works to restore his fields. With higher water levels, the planter alleged that the government's project denied him fresh water, free of salt water pushed inland by the tides, that previously arrived at his property and which he had used for irrigation over the years. The court found, however, that the planter was taking water for irrigation purpose that did not belong to him. Thus, the loss of that water was damage without injury. And the government's modification to the Savannah was for navigation—"the most important uses of the public." Ultimately, the appeals court determined that "all the right they [the plaintiffs] have in the ebb and flow of the tide of the Savannah river is subordinate to the control of the government over that navigable stream, for its free navigation by the public."[70]

By 1910, southern officials were demanding additional modifications or resumption of maintenance where federal assistance had been terminated.[71] And in response, the Corps became firmly ensconced in navigational maintenance across the southeastern coastal plain.[72] To justify its expenditures, the Corps began assembling information on the value of commerce and tallied the economic benefits generated by its work. As the twentieth century progressed, the larger projects tended to grow while some lesser projects dropped from the Corps's budget.[73] In 1937, a inventory of river basins revealed that most of the rivers that southern states had modified in the early nineteenth century were part of the federal water-ways system maintained by the Corps of Engineers.[74] Their presence was nearly ubiquitous across the South.

In addition to navigational improvements, federal authorities inserted authority over the fluvial landscapes of the South through the construction and approval of hydropower projects—some in association with navigational improvements. Southern states began inventorying their hydropower potential in the late nineteenth century, looking forward to an industrial renaissance.[75] Local power producers tapped streams across the Piedmont, providing the initial basis for expanding power conglomerates such as Duke Power.[76] Between private and federal projects, the southern landscape acquired hundreds of impoundments (fig. 5.2). Early twentieth-century decisions limited the expansive federal jurisdiction over navigable waters. One ruling held that Congress could not dam a navigable river solely for power production.[77] Nonetheless, the first of the major federal projects in the South was the Wilson Dam built on the Tennessee River to provide power for munitions plants during World War I. Although completed after the war, this hydropower project contributed to the growth of a chemical industry fueled by hydroelectric power at Mussel Shoals, Alabama.[78] It also became a part of the subsequent expansion of New Deal hydropower projects. Both the numerous dams built as part of the Tennessee Valley Authority and other lesser, but locally significant projects, such as the Santee-Cooper complex in South Carolina, stand as obvious monuments to a new federal authority over navigable waters in the South as much as a visible reminder of the urge to maximize the use of natural resources with multi-use projects. Opposition by yeoman and minority farmers in the Tennessee Valley and by local elites seeking to hold onto the Lost Cause in South Carolina could not deter these projects.[79] The many private hydroelectric dams required federal permits and thus asserted federal authority over rivers with hydropower potential. A key decision was *United States v. Appalachian Electric Power.*[80] In this case, the U.S. Supreme Court ruled that the New River was navigable, despite its many rapids, given that improvements could render it passable. This 1940 decision bolstered the role of federal government in defining navigability, opening such rivers to the federal permitting process, and thereby asserting its authority over an ever-expanding network of rivers. Subsequent decisions emphasized the role the federal government is entitled to play in interstate navigation issues, but also allowed for a certain amount of state autonomy in water resources management.[81]

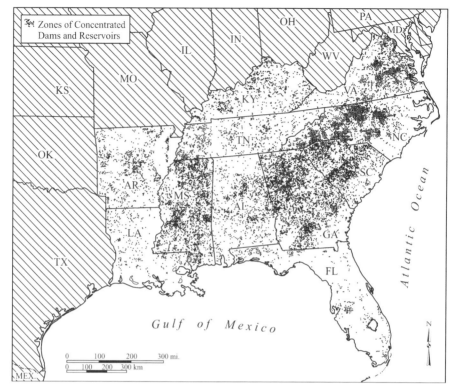

FIG. 5.2. Areas of concentrated dams. After U.S. Army Corps of Engineers, National Inventory of Dams [http://geo.usace.army.mil/pgis/f?p=397:12:], 2013. Cartography by Mary Lee Eggart.

In recent years, federal courts have repeatedly backed a definition of navigability that privileges national interests, particularly when the Corps of Engineers or federal laws are at issue. During the nineteenth century, the courts expanded the definition of navigability from rivers that were navigable in fact to those that were susceptible to being used as highways of commerce. By the 1940s, streams were considered navigable if reasonable improvements had rendered them fit for commercial activity.[82] Passage of the 1972 Clean Water Act extended federal jurisdiction to "nonnavigable intrastate waters whose use or misuse could affect interstate commerce."[83]

Examples of this trend abound along the South's federally modified waterways.[84] In *U.S. v. Tull*, the courts concluded that a private waterway may fall under the sway of the Corps of Engineers if it joined a navigable waterway and an obstruction impeded federal maintenance of navigation.[85] Tull had filled in a portion of a navigable channel without a permit from the Corps and thus had created an illegal obstruction in the eyes of the federal authorities. Flood-control projects on navigable waters by the Corps of Engineers did not entitle riparians to compensation when structures denied them use of water.[86] In 1981 the courts determined that federal courts were the final arbiter of navigability, although other federal agencies and their policies had a powerful influence on the courts.[87] Additionally, the Rivers and Harbors Act gave the Corps the widest possible authority in determining navigability.[88] Southern authorities eagerly had sought Corps projects to improve navigable waterways, but as these cases illustrate, an unforeseen outcome was that southern states relinquished a portion of their authority over defining navigation within their boundaries.[89] Thus, the states' actions indirectly limited their own management of riparian environments.

In one recent, highly contested water battle, observers speculated that navigation interests would prove pivotal.[90] At issue was water stored in Lake Sidney Lanier, a reservoir on the Chattahoochee River in north Georgia. In 1960, the Corps completed the dam that impounded water in this reservoir as part of a navigation project authorized by Congress in the 1940s. The reservoir's purpose was to store and then release water as needed to maintain sufficient water depth for uninterrupted downstream navigation throughout the year. Increasingly, Atlanta has requested and received a larger share of its potable water supply from this reservoir, thus reducing the water available for navigation. This situation became highly visible during the drought of 2007 when the news media carried frequent images of the extremely low levels of water in Lake Lanier. The drought merely highlighted a long-standing conflict over the limited flow of the Chattahoochee.

For several years prior to the serious drought of 2007, the states of Alabama, Florida, and Georgia (which all share an interest in the Chattahoochee) had been seeking a formula to sustain their individual interests. Alabama sought water for power and navigation—traditional uses of the water and those that justified construction of the dam and reservoir in the first place. Florida initiated claims to maintain adequate flow to preserve endangered species and also its commercial fishery in Apalachicola Bay near the river's mouth. Georgia was most concerned with supplying drinking water to its major metropolis and, to a lesser extent, with downriver withdrawals for irrigation agriculture.

Prior to authorization of the Chattahoochee River project, the Corps's 1939 report to Congress provided justification for funding and emphasized the importance of navigation and power to be derived from a series of locks, dams, and impoundments. It observed that "there is apparently no immediate necessity for increased water supply in this area though the prospect of a future demand is not improbable."[91] A follow-up report by the Corps provided more detail on the location of reservoirs and acknowledged Atlanta's desire for a reservoir north of the city that would supplement the city's water supply during times of shortage.[92] During construction, the Corps reported that by regulating flow of the Chattahoochee, the project provided Atlanta with a more dependable flow in the river and thus a more consistent supply of water to be taken from the river below the dam—not from the reservoir.[93] The Corps did not plan for water withdrawals from the reservoir and made no allocation for that purpose in its initial designs.

By the 1970s, following rapid growth of Atlanta, the Corps began to allocate water to the urban area. After droughts in the early 1980s, the Corps formally added water supply as a priority for the Lake Lanier reservoir—a change from its initial mandate.[94] The U.S. district court ruled in July 2009 that the Corps's reallocation of water in the reservoir to municipal water supply was not authorized by Congress. The judge concluded that such a change required congressional review and approval. Thus, in this decision, the traditional uses of the river for power and navigation took precedence over recent urban demand, although they were not the reason specified for the decision. An appeals court overturned this ruling in 2011, however, when it determined Atlanta's use of river water had authorization.[95] Both the district court and the appeals court's rulings largely ignored navigation and in turn focused on more fundamental separation-of-powers issues. In effect, the decision illustrates that the complexity of this case, and many others for that matter, far exceeds traditional common law concepts built around navigable waters. Nonetheless, by resituating riparian issues in constitutional or federal environmental laws, local ability to determine navigability is further diminished when decisions revert to Congress. And at the core of this issue were shortages, made evident by drought, that have prompted decades of litigation among states over a shared waterway.

Conclusions

Southern states embraced the authority to define navigable waters and the attendant opportunities to manage riparian environments through such actions as authorizing stream alterations for transportation or milling. During the early nineteenth century numerous southern navigation companies modified waterways that aided fall-zone urbanization and the expansion of inland agriculture. Cultivation, in turn, contributed to erosion and sedimentation. This process, along with extreme weather events, strained the modestly financed navigation companies, most of whom were in ruins by the end of the Civil War, as well as undermined their adequacy to provide effective navigation. Courts backed the establishment of navigation companies, their transformation of waterways, and their ability to charge tolls on public waterways. While there were modest incursions on navigational primacy under the law, unlike in New England, an instrumental interpretation of riparian common law did not supplant more traditional interpretations.

In the century following Reconstruction, southern states petitioned for federal river improvements and consequently witnessed an erosion of their own authority over water resources. As the Corps of Engineers invested federal dollars in navigation structures and Congress enabled federal permitting for hydropower installations and passed numerous environmental laws, courts have ruled that these works take precedence over local riparian interests. Furthermore, these works also have produced more enduring environmental transformations than the nineteenth-century projects, transformations that extend the temporal impact of legal decisions impinging on navigable waters. As interstate conflicts over water, such as the Chattahoochee River case, demand congressional attention, states lose additional authority over their internal waters. Future water shortages due to climate change will exacerbate an already contentious situation, which will play out far removed from local stakeholders.

6

Conserving Water for Fishing

Introduction

Antebellum southerners heartily embraced the notion of the commons—
a territorial concept that granted use of field, forest, and waterways to all.
Livestock owners along with hunters and fishermen largely ignored private property lines and took full advantage of public lands that enabled
the expansion of the resource base for small holders and enslaved laborers.
Historians have engaged in lively discussions about the loss of the southern commons. Postbellum fencing laws gradually denied white yeoman
and African American farmers access to forest and fields where their livestock had grazed under customary rights. Whether driven by a fundamental cultural shift or by economic interests, the southern landscape underwent a piecemeal enclosure movement at the county level beginning in the
1870s and continuing into the 1950s.[1]

Infringement on traditional common rights to hunting and fishing accompanied the realignment of property rights for grazing but through very
different means. Custom across the antebellum American South allowed
free and enslaved residents the privilege to hunt and fish on the property
of others, and common law provided the right to take fish from navigable waters. After emancipation, southern landowners supported restricting access to wildlife on their property couched in terms of conservation.
Steven Hahn has argued that conservation practices implemented during
the late nineteenth century were an indirect means to control labor, while
Scott Giltner concludes that they served a broader purpose of restricting
the freedoms of recently freed blacks.[2] Their interpretations provide a dis-
tinctively southern rationale for wildlife management practices that had
parallels with policies in other regions but that did not share the same underlying social and economic conditions. Restricting the commons artificially impinged on the naturally occurring abundance of water and the
aquatic life that lived there.

My concern here is with the transition of the fluvial commons in the
American South as a fundamental realignment of the geography of water
bodies and the natural resources they contain. These adjustments reflect

growing pressure on once-abundant aquatic resources, and as states faced perceived limits to abundance, they modified fishing rules and policies relating to access to waterways. Scholarship on the shifting legal status of the commons in other regions suggests some parallels and some obvious differences with the South. New Englanders redefined the commons through conservation laws; however, their efforts increasingly protected private investments—namely fish propagated by individuals. In the American West, locally managed commons eventually gave way to oversight of public lands by federal agencies.[3] Examples of state policies in the South bear remarkable similarity to the restrictions on fishing employed by conservation agencies in New England, albeit with a different intent. Likewise, although the South did not have the expansive federal land holdings that existed in the West, a growing federal role in defining the southern commons offers a slightly distorted reflection of the pattern that unfolded in western states. From support for protecting marine fisheries, to development of state parks, to funding for hatcheries for sport fish, to wild and scenic river designations, federal influences have permeated southern states' management of the aquatic commons.

Common-law traditions, rooted in Roman legal precedent and continued by southern jurists, held that fish in navigable waters were the property of the state and that all citizens had a legitimate right to harvest that resource.[4] Through various conservation policies enacted during the late nineteenth and early twentieth centuries, states began regulating fishing. These policy adjustments had multiple impacts. They offered a means to restore or perpetuate certain fish populations, they altered the social and legal contexts for taking fish, and they realigned the geography of water bodies. Through programs and policies designed to ensure recreational fishing, southern policy makers impeded the continuation of a once-thriving commercial freshwater fishery. While protecting the commons for the "public"—narrowly defined—conservation policies restricted access to some waterways and hence the fluvial commons became increasingly uncommon and access inequitable. Recent policies have tended to impose greater impediments on commercial activity while privileging sport activity in fresh waters and this has steered American policy back toward its English precedents that sought to preserve wildlife for the sport of the elite.[5]

Setting aside territories for protecting wildlife has European roots in the preserves of the aristocracy, but preserves for the common folk is more of an American institution. One of America's foremost conservationists,

Gifford Pinchot, received training in Europe, but when hired to manage the Biltmore Forest, he found his formal education hardly prepared him to deal with the large denuded tracts he encountered in western North Carolina.[6] Before conservation practices took root in the United States most game and fish policies permitted intensive exploitation. Conservation policies, however, redirected efforts to protect desirable species and their habitats. Reducing public access was one means to accomplish this, and states modified fishing regulations and created protected fluvial territories.[7] American states explicitly sought to provide access to common sportsmen, but they curtailed commercial fishing in certain waters. State parks, while limited in size, further restricted commercial fishing by setting aside areas specifically for recreational anglers, while wild and scenic rivers also accommodated recreational pursuits.

From Common to Scarce

Public rights to fish in waterways have their roots in common-law definitions of navigable waters (see chap. 5).[8] Submerged within the concept of navigable waters was the notion that the public had the right to take fish from those waters—although navigation rights generally took priority. There were restrictions to access, however, on lakes and non-navigable streams—with some exceptions such as certain lakes in Massachusetts and North Carolina. State courts across the South consistently upheld the principle of state ownership of fish and the public's right to both seek and harvest nature's bounty.[9] While public access to fish remained subservient to navigation rights, legal fishing rights flowed through the same channels as navigable waterways.

States, however, could limit access to fish, and they drew on European concepts to frame their regulatory approach. In some states, legislatures awarded monopolies to commercial fishermen. Recognizing the hardships this practice could impose on a limited number of citizens who relied on this formerly public resource for sustenance, a few states imposed conditions on the monopoly holders that forced them to provide free fish to the poor who could no longer legally fish on their own. Virginia maintained the public property status of waterways to allow poor citizens legal access to public waters and their aquatic resources. While restrictions might place less pressure on a resource and serve as-yet-unarticulated conservation goals, legislatures established monopoly rights to derive revenue and also to minimize any necessary monitoring and enforcement.[10]

Recognition of resource scarcity commonly prompts legal adjustments from customary rights to administrative regulation.[11] The earliest resource protection efforts sought to protect migratory species. Virginia's colonial legislative body required mill owners to build fish slopes to enable the seasonal fish runs to continue.[12] Other eastern seaboard states enacted similar legislation to protect fish for subsistence by upcountry farmers. North Carolina legislators, while seeking to maintain common access to fish, allowed for the expansion of commercial fisheries near the coast that ultimately destroyed inland fishing and virtually wiped out a once rich resource.[13] Depletion of both aquatic and marine life in public waters offers a further example of a recognized scarcity that prompted adjustments. Maryland and Virginia signed a compact in 1785 pledging to preserve the fish populations in the shared, interstate waters of the Potomac River.[14] By the late nineteenth century, the two states had modified their pact to outlaw the use of seines during restricted seasons.[15] Their actions reflect two of the fundamental tools used by states to protect threatened resources: restrictions on the devices used for collecting fish and excluding fishing from specific areas. Additionally, restricting fishing to specific seasons was a common conservation tool.[16] Colonial and early nineteenth-century efforts were aimed at protecting commercial and subsistence fishing, treating aquatic life as a common economic resource.[17] Although an inland state, Kentucky explicitly attributed its early conservation practices to Anglo-Saxon legal traditions and proclaimed fish belonged to the collective population, not individuals.[18]

Virginia authorities reported on reckless harvests of shad and rapid depletion of oysters in the late nineteenth century.[19] To offset these scarcity-creating situations, the state fish commission sought to restore shad populations biologically by propagation and restocking. It promoted a more geographical approach for the immobile oysters. Stating that "oyster planting is farming," the state's commissioner underscored the obvious, that cultivation on fixed tracts of ocean bottom was the key to restoring this fishery. While the legislature was unwilling to prohibit small-scale collecting of oysters, it passed legislation that distinguished between public commons and leased bottoms with exclusive rights to the leaseholder. The state surveyed and marked the "Baylor Line" to visibly demarcate the boundary between private and public oyster beds.[20]

Oyster conservation practices in Louisiana also exemplify the closure of public territory to unrestricted harvest. The state enacted policies to protect this highly valued and rapidly disappearing resource. After several failed attempts to protect oysters, the state clearly asserted ownership over the state's coastal "waterbottoms" in 1902. The legislature created an Oyster Commission that would lease water bottoms and exclude nonresidents from harvesting oysters in the state's waters.[21] Additionally, the 1910-authorized Conservation Commission sought to exclude out-of-state shrimpers and also the "Chinamen" which it considered a threat to local fishermen.[22] The state claimed that lack of conservation led to a decline in the valuable shrimp fishery and predicted a tenfold increase in shrimp landings with the extension of protections.[23] Its regulatory efforts restricted access to one threatened species of the marine commons. More importantly, such early efforts established conservation-oriented branches of government and extended the customary and common-law foundation through more explicit regulations that were part of an expanding national conservation impulse.

North Carolina saw its shad population dropping in the early twentieth century and attributed it to increased fishing intensity to satisfy a burgeoning market. To protect the shad fishery, the legislature prohibited the use of nets near the mouths of streams used by these migratory fish in 1905. This first legal step sought to maintain open passage between salt and fresh water and to restrict the use of certain fishing gear in specific locations. In 1909 the legislature expanded the territorial authority of the fish commission by calling for the survey and marking of coastal waters where it prohibited certain equipment.[24] The commission also advocated closing oyster-producing areas to general access and leasing "bottoms" in order to bring order to the oyster fishery while also ensuring the state revenue from this activity.[25] Each of these steps followed pronouncements of a loss of abundance and the need to restrict the commons through the overlay of state laws on traditional local fisheries management.

The Virginia Commission of Fisheries lamented the growth of the fishing industry and the depletion of marine resources despite increased regulation. Nonetheless, it observed that the salvation of the commercial fishery resided with oyster "planters," who were saving the resource by cultivating their leased beds.[26] In the commission's view, protected and carefully managed territories offered redemption to an aggressive economic pursuit. To put this principle to work, the state surveyed the oyster-producing areas and imposed different regulations to the public grounds and the leased bottoms where oyster cultivation was taking place. The Baylor Line was the boundary between these two distinct areas that oystermen worked in different ways and followed fundamentally different economic strategies. In the public waters, oystermen could not dredge the beds, they had to return small oysters to the water, and fishermen had to replace shell material to serve as beds for future generations of oysters. Planters, in contrast, were able to dredge their cultivated oyster beds.[27] But, despite steps to protect the oyster grounds, by 1927 the commission was sharply criticizing those working the public beds for exhausting the resource. The tonger, it complained "has abused his birthright and pillaged it for a mess of porridge today, forgetful of the morrow . . . tomorrow has come and we find depleted public beds." Meanwhile, it hailed the planter as saving the industry for Virginia.[28] Thus, the Baylor Line allowed conservation to emerge from private efforts regulated by the state and in marine waters, and conservation explicitly protected commercial fisheries. Virginia's conservation policies sought to protect private-sector oyster cultivators.

Intensive harvest of oysters in Chesapeake Bay prompted Maryland officials to grapple with early conservation measures as well. As northern dredgers hauled oysters to New England consumers, Marylanders sought to promote cultivation as a means of sustaining the bay's yield. Drawing on the success of leasing oyster bottoms for aquaculture in Connecticut, Maryland officials and scientists struggled to privatize oyster production. Their efforts met with stern resistance from the oystermen and the sizable block of coastal legislators. Legislated efforts that authorized state-run programs to restore oyster beds or move seed oysters to protected areas proved futile during the 1910s and early 1920s. Unlike other southern states, including its immediate neighbor, Maryland lagged behind in establishing oyster leasing and restricting the commons to the politically effective watermen.[29]

Protecting Freshwater Commons

Protective measures initially focused on the most lucrative fisheries in marine and estuarine waters, but they did not end at the upper limits of tidal waters. A first step commonly involved creating a state fish-and-game commission with responsibilities to protect aquatic and terrestrial wildlife. Virginia was among the first states to create a fish protective force in the 1880s which had responsibilities over oysters in marine waters and also migratory fish that followed tidal streams inland. This early agency had responsibilities that extended from the tidewater to the headwaters of inland rivers. The Board of Fisheries sought to carry out its legislated mandate, but commercial fishermen refused to comply. According to the fish commission, use of pound nets on tidal streams resulted in the slaughter of migrating trout. State law prohibited the use of pound nets in May, but there was no penalty attached to the act and fishermen ignored the law. Additionally, there was a tax for use of pound nets during the legal season, but when inspectors attempted to collect the taxes, they met open resistance. Rebuking wardens with firearms, fishermen declared they would not pay the taxes or submit to arrest.[30] The commons temporarily remained open at the threat of violence.

Florida fishermen also recognized weaknesses in state legislation and openly defied regulations. In 1913, the state created the Department of Game and Fish. It was not met with enthusiasm among freshwater fishermen, which led to an eventual lapse in legislative support. The state agency reported that fishermen were ignoring laws and that it was "almost impossible to convict violators after they are caught . . . and it is a well known fact that a large number of these men have organized in rebellion against the Fish Laws and have agreed among themselves that when one is caught and fined in the courts for violations that he serves a sentence instead of paying a fine in cash."[31] Such encounters hardened the attitude of fisheries agency personnel toward commercial enterprises on fresh waters. Commercial fishermen won the initial round in Florida when the legislature dismantled the freshwater portion of the enforcement agency in 1915. Only in 1927 did the state reinstitute an organization with authority over fresh waters.[32] With the formation of the Department of Game and Fresh Water Fish, the legislature repealed all local conservation laws in an attempt to create one consistent, statewide authority and to empower the new state agency. In the late 1920s, fisheries personnel resumed their attack on commercial activity on inland waters when they reported a declining number of black bass at a time of increasing interest in sport fishing. They advocated restrictions on the interstate sale of this valued game fish and also a process that would permit commercial fishermen to take "rough" fish—or those not desired by sport anglers. By 1932, the state fisheries body proclaimed that "it is the commercial net that has depleted Florida's supply of the choicest of sport fish [black bass]."[33] Sport fishermen found some relief to the stiff competition for black bass when the state legislature banned interstate sales in 1935.[34] Overall, state regulations narrowed the commons by leaving black bass to sport anglers and restricting commercial fishermen to rough fish.

Bifurcation of authority between fresh- and saltwater, as in Florida, appeared in Virginia and North Carolina, and the distinction between coastal and inland counties was obvious in legislation and regulation. States clearly differentiated between the very different scale of operation off their coasts and on inland waters. Coastal counties in Alabama, where there were established commercial fisheries, opposed fishing regulations in the early twentieth century. Meanwhile, the state game and fish commissioner reported that ineffective regulation contributed to declining fish stocks in inland counties.[35] With guidance from the commissioner, the legislature gradually enacted restrictions on commercial fishing gear such as seines on inland waters, along with provisions to stock rivers with game fish. These actions underscore the divergent approaches to different environments. Overcoming resistance to conservation practices on inland water is also reflected in more effective enforcement. Alabama authorities reported better cooperation from the courts and substantial increases in convictions—from an average of 184 per year between 1918 and 1922 to 1,344 per year between 1927 and 1930.[36] This remarkable expansion denotes the declining influence of commercial fishermen on inland waters. By 1930, state authorities further refined its policies that parceled nature. The Carmichael Act defined public and private waters and also specified game and nongame fish. These distinctions enabled the state to require fishing permits even on private waters and also placed additional restrictions on the sale and export of game fish.[37]

Improved enforcement in southern states stems in part from increased revenues from the sale of fishing licenses—another key plank in the rationale for fishing regulations. As early as 1913, Florida officials lamented the lack of license fees for sport fishing while similar fees applied to hunting.[38] Fishing permits or licenses limited legal access to wildlife, and in the South this all too often excluded poor blacks from the commons. States, however, argued that the revenue funded conservation programs that perpetuated sport fishing.[39] Tennessee by 1950 was able to sell a hundred thousand licenses to out-of-state fishermen and largely defer the cost of its agency to nonresidents.[40]

Agency staff in Louisiana consistently sought to justify restrictions on what they characterized as predatory commercial fishing and the creation of protected spaces by arguing that sport fishing was the ideal use of fresh water. Louisiana's Conservation Commission began a limited effort to restrict freshwater seining—associated with commercial fisheries. In its 1912 annual report, the Conservation Commission disparaged the commercial fishermen: "Unfortunately, the class of citizens which it [conservation law] seeks to control is the most independent and most improvident of all citizens. After one hundred years of effort they have nothing to show for all their labor but the direst poverty, for the simple reason that the State has neglected them and the marvelous possibilities of the food supply they handle."[41] The agency cautioned that fish resources were disappearing due to large-scale exploitation and that they had value beyond commercial fishermen and fish markets.

Commercial fishing was a major economic activity on Louisiana's inland waterways and one that the Conservation Commission did not want to extinguish. An early report underscored its vitality and the opportunities to expand it through conservation practices: "The fisheries of the state are capable of indefinite extension. We believe the State ought at once to build and equip one or more catfish and game fish hatcheries on the Achfalaya [sic] and other rivers, so that fully two hundred and fifty millions of the young of such fish might be placed in the rivers and streams of the State annually. This would mean returns of millions of dollars from the markets of the world."[42] Ultimately, the commission accommodated commercial concerns when it pointed out that the Mississippi and Atchafalaya rivers, both undeniably navigable waters, were so large that intensive harvests would not deplete resources there. In the commission's view, the major waterways should remain exempt from most restrictions. A dual regulatory strategy that protected commercial activity on the major waterways and privileged sport fishing on smaller stream and lakes created a geographical distinction in terms of conservation practices. But by the 1920s, the commission was restricting fishing even in large rivers during the breeding season to offset declining numbers of the two dominant commercial species—catfish and buffalo fish. It had also undertaken a cooperative effort with the U.S. Bureau of Fisheries to propagate buffalo fish as further insurance against declining numbers.[43] Federal guidance and involvement was key to this effort and reflects an increasing federal role in waterways and fisheries management.

Louisiana's conservation efforts were not entirely uncontested. Commercial fishermen resisted the imposition of closed fishing seasons and the state's courts ruled a 1908 conservation law unconstitutional. The conservation commissioner lamented

> great quantities of fine game fish dumped onto the markets, which fish we felt reasonably certain had been caught with set seines, trammel nets and other unlawful and unlicensed means of catching fish during the breeding season. Whenever, we investigated these catches we were

informed that they had been caught with rod, hook and line and were utterly unable to refute the declarations. Our decisions kept great quantities of such fish out of the market and on that plea we do not regret our action . . . the professional fisherman with the half mile long net of one inch mesh, working the waters during all the breeding seasons is a serious menace to the existence of the fish and needs your most careful attention.[44]

The commission appealed to the legislature to restore restrictions: "We earnestly beg of you to urge the General Assembly to declare the breeding seasons of all game animals and fish absolutely sacred, so that our children and the unborn generations to come after us may find this fair Louisiana, fairer and better for this present generation having been wise enough not only to have seen the possibilities of the land, the rivers and the sea, but to have adjudicated the trust sacredly and solemnly on the platform of the greatest good to the greatest number."[45] And indeed, a 1912 act prohibited taking catfish and buffalo fish during their breeding seasons.[46] By 1914, the commission reported that effective laws and their enforcement were contributing to healthy fish populations and that conservation had not driven fishermen out of business.[47] Nonetheless, restrictions impinged on commercial activities and placed limits on the commons.

Texas fish management dates to the 1870s, when the legislature prohibited seine and net fishing on the state rivers. Those restrictions were followed by legislation that mandated the construction of fish ways around dams. Collaborative efforts with the U.S. Fish Commissioner to stock Texas ponds and stock tanks with carp eventually stalled when the legislature terminated the state Fish Commission in 1885.[48] Not until conservation practices emerged on the national scene and growing dissatisfaction with commercial fisheries provided a rationale for new state actions did Texas reinstate an agency authorized to manage fish populations. As early as 1912, the Game, Fish, and Oyster Commission observed that commercial fishermen were mocking conservation laws.[49] A decade later, the commission charged that "seiners" were contributing to the depletion of fish stocks during a drought and urged the extension of state fishing regulations from public to private waters to ensure viable fish populations. Exhibiting the true fisherman's zeal, the commission urged additional restrictions on commercial fishing practices, proclaiming that a "stream without fish is a miscarriage of social justice." Policy had begun to cater to the sportsman in the state's fresh waters by the 1920s, yet there was a more democratic cast to the regulation of waterways than in England. Policy makers noted that access to public waters was a response to those who could not join exclusive fishing clubs.[50]

In North Carolina, the state conservation commission began operations in 1926 and undertook responsibility for "state lakes" that had been set aside by colonial law as public waters. As early as 1827, legislators excluded these distinctive, shallow, obliquely shaped lakes from sale. In the early twentieth century, the legislature dedicated them to the benefit of the state and in 1929 placed them under the supervision of the conservation commission.[51] The lakes eventually became units of the state park system and received special status under its conservation policy. Although sale of the lakes themselves was not permissible, private citizens had secured title to most of the property surrounding the more popular water bodies. This created serious access problems for the general population. Access and interest in commercial fishing practices in these lakes produced conflicts between local residents and those lured to the areas for recreation. To address the public access issue, state officials argued for acquisition of public boat launching areas. Efforts to remove large private structures over the state lakes, to require permits for boats and docks, and to eliminate pollution sources reflect the extension of state administration over these public waters. To enhance the lakes' value for sportsmen, the state initiated a restocking program in 1928 and also excluded fishing from certain sections of these lakes. It assigned wardens to ensure "firm, yet courteous enforcement of the regulations."[52] In addition, the state experimented with permitting local fishermen to use trot lines to so that they could provide food for their tables. This effort also was seen as a way of helping eliminate "scavenger" or undesirable fish.[53] Overall the state fisheries organization proclaimed, optimistically, that fish laws were gaining public support due in part to the "growing realization that fisheries regulations are not intended to curb individual enjoyment of fishing as one of the greatest of all sports, but rather they represent the State's efforts to continue and increase the attractiveness of fishing in order that it may be as fully or more fully in the future."[54] Inland fishery regulations included requiring licenses, restrictions on equipment, and closed seasons.[55] These regulations, and an active enforcement program, impinged on commercial activity while promoting sport fishing in public waters. The state's policy embraced conservation ideals: "Any restrictions on the free use of this resource is intended only for the purpose of preventing wasteful destruction of a common inheritance, in which every citizen of the State has a definite property interest, by a few who would deprive the majority of their share of the benefits."[56] Regulation sought to stave off the tragedy of the commons, but angling, with some subsistence fishing, was the desired outcome on inland water bodies, not commercial fishing.

Tennessee also acquired lakes that came under state authority. Its first acquisition in 1912 was Reelfoot Lake, a large water body claimed by the West Tennessee Land Company. One entrepreneur leased much of the lake and operated a monopoly on commercial fishing, enforced by a group of so-called "night riders" who meted out punishment to anyone who defied the exclusive marketing arrangement.[57] The state stepped in to wrest control of the lake from the market fishermen and hunters in order to establish public access to the lake and its aquatic and avian life. State acquisition proceeded through a contentious battle that culminated in the state's purchase of the lake and explicit declarations by the legislature that it was a public and common fishery and game preserve. Ultimately, the state supreme court ruled it was navigable water, hence public, in 1913.[58] Nonetheless, state administration of the lake remained ambiguous for several more years. Guides and fishermen continued to inhabit its shore, and according to the state game and fish agency, the fishermen considered the fish in the lake their property.[59] Eventually the state imposed a permitting system for commercial fishing that allowed market fishing to continue, but fishermen had to purchase licenses to carry out their trade.[60] While the state did not entirely rid the lake of the possessive commercial fishermen, it opened the lake to sport fishing by tightening access to the commons.

Beyond Reelfoot Lake, Tennessee gradually shifted its tolerance on commercial devices on rivers. In 1920, the game and fish department argued that local laws threatened the riparian rights of upstream or downstream users by permitting traps or seines that impeded fish migration. At the same time, it supported the rights of riparian landowners to use basket traps or nets to obtain "rough" fish for domestic consumption since, it argued, this would not reduce game fish populations. Furthermore, the department advocated the extension of market fishing to all the large streams of the state—not just major rivers like the Mississippi—with restrictions on wing and trammel nets.[61] This position shifted over time, and the head of the Game and Fish Commission began regular attacks on the use of nets, except on the largest rivers. By the 1950s, additional lakes had come under state supervision, where it maintained the water bodies, stocked them with fish, and enforced fishing regulations. These management practices ensured the state's residents that there would be locations where sport fishing was protected and also reduced the fluvial commons.[62]

To some extent, commercial fishing was largely the domain of whites. The lawlessness of those who resisted conservation laws created dangerous settings for African Americans on remote stretches of river. Although poorly documented, accounts of fishing and houseboat dwellers in the Ohio River basin suggest few blacks relied on the river for a livelihood. Nonetheless, loss of tenant farm homes forced some African Americans to take up dwelling on houseboats and fishing in the South during the 1930s.[63]

Mississippi enacted conservation legislation somewhat later than its neighbors, but in effect, created a series of lakes designated as public waters for fishing—both sport and commercial. The state drew on model legislation prepared by the Isaac Walton League when it established its Game and Fish Commission in 1932. Since the state was influenced by the leading national sport fishermen's organization, it is no surprise that by 1933, it reported prosecution and convictions of fishermen using unlicensed commercial nets and also for selling game fish.[64] In addition to constricting the commons for commercial practices, the state's conservation law enabled the state to acquire and manage land for parks, refuges, and fishing waters. With assistance from the federal WPA program, Mississippi developed six lakes for public fishing and recreation. Fishing on those water bodies had to conform to state conservation regulations and accommodate both sport and commercial activity.[65] By the early 1950s, the state reported that these lakes primarily served sport fishermen, and it had undertaken an aggressive program to remove "commercial or rough" fish from one of them, Moon Lake.[66]

In terms of drawing the regulatory net ever tighter around specific areas, Louisiana began authorizing the creation of parish (county) game and fish preserves. Between 1912 and 1940, the state legislature approved twenty-five locally administered protected areas. Delegating supervision to parish police juries parallels the "local option" practices seen in fence laws. Parishes had little expertise in wildlife management, although they did take some steps to protect the resources they were responsible for. Caddo Parish jurors, for example, requested the assignment of a deputy sheriff to patrol the lake and funds to outfit the law enforcement personnel with a boat to patrol Caddo Lake. The compelling reason to invest in enforcement was to restrict practices associated with commercial-scale fishing on the parish's new fish preserve. Its rationale for enforcing existing laws reveals a one-sided bias toward sport fishing: "The Commission feels that if the laws against seining, netting and dynamiting are rigidly enforced, that in a very short time Caddo Lake and its tributaries will be filled with fish of every description and will become the finest fishing resort in the South."[67] Thus, local bodies, in collaboration with the state legislature and conservation agencies, set aside certain water bodies as protected territories. They could focus enforcement efforts on these relatively small spaces and effectively fence out what they portrayed as destructive fishing practices. In addition, although this was unspoken, conservation to support fishing by sportsmen largely excluded blacks. Ultimately, these policies reduced the fishing commons.

Regulating Protected Areas

Across the South, with the push of national organizations, states carved out additional territories where agencies could establish limits on wildlife pursuits. Encouraged by the National Conference on State Parks and with guidance from National Park Service experts, states across the country were creating and expanding park systems in the 1920s. During that decade Raymond Torrey observed the uneven national progress. He comments that the Northeast, Middle Atlantic, upper Mississippi and Ohio river basins, and the Pacific coast states were making good progress. Yet, he laments that the southern states, which were experiencing rapid population growth, lagged behind. Nonetheless, he notes that Texas, Florida, Alabama, Arkansas, Oklahoma, and Tennessee had made "excellent beginnings."[68] His state-by-state summary exposes the relatively small acreage dedicated to parks and the prevailing emphasis on historical monuments over outdoor recreation parks (table 6.1). Nonetheless, two of the larger territories within the emerging state park system were the "state lakes" in North Carolina and the sizable Reelfoot Lake in Tennessee.[69] These water bodies already were protected under state fishing regulations and represented an initial stage of encroachment on the traditional commons.

There were two explicit reasons proffered to justify creating protected areas: depletion of wildlife and, somewhat ironically, the encroachment of private preserves on the public commons. Private efforts to establish game preserves in the coastal wetlands in Louisiana set aside thousands of acres in preserves before 1920.[70] Largely established for waterfowl conservation, they represent an effort to impose state regulation of wildlife taking by the general population and to serve sportsmen. As the state sought to exclude market hunters, trappers, and fishermen from their traditional wildlife

TABLE 6.1 Southern State Parks and Protected Areas, 1926

State	Number Parks/ Protected Areas	Acreage
Alabama	8	50
Arkansas	1	80
Georgia	0	0
Florida	5	4,100
Kentucky	6	2,000
Louisiana	2	2,300
Mississippi	0	0
North Carolina	2	1,600
South Carolina	0	0
Tennessee	1	15,000
Texas	54	31,000
Virginia	0	0

Source: Raymond Torrey, *State Parks*, 1926.

harvesting areas, the displaced professionals expressed their reluctance to comply with new regulations and threatened violence against state authorities.[71] The rationale for preserves was extended to parks as places that would preserve public access to untrammeled territories dedicated to recreation.[72] In Georgia, private interests were purchasing land in the coastal counties and creating private preserves. According to Beatrice Nelson, the "resulting restriction on the right of the natives to hunt and fish has led to the provision of public opportunities for hunting."[73] North Carolina authorities likewise were concerned with private ownership around their state lakes and took steps to provide greater public access.[74] Almost without exception, when southern states created park systems, administrators touted the fact that parks would provide the benefits of outdoor recreation to all citizens—within reach both financially and geographically.[75]

National efforts to encourage state parks during the New Deal era found proponents across the country, but there were an inordinate number of Civilian Conservation Corps (CCC) project projects in the South and they proved most effective in establishing park systems throughout the region.[76] Parks were seen as a way of reducing regional distinctions and drawing southerners into the national fold. Professionals employed by the National Park Service were instrumental in shaping the landscapes and the practices of this emerging park network. While southern efforts may have lagged behind other sections of the country, states in the region gradually created park commissions during the 1920s. As they acquired property—often as gifts—and created parks, they imposed conservation-oriented regulations on those territories. Consistently, state parks prohibited hunting with firearms, but promoted regulated fishing. One prominent limitation had to do with race and not the perennial conflict between market and sport fishing. Southern states were resistant to creating parks for African Americans, and this group of citizens was excluded from most parks before the civil rights movement.[77]

States like Alabama, Tennessee, and Texas all readily acknowledge the essential role of New Deal funding and CCC work crews in establishing their park systems.[78] To secure assistance from National Park Service personnel, states had to develop conservation plans which meshed with the New Deal notions of environmental stewardship. Alabama passed its conservation act in 1939 and set to work deploying the Civilian Conservation Corps teams to develop five state park sites.[79] In Tennessee, the TVA was the most influential federal influence. After nearly a decade of deliberating parks, the Tennessee legislature enacted a conservation policy that closely followed TVA recommendations. Sport fishing on the many lakes created by the giant hydropower/flood-control project was a key feature of park development, and conservation of fish was central to managing park properties.[80] Likewise in Texas, the state sought professional assistance from National Park Service staff and financial assistance in the form of CCC work camps to push its state park system forward. Local politicians, such as the eventual president Lyndon Johnson, worked assiduously to direct CCC efforts to expand the state parks.[81] As in other states, conservation practices formed the backbone of wildlife management policies in those territories.[82]

The Louisiana parks commission explicitly sought to protect wildlife. Following the guidance of the National Resources Board, its rule number 9 stated: "Wildlife of State Parks is under strictest protection and must not be destroyed or unnecessarily disturbed."[83] This did not exclude fishing, however, and indeed fishing was one of the recreational activities touted by the park system (fig. 6.1). Over the years, the park system grew to include lakes where fishing was a principal attraction, and by the 1940s the agency was taking steps to eradicate predatory fish and thereby encourage

FIG. 6.1. Fishing on Toledo Bend Reservoir, Louisiana. Used with permission of the Louisiana State Library.

the propagation of species desired by sportsmen.[84] Overall the territory circumscribed by park boundaries was modest in southern states. Nonetheless, these newly designated territories promoted recreational fishing exclusively.

Mississippi established its Board of Park Supervisors in 1936 to manage parks constructed by the Civilian Conservation Corps. Without the federal government's involvement, the park system might have taken much longer to establish, and indeed the park supervisor pointed out that "all credit or blame for their development must rest with the Federal agents." Most of the parks included a public water body, whether a stream or lake. Park rules explicitly stated that state game laws applied and that "no person shall take more than 15 fish of any and all species per day from the waters within the park." Thus, the daily limit excluded commercial fishing in parks.[85]

Virginia assigned multiple agencies to maintain sport fishing in its parks in the late 1930s. The Game and Inland Fisheries Commission stocked the rivers and lakes, while the Department of Conservation promulgated rules and regulations for fishing. Although fishing was allowed, hunting was expressly forbidden in parks.[86] Likewise South Carolina did not permit the use of firearms in parks, but allowed fishing under strict regulations.[87] Following a similar course, Florida's Park Service sought to "develop, maintain and operate State Park lands so as to enable our people to use and enjoy their treasures without depleting them." Fishing was one of the prime activities in parks both for state residents and for the large number of seasonal visitors.[88] Farther west, water covered 24 percent of the property in Texas's state parks and the administrators considered water as a key enhancement to a park's value. Managing water for sport fishing was a primary concern; state biologists provided conservation-oriented planning.[89] Within park boundaries, stocking and careful management of fish populations perpetuated the ecologies that conservation biologists sought to produce for visitors, and regulations placed limits on the type of fishing, clearly favoring sport over commercial use.

While state parks across the South were limited in size and placed only modest river or lake waters under their fishing regulation, the 1960s movement to create wild and scenic rivers extended the reach of protected areas with fishing limitations. Congress passed the Wild and Scenic Rivers Act in 1968 (PL 90–542), which enabled state and federal agencies to designate certain river segments as free-flowing and prevent dam construction. By classifying these rivers as wild, scenic, or recreational, the law promoted and privileged sport over commercial fishing. Southern states, however, did not embrace the Wild and Scenic Rivers Act largely due to apprehension among rural landowners about potential infringement on their property rights. By 2000, only a modest number of streams in the southern states bore one of its classifications (fig. 6.2). Similarly, the Heritage Rivers program, launched by executive order in 1997, prioritized certain river segments for restoration and with that conservation of fish populations, but few southern states promoted rivers within their boundaries for this designation in subsequent years.[90] Consequently, fishing restrictions on southern streams experienced minimal change from this federal policy. However, even for those few segments, there is concern that wild and scenic designations might allow the federal government to claim water rights previously unavailable to them for upriver areas. At the core of the concern is that "reserved rights" could enable the national government to impose restrictions on upstream riparians in order to sustain sufficient flow to ensure that a wild or scenic river meet that designation during a low flow period.[91] Concern over federal intrusion on local riparian rights merely exacerbates southern resistance to wild and scenic designations.

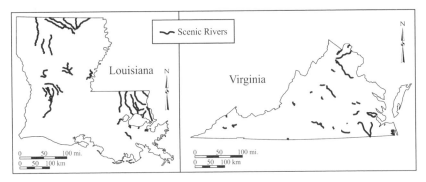

FIG. 6.2. Virginia and Louisiana Wild and Scenic Rivers. After Virginia Department of Conservation, Virginia Wild and Scenic Rivers [http://geo.usace.army.mil/pgis/f?p=397:12:], 2013; and Elaine Yodis and Craig Colten, *Louisiana Geography* [New York: McGraw-Hill Primis Custom Publishing, 2012].

One prominent exception is the Buffalo National River in Arkansas. Created by Congress in 1972, it represents a far more ambitious designation than merely classifying a stream segment as a protected channel under the Wild and Scenic Rivers Act; this came about with strong local support. At the behest of local residents and politicians, Congress passed legislation that enabled the National Park Service to assemble some ninety-four thousand acres along over 130 miles of the Buffalo River and placed it under the park service's jurisdiction. Controversy surrounded the creation of the park and pitted advocates of multipurpose dams against those seeking to preserve a free-flowing river as a national park. After the Corps of Engineers shelved a proposed dam, landowners resisted federal acquisition of their family farms. The small number of riparian property owners was outnumbered by advocates for the national river, and supporters ultimately witnessed the creation of a park. In a nod to traditional practices, the Park Service acquired a sizable buffer zone around the river, and by allowing some limited hunting in adjacent areas, it accommodated outdoorsmen. Additionally, the legislation creating the park gave the Secretary of the Interior authority to close certain areas to fishing (PL 92–237, sec. 3), and the rules imposed on the river within the park prohibited commercial fishing.[92] Thus, the establishment of a protected river reduced the opportunity for commercial fishing.

Riparian landowners, particularly in the South, were highly suspicious that the wild and scenic rivers program might deliver recreational boaters to their property and result in unwanted trespassers damaging crops, forests, or livestock. The rejection of the federal program reflects these apprehensions of property rights advocates. Nonetheless, across the South state legislators created scenic river programs which shared the objective of preventing future dam building with the federal initiative. Based in state agencies, they were more palatable to local constituencies—at least in some states. Tennessee, Georgia, and Florida, with an abundance of scenic waterways, created programs by the early 1970s, but followed up with few river segment designations. In contrast, Louisiana and Virginia overlaid scenic designations on many waterways. Louisiana established its system in 1970 and has placed sixty-four rivers with about three thousand miles of waterways within its system (fig. 6.2).[93] Louisiana limits reservoir construction, forestry, and re-channelization on these protected waterways, but allows fishing to continue. The legislation permits commercial activity with a state-approved permit.[94] Virginia boasts a scenic rivers system with twenty-eight river segments containing 610 miles of waterway.[95] As with the federal program, it prohibits construction of dams in designated stream segments. The state program explicitly avoids imposing any regulations on adjacent land uses. It also works within the framework of the state inland fisheries agency to manage fish populations and regulate fishing. Thus the state programs have deflected the touchy issue of property rights, while avoiding new fishing restrictions. Market fishing on many of the smaller rivers has virtually disappeared, and although the scenic rivers designations emphasize recreational uses, they do little to impact a nearly nonexistent commercial activity.

Conclusions

The southern fluvial commons underwent several deliberate demarcations and came under increasing regulatory supervision by state agencies during the early twentieth century. State conservation/fish and game bodies established preserves where they extended protections—largely to waterfowl and terrestrial species. In the face of perceived shortages, fishing protections first encompassed marine waters and sought to protect commercial species such as oysters and shrimp from overly aggressive collection. By requiring licenses, limiting the seasons, restricting fishing equipment, and even leasing oyster beds, state bodies imposed authority on marine fisheries and thereby limited the commons.

In response to reported declines in freshwater fish or threats to public access, states instituted conservation practices and established protected territories. With a clear emphasis on restraining unchecked commercial fishing, states imposed restrictions on freshwater fisheries similar to those they placed on marine waters, but also took steps to restrain commercial fishing. In line with marine restrictions, they limited the seasons and required permits or licenses. Targeting commercial activity, some states excluded game fish from the market fishery, but allowed taking "rough" fish. Selected propagation efforts, coupled with programs to remove nongame fish, further enhanced sport fishing. While states with massive waterways and sizable commercial fisheries, like Louisiana and Tennessee, accommodated both sport and professional fishermen, conservation tools clearly privileged sportsmen and geographic limits shifted commercial activity to major rivers. There were considerable barriers imposed on market fishing. Additionally, state lakes or preserves came into existence to address declining game fish stocks and to ensure public access. State parks provided another measure of state limitations on commercial fishing. Parks commonly excluded commercial activity and provided a sanctuary for the recreational angler. Scenic waterways extended limits on complete public access. Under the guise of perpetuating public access and conserving sport fish, southern states made the commons increasingly uncommon by the late twentieth century.

7

Inadequate Quality

Introduction

Howard Odum, the noted authority on the South, waxed poetic about the region's water riches in the 1930s. He observed that the "abundant rainfall of the Southeast, its ever-flowing streams" constituted a portion of "the regional abundance which is so commonly taken for granted." He characterized the region's extensive coastlines, "fringed with inflowing rivers and rivulets, brooks and branches, springs and freshets," as "natural wealth of the first order."[1] His portrait exemplified the belief that the South and its future success—agricultural or industrial—would benefit from the ample supplies of pure water.

Yet perpetual abundance of usable water was not guaranteed. In the absence of discussions of climate change, even in the face of serious droughts that had impacted not only the Great Plains but the South as well, loss of abundance could result from human-induced degradation of the water supply. Water pollution had emerged on the national scene in a prominent way in the 1930s, although the South's rivers had not suffered like their counterparts in the more industrialized sections of the country.[2] The loss of water quality, while not eliminating a single gallon of water, could reduce the available water supply for human consumption and industrial processing. This chapter considers the human-induced shortages that resulted from casual use of waterways as waste sinks. The consequent diminishment of water quality reflects the political drive to transform the region into the New South coupled with an environmental resource base that could not expand in tandem with population and industrial growth. The public opposition to pollution that ensued is evidence of a strong impulse to protect fishing activities more so than public health. The conflicts between sportsmen and torpid water pollution abatement agencies expose a fundamental disjunction between the drive toward a New South and the protection of traditional practices. Concern and conflict also arose over groundwater supplies and further illustrate that the region's populace was less tolerant of pollution than their governing bodies, albeit public health was an important motivation behind the groundwater issue.

Southern Environmentalists?

Historians and geographers have long portrayed southerners as abusers of a once bucolic landscape. A cornerstone of this argument is that abundance of virgin soil and flowing water fostered attitudes that promoted degradation. Avery Craven recounted agricultural practices in Virginia and Maryland that left soils exhausted and set in motion field rotation and the expansion of destructive cultivation practices.[3] His work set the stage for Stanley Trimble's account, which argues that the susceptible Piedmont suffered serious erosion due to poor farming practices.[4] James Cobb and Albert Cowdrey take the discussion from the farm to the factory, contending that southern states accommodated industrial development in the twentieth century at the expense of the environment. While southern states actively recruited industry and enacted lenient policies, Cobb and Cowdrey's examination of government environmental records neglects to consider how the public responded to environmental damage. Lethargic government efforts to address pollution contrasted sharply with popular efforts by southerners to protect valued aquatic resources such as fish and, to a lesser extent, public health within the context of a much smaller scale of urban-industrial pollution that varied considerably across the South. While government bodies tended toward lenient environmental policies, sportsmen, farmers, and others vigorously objected to pollution in numerous instances. Their complaints, while not necessarily in alignment with national environmental organizations, prompted a series of federal enforcement actions in situations where states failed to intercede in interstate pollution cases emanating from outside their boundaries.[5]

Southern states, like their counterparts across the country, had pollution laws on the books from the early twentieth century. For example, a 1905 survey characterizes pollution restrictions in the South as "partial;" that is, legislatures had forbidden poisoning wells or drinking water. This report labels restrictions in states across the Midwest and Northeast as "general" or "severe"—that is, laws that applied stringent and novel methods to protect and restore water quality.[6] A subsequent survey of state laws in 1939 indicates that most southern state legislatures had given regulators "incomplete control" over pollution.[7] States that assigned only partial or ineffective control to a state agency earned this designation. Overall, southern regulations during the early twentieth century were in a position to respond to pollution incidents rather than to restrict activities that might contribute to a public "nuisance."

James Cobb, a leading historian of southern industrialization, reports that "prior to the late 1960s few if any southern leaders gave thought to the long-term environmental implications of industrial development."[8] He illustrates his point with a South Carolina example where local boosters promised to cover legal costs due to any pollution suits if a potential manufacturer built its facility there. Ironically, his evidence contradicts his assertion by documenting that local leaders foresaw potential problems and took steps to minimize future legal penalties for environmental damage. Albert Cowdrey's fine environmental history of the South also points out that the southern states' quest for industrial jobs and accommodating governments contributed to adverse environmental impacts. He states that "the petrochemical industry joined upstream companies and agriculture in pouring massive discharges of pollutants into the Mississippi River, the air, and the land—until the 1970s with utter lack of restraint."[9] He failed to consider the massive 1960s pollution incidents that sparked a strong public response and forced the diversion of agricultural chemical wastes from the river at Memphis to land disposal sites by the mid-1960s.[10] Both these historians cited a limited number of examples and focused on state governments' responses to industrial effluents without including popular sentiment or federal intervention. In addition, Richard Bartlett's detailed examination of paper mill pollution in the Pigeon River reports that North Carolina law explicitly protected the manufacturer against pollution liabilities—exposing forethought about pollution and steps taken to protect a polluter.[11] More recently, environmental historian Martin Melosi argues that southern states' pollution abatement efforts lagged behind that of their counterparts in the Northeast and Midwest.[12] Actions taken to remedy pollution that reflect late twentieth-century environmentalism have emerged, but largely after the enactment of similar policies in other parts of the country.[13]

Yet, popular opinion, scale, and regional variations are important distinctions in discussing southern environmental stewardship. Carville Earle disabused the notion that southern farmers were soil miners across the entire span of that region's history and territory.[14] Likewise, there is ample evidence that citizens in the South objected to pollution caused by the newly arriving industries during the twentieth century. Indeed, rural farmers in Georgia, who sought redress for damages to forest and fields caused by the smelter smoke issuing from neighboring Tennessee, initiated one of the earliest interstate pollution battles that rose to the U.S. Supreme Court.[15] Downstream residents in Tennessee objected to the serious pollution flowing from the legally protected paper mill in North Carolina. Farmers, despite ineffective state agency intervention, appealed to federal authorities to halt air pollution in Florida. Fishermen joined a chorus of complainants when toxic chemicals caused massive fish kills on the Mississippi River in the mid-1960s. Texas sportsmen prodded state authorities to take action against polluting oil fields; and during the wartime industrialization of southwest Louisiana, sport anglers challenged factory discharges. Amendments to the Federal Water Pollution Control Act in 1956 enabled federal intervention in interstate pollution incidents without a state's invitation and allowed sportsmen in rural Claiborne Parish, Louisiana, to trigger the first hearing under that law. Beyond this action, there had been several lawsuits and other actions taken to halt damages caused by industries fouling favorite fishing waters in Louisiana before the late 1950s.[16]

The present chapter traces the emergence of concern with water pollution in several river basins in the American South: Corney Creek, the Potomac, the Chattahoochee, the Pearl, the Coosa, the Perdido, and the North Holston.[17] Evidence of lax government oversight comes from federal surveys of river basins in 1937, 1951, and 1958. These national tabulations of stream conditions expose persistent recognition of pollution but uneven responses. Eventually, each of the basins considered here became the scene of an interstate pollution enforcement action in the 1950s or 1960s. Attracting that level of scrutiny and response required loud and sustained local objections. By revealing both a protracted state government response to pollution and popular criticism of foul waters, this chapter supports the long-standing historical interpretation that states tolerated diminished water quality in exchange for jobs, while also showcasing popular sentiment that contrasted with state policies. These southern pollution enforcement efforts differ from those in other regions of the country during that time because they emphasized protecting water quality to sustain fish populations, but minimized public health.[18] To conclude that policy represents the full measure of southern environmental attitudes is inappropriate, although it is also incorrect to see the southern response to pollution in the 1950s and 1960s as part of the same emergent environmental movement driving enforcement in other regions of the country. The opponents to pollution were not environmentalists by any stretch of the imagination. Nonetheless, fishermen took steps to offset the manufactured shortages of suitable water quality. In the case of groundwater, southern government bodies participated in early investigations, although a significant class-action suit against an industrial polluter provides a parallel with public opposition to surface water degradation.

Mapping the Loss of Abundance

Industrialization and urbanization of the American South were very much a part of both national and regional efforts to foster the emergence of a New South. Export of staple crops had fueled the intensive agricultural development of the southern states in the early nineteenth century, and industry arose in the South to process the most abundant natural resources in the region—minerals (coal in Maryland, copper in Tennessee, phosphates in Florida, oil in Texas and Louisiana) and timber products (naval stores, lumber, and paper products) from across the Atlantic and Gulf plains and Appalachia. Textile mills flourished as industry migrated from New England in the twentieth century to tap low wage workers near the source of cotton. Capital transferred from New England and the Midwest fueled much of the industrial-scale natural resource exploitation that began in the late nineteenth century and continued well into the last century.[19] Thus, the fortunes built in northern commercial centers provided the financial base for much of the twentieth-century expansion of cities and manufacturing in the so-called Sunbelt. And although manufacturing emerged as a prominent economic engine later in the South than in the North, it had ties to the same sources of capital and technology tapped by polluting industry elsewhere.

By the 1930s, there was a rising national concern over deteriorating water quality—or emerging shortages of usable water. What has been largely invisible during wet years became obvious during drought. The same dry conditions that contributed to the Dust Bowl on the Great Plains reduced the flow in many streams well beyond the country's midsection and transformed what had been manageable amounts of sewage and industrial wastes into serious threats to public water supplies. The emerging national interest in pollution during the post–World War I years provides a suitable starting point for this discussion. Partly in response to a shrill public outcry over obvious degradation of coastal and river waters by industry during the boom years of the 1920s, congressmen introduced several bills to address pollution in the following decade, although none became law. As part of a national inquiry into water quality President Franklin Roosevelt created the National Resources Committee (NRC) composed of water resources experts, including geographer Gilbert White.

The president directed this committee to survey river basins and report on the status of flood control, irrigation, water power, soil conservation, pollution, and water-based recreation. The NRC issued a series of individual basin reports and a summary report. For each basin, state-level authorities in public health and sanitary engineering, hydrology, regional planning, and wildlife and forest conservation developed reports following a template from the national committee.[20]

The NRC's summary document proclaimed that pollution was "with a few exceptions, a major problem only in the heavily populated manufacturing areas of the Northeast"—a territory it labeled the "pollution belt" (fig. 7.1).[21] Of the stream basins considered here, the 1939 report characterized pollution in the Potomac as "serious." The Chattahoochee, Coosa, and North Holston basins all fit within its "less serious" designation. Pollution in the Pearl and the Perdido basins was of "minor importance." And although the report does not specify tiny Corney Creek, it labeled the larger basin's pollution situation as "less serious, but still important."[22] Thus the federal government's initial mapping of pollution indicated the problem was less significant across the rural and less industrialized South, although basins in this region reflect the full range of water quality and development. State policies in the South reflected a low priority given to pollution control. With the exception of Maryland and Florida, the southern states these rivers passed through had laws that provided for "incomplete control" of water pollution.[23]

Looking closely at the seven basins, the Potomac had the most pronounced pollution problem in the 1930s. It drains the ridge-and-valley province of West Virginia and western Virginia and areas in Maryland where considerable coal mining and forest removal had occurred in the late nineteenth century.[24] It forms a portion of the Virginia-Maryland border before emptying into Chesapeake Bay. In addition, the basin then contained a considerable population in the upper reaches and even greater densities in the lower course near Washington, DC—about half of the 1.2 million people lived upriver from the nation's capital. Effluent entering the river flowed from coal mines, gas and coke works, paper and pulp mills, tanneries, and chemical plants, plus municipal sewage treatment plants. By 1937, Congress had authorized the creation of an interstate conservancy district to address interstate pollution issues in this basin—reflecting the seriousness of the problem and also the complications encountered cleaning up interstate streams. Of particular significance in terms of policy, Washington, DC, was both the principal water consumer and the major

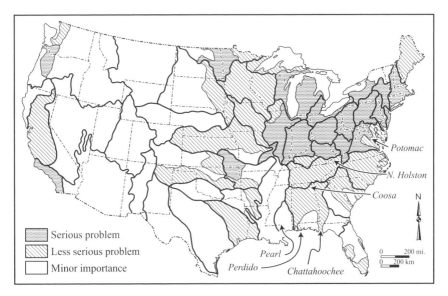

FIG. 7.1. River Basins and Pollution Status. After National Resources Committee, *Water Pollution in the United States*, U.S. Congress, House Doc. 155, 76th Cong., 1st sess., 1939. Cartography by Clifford Duplechin.

effluent source. Upstream pollutants threatened the city's potable water while sewage flowing from the nation's capital endangered downstream aquatic resources—but few communities. Recommendations in the 1937 survey sought to address the geographic reality and specified that natural resource degradation merited attention.[25]

Originating in the southern Appalachians, flowing through the Atlanta urban area, and forming about half of the boundary between Alabama and Georgia, the Chattahoochee River is a very different waterway from the Potomac. In the 1920s and 1930s, its largest urban center released substantial effluent into the upper stretches of the river, and several other communities discharged untreated sewage and wastes from textile mills. Unlike the Potomac situation, the largest source of effluent on the Chattahoochee, Atlanta, was well upstream from other smaller sources, and it also discharged its by-products above numerous small water-using communities. Although its wastes eventually reached the sea, it presented a problem to many users along the way, not just marine life. The authors of the basin survey indicated that "industrial wastes at present causes *local* [emphasis added] concern," but did not merit state, regional, or national attention. Soil erosion in the middle and upper reaches was a greater concern than municipal or industrial pollution, along with downstream sedimentation and malaria control, which the survey identified as the most critical issues.[26] Public health was a concern, but not in association with pollution, rather with the mosquito-breeding wetlands found along the river and exacerbated by sedimentation. About half of the Alabama and Georgia communities discharged untreated sewage into the river, but since many communities relied on groundwater for their municipal supplies, the threat of waterborne diseases was minimal, and hence there were few public health concerns.[27]

The Coosa River flows from northwest Georgia into northeast Alabama and drains into Mobile Bay as part of the Alabama River system. While Rome, Georgia, and Gadsden, Alabama, were emerging as regional industrial centers, agriculture was the dominant land use in the basin. Severe erosion and gullying had impacted a sizable portion of the basin by the 1920s and contributed to substantial sedimentation in the Lake Martin Reservoir near the confluence of the Coosa and Tallapoosa rivers. In the 1930s municipalities and industries both discharged untreated sewage into the river, which created a "constant menace" to downstream communities. Drought produced low flow in 1934 and 1935 and made water quality issues all the more obvious. Federal authorities recommended that the Alabama legislature should enact legislation to control waste disposal.[28] Yet, with only modest-sized cities along its banks, biological pollution in the Coosa did not constitute as serious a threat as in basins with larger cities.

The 1937 federal survey did not point out pollution on the North Fork of the Holston, a small tributary of the upper Tennessee River that drains the western flanks of the Appalachians. With ample precipitation and stream flow under normal conditions, most communities and industries in the basin used waterways to transport untreated wastes downstream. In reference to the larger Tennessee River basin, the report indicated that "the discharge of wastes from textile and pulp and paper mills has created a serious pollution condition." It went on to claim that installation of waste treatment systems was "greatly needed."[29] Yet, both the communities the report identified as needing treatment equipment had their respective projects "deferred" during a time when abundant WPA funds provided a critical boost to local sewage treatment projects. Along the North Holston, there were no large cities and only one sizable industry. Yet, as early as 1924 the Mathieson Alkali Company works in Saltville, Virginia, had created a sizable pollution problem when its waste lagoon ruptured and impacted water quality over four hundred miles from the release.[30]

Such incidents apparently did not register as chronic problems in the view of the NRC report.

The Perdido River drains a small basin which had a low population density in the 1930s. Pine forests covered much of the area, although logging and expanding agricultural uses had contributed to deforestation and subsequent erosion. The 1937 survey notes that the small number of larger towns in the adjacent and more populated Escambia basin minimized the pollution problem, although it observes that there were few sewage treatment facilities and the flow of untreated biological wastes threatened coastal shellfish beds. The report makes no specific reference to the Perdido but mapped it as part of the Escambia basin. Other than pulp mills, no mention of industry appears in the basin's overview. Yet, the report emphasizes the importance of recreational and wildlife possibilities. It indicates three national forests existed in the basin and that bathing beaches were susceptible to future pollution if cities and industries did not provide adequate treatment. As in other basins in the South, the chief public health problem was drainage for malaria control.[31]

Draining much of Mississippi and a small section of Louisiana, the Pearl River had a relatively small, rural population.[32] Agricultural and forest land uses predominated in the basin. NRC investigators noted that sewage pollution was a minor problem, although industrial wastes seriously impacted water quality in some locations. Reliance on rich groundwater resources minimized demand on river water for public supplies. Consequently, Jackson, the largest city in the basin with sixty thousand residents, was able to use the river for its sewage removal. The largest industrial concentrations existed in the lower basin near Bogalusa, Louisiana, and nearby Picayune, Mississippi. Damage to coastal shellfish by the industrial effluent was the principal concern and prompted the authors to declare that "preparation of pollution-abatement plans are urgently needed." Malaria control was another prominent concern in the coastal wetlands.[33]

Tiny Corney Creek did not register in the 1937 basin survey, but it was part of the larger Ouachita River basin. Federal authorities reported oil field wastes as the principal pollution source there, but observed that brine discharges would decline as pumping depleted local reserves. Federal personnel also noted, with some caution about future growth, that dilution was the best remedy for industrial pollution at the time. Crude oil production was just commencing in the Corney Creek basin in the late 1930s, and despite dry conditions during much of that decade, brine waste had yet to make a significant impact.[34]

These river basins offer sharp contrasts. The Potomac basin had the densest concentration of industry and people, and consequently it had the most critical pollution problems, principally because there were numerous manufacturing operations above the basin's largest city, Washington, DC (663,000 residents in 1940), near the river's mouth. While Atlanta's 302,000 residents (as of 1940) discharged municipal effluent into the upper reaches of the Chattahoochee, soil erosion from the Piedmont and malaria control were more prominent concerns at the time because downstream communities relied on groundwater, thereby greatly reducing the threat of waterborne diseases. Scattered industrialization and urbanization were occurring along the largely rural courses of the Coosa and North Holston and causing water quality to decline. With low population density and few industries, there were minimal problems along the Perdido, although pollution could impact shellfish and recreational beaches. Along the lower Pearl River, industrial wastes presented a serious problem to marine shellfish, while domestic sewage from Jackson and several smaller upstream towns was not a threat since downstream communities consumed groundwater. Rural and thinly populated Corney Creek basin was on the cusp of an oil boom and the release of brine and oily wastes. The one thing the basins shared is that WPA funds had financed the installation of municipal sewers by the end of the 1930s. Nationally over half the volume of municipal sewage received treatment by 1939, but for communities in these basins which remained without treatment works, installation of sewer lines increased the flow of municipal wastes to rivers at the same time that the economic downturn reduced industrial discharges.[35] As the Great Depression ended and industrial activity expanded during World War II, combined municipal and industrial waste loads increased in tandem and reached quantities well above pre-1930 levels.

Controlling Pollution in the 1950s

Following the end of World War II in 1945, there was renewed public and government interest in water pollution. Voluminous and unchecked industrial waste discharges during the conflict had left many streams across the country in deplorable condition. Consequently, most states revamped their pollution laws, and Congress passed the 1948 Federal Water Pollution Control Act, which provided funds for improving municipal waste treatment and researching industrial waste management. Primary authority for pollution abatement resided with states, and southern legislatures commonly created pollution control commissions, following models established in northern states. These bodies had the authority to issue rulings on pollution disputes and also to permit urban and industrial discharges. Postwar legislation and scrutiny of water quality prompted a series of river basin assessments in the 1950s that provide a contrast with those compiled in the 1930s.[36]

The Potomac River basin witnessed a massive population increase, particularly in its lower reaches, from 1.2 million residents in 1932 to 2.3 million in 1950. Mining and timber removal were still present, although somewhat diminished by midcentury, and notably chemical production had increased during the war years, as had pulp and paper making, and leather tanning. Approximately 70 percent of municipal sewage in the basin received treatment, yet the federal survey reported that only 46 percent received "adequate" treatment. Meanwhile at least a third of the industrial facilities provided no treatment, and just under half of those operated "satisfactorily." The 1951 survey indicated most municipalities needed new or enlarged plants to meet the requirements of the basin's growing population. In the upper basin, there appeared to be little progress with treatment since the late 1930s (fig. 7.2). Numerous communities identified in the 1937 report still did not have treatment facilities. The pace of construction had been slow, particularly with the diversion of materiel and engineering expertise to the war effort. By the late 1950s numerous communities had added sewage treatment facilities, particularly in the lower river basin (fig. 7.2). These efforts provided some protection to the more than 180 community water supplies drawn from the Potomac River. Revealing a basic level of surveillance over these water supplies, the Potomac River basin states were able to provide federal investigators with information on both sewage and industrial waste treatment facilities. Meanwhile, most manufacturing concerns provided only primary treatment—some form of mechanical screening or settling of waste solids (fig. 7.3). While this rudimentary treatment represented an improvement since 1951, it did little more than address the biological load dumped into the waterway. By the early 1950s, human-induced shortages due to deteriorating quality of process water forced industries to seek alternative water sources or locate outside the area.[37] Poor water quality was having an impact beyond fouling drinking water supplies and was adversely impacting economic development in this urbanized and industrialized basin.

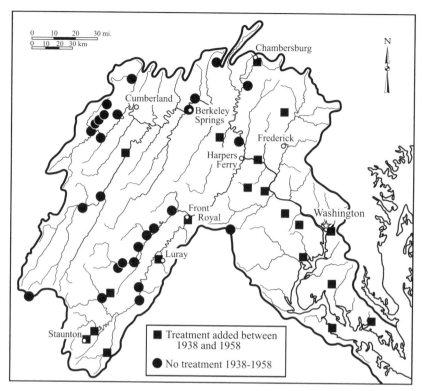

FIG. 7.2. Potomac River Municipal Waste Treatment, 1957. After U.S. Department of Health, Education and Welfare, *1957 Inventory: Municipal and Industrial Waste Facilities, Regions II, III and IV* (Washington, DC: U.S. Department of Health, Education, and Welfare, Public Health Service, 1958). Cartography by Clifford Duplechin.

The Chattahoochee River basin presents a more perplexing situation. Ineffective record keeping by local authorities impedes tracing developments between the 1930s and 1950s. Georgia's virtual absence of municipal or industrial waste treatment data in the 1930s suggests a lack of state attention to pollution problems. Alabama performed slightly better than its neighbor in terms of tabulating treatment facilities in the 1950s. It responded to the postwar federal inquiries but offered little specific information. For the most part, Alabama's responses indicated that there was an undetermined need for treatment by cities in 1951, and that lack of information lingered to 1958 when all but one of its communities still had no treatment facilities (fig. 7.4). Georgia, however, reported marked progress by the late 1950s. Although the state provided no data in 1937 or 1951,

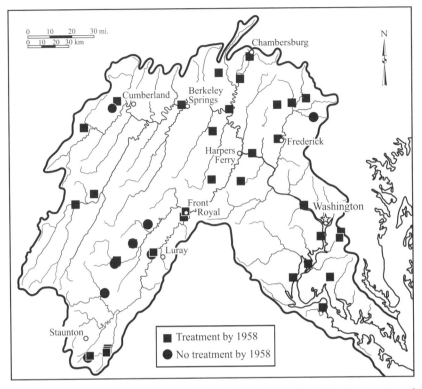

0   10   20   30 mi.
0   10   20 30 km

Chambersburg

Cumberland

Berkeley Springs

Harpers Ferry

Frederick

Front Royal

Washington

Luray

Staunton

N

■ Treatment by 1958
● No treatment by 1958

FIG. 7.3. Potomac River Industrial Waste Treatment, 1957. After U.S. Department of Health, Education and Welfare, *1957 Inventory: Municipal and Industrial Waste Facilities, Regions II, III and IV* (Washington, DC: U.S. Department of Health, Education, and Welfare, Public Health Service, 1958). Cartography by Clifford Duplechin.

it reported in 1958 that several suburban communities had begun sending their effluent through the Atlanta sewage treatment facilities. Numerous other communities had mixed treatment facilities—offering multiple forms of treatment. While basic record keeping is a weak measure of a state's pollution policy, in this case it represents a fundamental shift in state practice and the allocation of at least minimal resources to address water quality. Neither Georgia nor Alabama provided much information on industrial waste treatment to the USPHS for its 1958 report—far less than the comparable report for the Potomac River. Urbanization brought with it greater pollution-control facilities, while smaller downstream towns and manufacturers remained without treatment.[38]

For the upper Coosa River basin, Georgia again offered no information

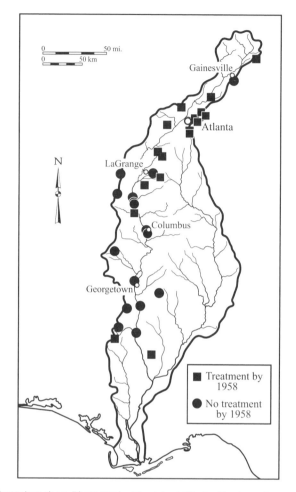

FIG. 7.4. Chattahoochee River Basin Municipal Waste Treatment, 1957. After U.S. Department of Health, Education and Welfare, *1957 Inventory: Municipal and Industrial Waste Facilities, Regions II, III and IV* (Washington, DC: U.S. Department of Health, Education, and Welfare, Public Health Service, 1958). Cartography by Clifford Duplechin.

to federal authorities in 1951. By contrast, Alabama officials reported that eleven of the twenty-one reporting communities along the waterway had adequate sewage treatment, yet the capacity of many remained undetermined. By 1958, most municipalities and industries had primary treatment, suggesting modest government response to a growing problem (fig. 7.5).[39]

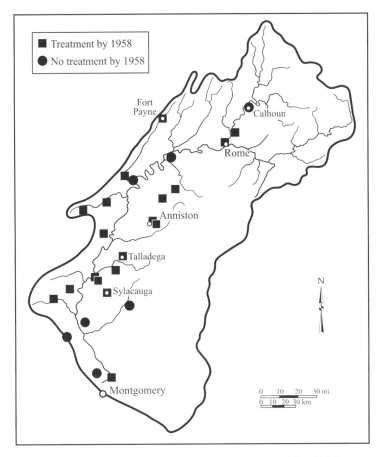

FIG. 7.5. Coosa River Basin Municipal Waste Treatment, 1957. After U.S. Department of Health, Education and Welfare, *1957 Inventory: Municipal and Industrial Waste Facilities, Regions II, III and IV* (Washington, DC: U.S. Department of Health, Education, and Welfare, Public Health Service, 1958). Cartography by Clifford Duplechin.

The 1951 federal report identifies only Saltville, Virginia, among the small communities along the North Holston. At that time, it had a new municipal sewage treatment plant and an industry that was a major polluter. Despite being the sole large manufacturer in the basin, this chemical plant had a considerable impact: "The water [of the North Holston] is unsuitable for public water supplies and other purposes due to inorganic dissolved solids discharged by industry."[40] A major fish kill during a drought in 1946 triggered public complaints, particularly from sportsmen, and the state agency took steps to stem intrastate pollution.[41] According to a company spokesmen, the industry impounded more wastes than normal in a waste lagoon as it awaited adequate river flow to dilute its toxic effluent. In the absence of rain to boost the stream's discharge, the manufacturer overloaded its waste lagoon, which eventually failed and allowed a massive release of chlorides that caused the massive fish kill. A second discharge in 1948 had similar results. By the early 1950s, the river was useless for sport fishing or municipal water supplies. State authorities, responding to sport fishermen, sought a solution, but the problem lingered into the 1960s.[42] It was not just drought that produced the environmental damage, but the continued reliance on a waste disposal system that could not adjust to low flow conditions.

The Perdido River served few communities and drained into a relatively undeveloped bay during the early 1950s. Most municipalities along its course relied on groundwater for their potable water supplies, minimizing the threat of waterborne diseases from biological pollution. One large manufacturer had constructed a paper mill on the Perdido since the 1930s investigation, and it included a treatment system in its initial design. By 1958, Alabama municipalities along the Perdido were treating their sewage, but the one large industry in Bay Minette provided none (fig. 7.6). Downstream from the Bay Minette plant, a paper mill near Pensacola, which opened in the early 1940s, treated its wastes, but was not listed in the 1958 inventory.[43] In the Perdido basin, Florida was unresponsive to federal inquiries, while Alabama supplied better information, indicating uneven attention to water quality issues.

Jackson, Mississippi, the largest city in the Pearl River basin, provided no treatment to its effluent. It released the sewage of over one hundred thousand residents to the river, while several small upstream communities used community septic systems to provide limited treatment in 1958 (fig. 7.7). For the most part, downstream communities and industries did little to minimize the impact of their releases. The 1951 report noted that eleven of fourteen municipal treatment plants in the basin had unsatisfactory capacity. As in Georgia and Alabama, information on treatment was scanty at best, suggesting minimal oversight by government regulators. The 1958 inventory reported that most Mississippi industries had no treatment or that no information was available (fig. 7.8). Louisiana provided no industrial information for the Pearl River despite the operation of a major paper mill in Bogalusa.[44]

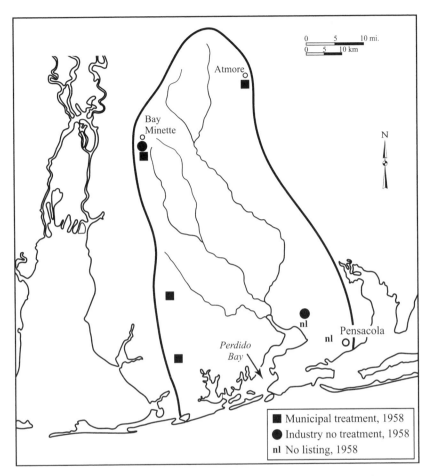

Atmore

Bay
Minette

N

Perdido
Bay

nl

Pensacola
nl

0   5   10 mi.
0   5   10 km

■ Municipal treatment, 1958
● Industry no treatment, 1958
nl No listing, 1958

FIG. 7.6. Perdido River Basin Municipal Waste Treatment, 1957. After U.S. Department of Health, Education and Welfare, *1957 Inventory: Municipal and Industrial Waste Facilities, Regions II, III and IV* (Washington, DC: U.S. Department of Health, Education, and Welfare, Public Health Service, 1958). Cartography by Clifford Duplechin.

Corney Creek, in north Louisiana, did not attract the attention of the 1950s reports, and there were no municipalities or manufacturers that relied on the creek for waste removal or water supplies. Local sportsmen had recruited federal authorities to help them stem a series of pollution incidents caused by brine wastes draining from oil fields in the neighboring state of Arkansas. Initial concern arose following a series of fish kills that

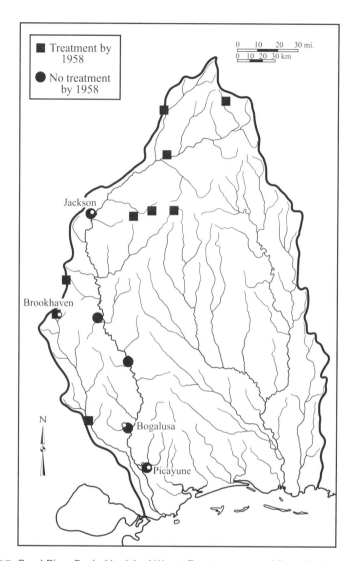

FIG. 7.7. Pearl River Basin Municipal Waste Treatment, 1957. After U.S. Department of Health, Education, and Welfare, *1957 Inventory: Municipal and Industrial Waste Facilities, Regions II, III and IV* (Washington, DC: U.S. Department of Health, Education, and Welfare, Public Health Service, 1958). Cartography by Clifford Duplechin.

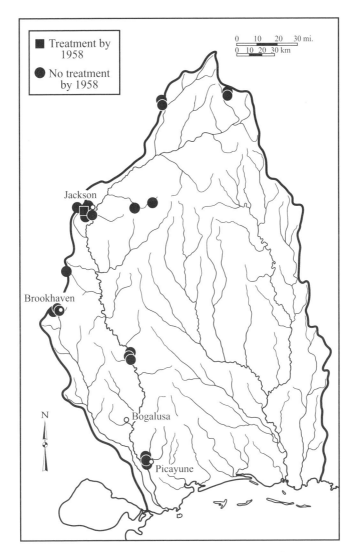

FIG. 7.8. Pearl River Basin Industrial Waste Treatment, 1957. After U.S. Department of Health, Education, and Welfare, *1957 Inventory: Municipal and Industrial Waste Facilities, Regions II, III and IV* (Washington, DC: U.S. Department of Health, Education, and Welfare, Public Health Service, 1958). Cartography by Clifford Duplechin.

resulted from the combination of low flow in the small waterway during a drought and increasing amounts of salt-laden discharges from oil wells. The creek was unable to accommodate the toxic salts, and Louisiana authorities had no jurisdiction over producers in an adjacent state. To seek a remedy, local officials went directly to their congressional delegation and pleaded for federal intervention.[45]

Public Opposition to Pollution

The 1948 Federal Water Pollution Control Act offered states a means to request federal intervention and mediation in disputes over interstate pollution incidents, although there was only one request received through 1955.[46] It was not until the 1956 amendments to the earlier legislation that federal authorities received the authorization to step in without an invitation from an aggrieved state, and only then did the interstate pollution conferences begin. Federal enforcement consisted of a multistage process. Following receipt of complaints from state or municipal authorities that an upstream state was harming interstate waters, the U.S. Public Health Service could convene a public conference. The purpose of the conference was to receive testimony from parties on both sides of the situation and to create a schedule for eliminating the problem. If the offending parties did not meet the schedule, more stringent steps, including court action, could ensue.

Intervention did not follow every indication of pollution. In order for the Public Health Service to initiate a conference, it required multiple complaints from the local level and subsequent investigations conducted by its field staff. The Public Health Service initiated enforcement actions at several locations outside the so-called "pollution belt" in the late 1950s, and generally stayed clear of the country's urban-industrial core.[47]

The premier federal intervention in 1957 was representative of southern pollution issues. Oil production in south Arkansas released brines into streams that flowed into northern Louisiana. A combination of declining yields in the oil fields, which resulted in increased brine production, and drought in the late 1940s and again in the 1950s diminished stream flow, which made the pollution all too obvious. In the wake of repeated fish kills, ad hoc local organizations battled for nearly a decade to secure federal intervention in the pollution of Corney Creek. Fishermen and farmers both objected to the damage to sport fishing—largely ignoring any decline in potable water quality. Citizens worked through local clubs, the parish governing body, and local congressmen, but not state agencies, to secure a pair of federal investigations, and ultimately this small waterway became the trial run for the federal interstate pollution conference process. Only after federal intervention and pressure on state agencies, and the end of a drought that had exacerbated the situation, did conditions improve.[48]

At the other extreme of enforcement actions in the South was the Potomac River—the first case brought before a public hearing on the fringes of the manufacturing belt. As "the nation's river," the Potomac was under a particularly powerful microscope and easily gained the attention of both the Public Health Service and Congress.[49] The chief pollution concern in the Potomac basin was not industrial wastes from upstream, but sewage from the Washington, DC, area. Between 1932 and 1954, the "sewered" population of the nation's capital nearly tripled, from 575,000 to 1.5 million, and the city was unable to expand its sewage works at that same pace. The Potomac's sluggish flow and the combined discharge of several population centers earned it descriptions of "malodorous" and "unsightly." Investigators measured a near absence of dissolved oxygen in the lower reaches and exceptionally high bacteria counts—all the result of heavy sewage loads released by overwhelmed treatment plants. No communities used water from this heavily polluted section of the river for their drinking water supplies; nonetheless, it was an important recreational resource and the site of commercial fishing.[50] Unlike the case with other public gatherings sparked by downstream parties who sought assistance challenging the releases of upstream neighbors, the U.S. Public Health Service convened the Potomac hearing in 1957 based on a series of public reports and ongoing observations. As an outcome of the public hearing, the states and municipalities agreed to timetables to initiate coordinated abatement efforts. When the Corps of Engineers revisited the river in 1962, it found the mean coliform bacteria count in most locations above the allowable level for chlorinated water supplies, particularly in the lower river.[51] Treatment had not kept up with increases in sewage and industrial waste discharges. In the Potomac, there was popular concern, but no popular uprising. Rather, multiple federal and state agencies scrutinized this river, and it is exceptional in that respect.

After years of unsatisfied complaints to state authorities, spawned in part by a deadly industrial waste release during a 1946 drought, citizens and downstream communities in Tennessee requested federal intervention in the North Holston River case. Virginia held several hearings during the mid-1950s to permit citizens, municipal authorities, and company officials to declare their respective positions on the continuing contamination emanating from the Saltville chemical plant of Olin-Mathieson Chemical Corporation. Specific complaints arose from a host of sources: sportsmen, farmers, businessmen, and community leaders. Their criticism centered on fish kills, destruction of agricultural and municipal water supplies, damages to farm equipment, and diversion of potential industrial activity from the basin. When Olin-Mathieson officials proclaimed there were no feasible technologies for reducing its wastes and Virginia state officials agreed, Tennessee business leaders finally prodded their Stream Pollution Control Board to take action. It appealed to the Public Health Service for an interstate pollution conference, which convened in October 1960.[52] Statements offered in the course of the proceeding indicate that small cities in Tennessee felt that the chloride pollution in the North Holston denied them the opportunity to attract new industry and participate in the economic boost promised by the Tennessee Valley Authority. Conservation groups from Tennessee and Virginia complained that state agencies had been unresponsive to their appeals to clean up the river.[53] Although conservation groups participated and voiced concern over destruction of aquatic life and the conference concluded that recreational uses were impaired, the central theme of the conference was the impact to downstream industrial water supplies.

A conference to consider pollution of the Pearl River convened in New Orleans in October 1963. Industrial wastes from the pulp and paper mill near Bogalusa, Louisiana, and the Crosby Chemical Company in Picayune, Mississippi, and their impact on fish spawning and the shellfishing industry near the river's mouth dominated the proceedings. Fishermen reported that their catches were declining.[54] Ultimately, the conference called for the two principal industries and the two cities in the lower river to improve their effluent treatment. Discharges from further upstream received very little attention. When a follow-up conference took place in 1968, it exposed that the polluters had failed to meet the goals set out during the first event. As in the initial gathering, shellfish and recreational uses dominated the discussion. Several sportsmen's groups participated and vigorously complained about Crosby Chemical's failure to clean up its discharges. In particular, the fishermen charged that tar from the chemical plant was destroying fish and in doing so was eliminating an important food source. Downstream landowners charged that chemical residue continued to foul a tributary of the Pearl, despite contradictory testimony from Crosby officials. Armed with petitions and photographic evidence of continued pollution, the fishermen made a compelling case.[55] On the lower Pearl River, locally based popular opposition to industrial pollution prompted federal officials to convene the conference, and concerns of sportsmen served as the centerpiece of the deliberations. The loss of abundance reflected diminished aquatic habitat.

The USPHS convened a conference on the Coosa River in August 1963. The impetus for this conference was frequent complaints that pollution was "interfering with recreational uses, retarding the development of potentially valuable lake shore property, and damaging the appearance and general aesthetic appeal of these rivers and upper Lake Weiss."[56] Several fish kills caused by industrial wastes in the early 1960s also contributed to the public discontent. Fishermen, wildlife organizations, and civic groups voiced strong objections to the damage Georgia industries were causing to Alabama stream conditions.[57] Elimination of the natural resource abundance, and not public health protection, provided the justification for the federal intervention in the Coosa River.

In 1966, the Federal Water Pollution Control Administration (FWPCA), which had absorbed the role of the Public Health Service's water quality program beginning in 1965 and was housed in the Department of the Interior, initiated a conference on interstate pollution in the Chattahoochee River. Participants in the conference reflect the anti-intervention position of most southern politicians, which took the form of adversarial posturing. Other than attendance by civic-minded organizations and individuals, the hearing record provides little evidence that there was strong public concern with pollution in this case. State agencies apparently shared this apathy. Alabama's representative, from the downstream state, expressed surprise that federal authorities would intervene in the matter and voiced resentment that federal authorities were dragging the state's Water Improvement Commission into the hearings as part of the national effort to define water quality criteria. Georgia's representative chastised the federal authorities for presenting outdated information about pollution sources and for the lack of advance notice to prepare for the hearing. Although members of the press, area academics, consultants, and members of the League of Women Voters attended, only industrial, municipal, state, and federal officials testified. There is no explicit record of conservation or environmental organizations participating. The fact that the federal government convened the conference when both states were reluctant participants suggests complaints came from other sources not allowed to speak at the conference. Damage to federal reservoirs likely contributed to the

FWPCA's uninvited involvement. One additional motivation for the federal government's calling the conference was to compel Georgia and Alabama to establish water quality criteria for bacteria—something required under the 1965 federal water pollution legislation, but not accomplished at that time.[58]

In opening the hearings, the FWPCA indicated its chief concern was with protecting the river as a "natural resource" and to protect reservoirs along the river, rather than protecting the water supplies of the several communities that used Chattahoochee River waters.[59] The reservoirs provided opportunities for sport fishing and recreation in addition to potable water. Protection of aquatic life and recreational activities took center stage and eclipsed discussions about public water supplies. Although sewage treatment capabilities in the basin had increased since the 1930s, still 78 percent of urban wastes that entered the waterway were untreated, along with 22 percent of industrial wastes. Considerable volumes of biological wastes placed heavy oxygen demands on the Chattahoochee and threatened aquatic life. Below Atlanta, dissolved oxygen levels in the river and reservoirs were below thresholds considered adequate for fish propagation. Inadequately treated sewage fed considerable bacteria colonies. All but one coliform bacteria measurement below Atlanta exceeded levels recommended for direct contact, and all but three exceeded safe levels for use as chlorinated water supplies.[60] With large-scale urbanization in its upper reaches, the Chattahoochee was beginning to compare with the Potomac in terms of its pollution load. State representatives seemed only mildly concerned, and the Atlanta newspaper editorialized about the impending costs of better sewage treatment and not local concern with the loss of resource abundance.[61]

The final conference covered in this chapter convened in January 1970 to consider pollution of Perdido Bay, at the mouth of the Perdido River in the Florida panhandle. Fundamental to this case was vigorous public displeasure with pollution from a single, but large, paper mill near Pensacola. Operating since the early 1940s, the mill's effluent exceeded the residents' tolerance threshold during the late 1960s. Florida and Alabama residents who had once enjoyed the typical amenities of waterfront properties along the lower river and bay, and fishermen who had formerly relied on the bay for a livelihood, joined forces to object to declining water quality. Ad hoc antipollution groups testified, and one citizen's organization submitted a petition with over a thousand signatures. Although the Perdido was one of the smaller basins that witnessed an interstate pollution conference, pollution there sparked a citizen response that was unusually prominent—reflecting in part a growing environmental activism nationally. Complainants supplied photos of visible pollution and charged the company with creating foul odors and health threats and with rendering the coastal estuary barren. Both sport and commercial fishermen were prime speakers in the hearing, underscoring the concern with damage to aquatic life. State officials claimed that St. Regis Paper Company, the principal offender, had been diligent in addressing pollution control needs, and the company touted its $800,000 federal grant to improve its waste treatment facilities. In this situation, the public had higher expectations than regulatory authorities and were less patient.[62]

Groundwater Concerns

Groundwater does not provide direct habitat for sport fish, and this in part explains the level of concern with this water supply in the first half of the twentieth century. But most rural households relied on groundwater for domestic and agricultural use, and there was an expectation of purity. Yet there was also value in impure groundwater. Nineteenth-century spas built around springs relied on mineralized water to draw visitors.[63] Naturally occurring mineral waters had medicinal and economic benefits and did not threaten other water supplies. Such naturally polluted waters were not only tolerated but highly prized. Impurities that garnered the attention of the nineteenth-century legislators and jurists were contaminants introduced directly to a well or even the inadvertent release of deleterious substances that could damage groundwaters. Even though the South remained a largely rural society and many households relied on shallow wells for household use, there were only minimal statutory protections. Only six southern states had laws that explicitly extended water quality protection to "springs, wells, or groundwater" in 1905.[64] In general southern regulation of groundwater quality lagged behind other regions.

With growing concern for natural resources in the late nineteenth and early twentieth centuries, state and federal authorities conducted an increasing number of inventories of all resources: geologic, biologic, and hydrologic. Among these inventories were groundwater surveys that appeared beginning in the 1910s, and they commonly contained measures of water quality. Typically, investigators were concerned with naturally occurring minerals and the suitability of water for industrial purposes, although geologists in Florida reported on saltwater intrusion in 1913.[65]

Mississippi investigators advised that shallow wells could become contaminated from surface sources.[66] Reflecting concern with pollution, some of the earliest and most influential investigations of bacterial pollution of domestic wells were conducted in the South. In the 1920s, a U.S. Public Health team carried out field experiments to trace the rate of contaminant movement in sandy soils on North Carolina's barrier islands.[67] The following decade, researchers from the Alabama Department of Health investigated bacterial movement in groundwater.[68] Researchers at both sites observed that soils impeded the long-distance migration of bacterial contaminants, but they also reported that chemicals could travel farther. With an emphasis on bacteria, these pre–World War II studies reflect the prevailing concern with the loss of suitable drinking water caused by pollution from outhouses, livestock, or cemeteries. Such concerns were not limited to the South, but its sizable rural population accentuated this problem.

Despite both the groundwater inventories and the public health investigations, and the fact that most southern states had experienced groundwater incidents, by 1959 the number of states with laws pertaining directly to subsurface water had climbed to only eight.[69] These state laws generally forbade the deliberate dumping of contaminants into wells, but also provided the basis for suits against unintentional pollution from neighboring properties. The relatively low number of states with groundwater protection laws reflects the relative portion of the population relying on groundwater. As of 1950, only about 8 percent of all groundwater withdrawals at the national level served domestic consumers, and the percentage fell to 6 percent by 1960. Nonetheless, across the South a very high percentage of rural dwellers relied on groundwater and a sizable number of municipalities did as well.[70] Indeed, saltwater contamination was prevalent in most urban groundwater supplies along the seaboard of southern states in the early 1950s (fig. 7.9). As urban populations grew and cities pumped more and more groundwater, water tables fell. This allowed salt water from the coasts to migrate toward the urban wells and foul the public supplies. Miami suffered saltwater intrusion to its municipal wells as early as 1939, and Baltimore had to close its harbor-area wells due to contamination by the 1940s.[71] Closing of select wells along with efforts to restrict pumping in the most vulnerable areas followed these incidents with urban groundwater pollution.

Public concern with rural subterranean water pollution erupted following a series of "blue baby" incidents in the 1940s and 1950s. Excessive concentrations of nitrates in groundwater can starve an infant of oxygen

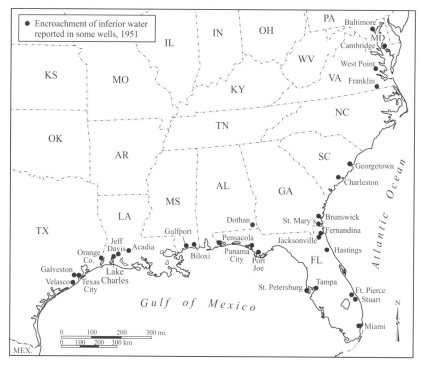

FIG. 7.9. Saltwater Contamination of Municipal Water Supplies, 1951. After Harold E. Thomas, *The Conservation of Ground Water* (New York: McGraw-Hill, 1951), 285–87. Cartography by Mary Lee Eggart.

in the blood; hence their skin takes on a bluish tint. Scientists attributed the presence of high nitrate levels to leachate from agricultural fertilizers, stockyards, cesspools, as well as to naturally occurring minerals.[72] Texas responded vigorously to the discovery of this syndrome for several reasons. It had a rapidly growing urban population and 580 municipalities that relied solely on groundwater for municipal supplies. In 1953, Texas used more groundwater than any other state, with the exception of California, and consumption had increased fourfold during the preceding in six years—albeit much of it for irrigation.[73] But the state's concern went well beyond rural consumers and agricultural users, and the public health of its growing urban population was central to its response. Although it had taken steps to address oil field wastes in the 1930s, Texas continued to suffer groundwater pollution caused by brine leaching from surface disposal pits that dotted its rural landscape.[74] With a troubling outlook on its future groundwater supplies, the state launched a series of investigations in the early 1950s. Researchers working for the Texas Board of Water Engineers documented the presence of chlorides (salts) and nitrates as two key measures (fig. 7.10). Many of the county-based surveys centered on the high plains of north central Texas, where a drought during much of the early 1950s accentuated semi-arid conditions aggravated by growing demands on subsurface water. The surveys provided vital information, but only enabled the state agency to recommend modified practices to the polluters causing the problem.[75] Meanwhile, the neighboring states of Louisiana and Arkansas suffered from similar oil field related problems.[76]

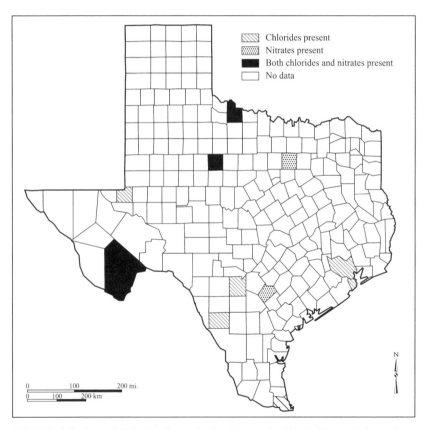

FIG. 7.10. Nitrate and Chloride Groundwater Contamination in Texas during 1950s. Compiled from numerous Texas Water Development Board reports. Cartography by Mary Lee Eggart.

Diminishment of groundwater can have much longer lasting consequences than surface water pollution. Introduction of contaminants to the surface may not appear in wells for decades, and even after their discovery, it can take an equally long time for deleterious pollutants to move through an aquifer. Consequently, the cessation of pollution practices above groundwater-bearing geologic formations does not terminate the impacts, as southern states came to find out.

The Velsicol waste disposal pit incident in western Tennessee exemplifies this persistent condition and the arrival of industrial impacts to the countryside. After its chemical wastes contributed to a massive fish kill in the Mississippi River in 1963, Velsicol's Memphis operation redirected its wastes to a series of disposal trenches in sandy soils in a nearby county in a classic example of what Joel Tarr refers to as the search for the ultimate sink.[77] The agricultural chemical wastes soon contaminated the aquifer that supplied local domestic wells.[78] Local landowners filed a class action suit and won a substantial settlement, but it took twenty years for the litigation to run its course and the decision did not clean up their wells.[79] Public outrage drove the protracted litigation.

The disposal of industrial wastes near Pensacola also produced a long-lasting problem. For more than seventy years, a manufacturer dumped concentrated acid wastes into infiltration ponds designed to allow the effluent to leach into the ground. Traveling through a largely sandy aquifer, the diluted acid eventually reached a city well more than a mile from the disposal site. Contamination of the well forced municipal officials to close the well to prevent harm to its citizens and its water delivery system.[80]

Although water specialists recognized the South as being richly endowed with surface water, they also noted its abundant groundwater supplies. In 1960, the U.S. Geological Survey referred to the coastal plain region as the "sleeping giant" among the nation's water supplies.[81] By the 1950s, southern states began noticing human-induced shortages being imposed on subsurface supplies in rural areas. During the next decade, urban industrial impacts were becoming more common. In contrast to surface waters, there appears to be a more vigorous response by state agencies to groundwater pollution, albeit in an era of growing national environmental concern and increasing federal involvement. Rural dwellers in Tennessee, however, filed suit independent of the state, after an industry fouled their aquifer. By the 1970s a survey of groundwater pollution in the central southern states emphasized the range of concerns and actual contamination incidents. Oil field brines, municipal landfills, feedlots, septic systems, and industrial waste lagoons all had impinged on drinking water supplies.[82] The impacts of urban expansion and industrial growth were slowly inducing shortages on the groundwater portion of the region's water wealth.

Conclusions

The role of natural resource protection and public opposition to the loss of abundance in quality water ranged considerably across the region. State regulators, however, showed little concern with impending surface water shortages, as historians have reported. Poor record keeping of pollution abatement facilities, lethargic responses to constituents' complaints, and the persistence of sanctioned discharges of untreated municipal and industrial wastes reflect a low priority given to surface water pollution by state regulators.

Government agencies within the Potomac River basin proved to be an exception. They maintained a more complete accounting of pollution sources and treatment facilities and cooperated within an interstate compact to reduce pollution. The existence of one of the country's earliest interstate compacts and censuses of treatment facilities reflect the sheer magnitude of the problem and early government attention to it. Thus, at the northern fringe of the South, public agencies played a significant role in detecting, defining, and addressing diminished water supplies due to pollution of the so-called "nation's river."

Citizen concern and opposition to loss of abundant fisheries called attention to the pollution problem in other smaller basins and prompted the all-important involvement of federal authorities to stem diminished water supplies and the associated natural resource damages. Beginning in the 1940s, local fishermen led the fight to halt oil field pollution in Corney Creek. Fish kills on the North Holston motivated initial concern with pollution in the 1920s, but by the 1960s deterioration of industrial water supplies and loss of potential employers inspired a vigorous response along the lower North Holston in Tennessee that highlighted water as a critical resource for economic development. On the lower Pearl River, state agencies reported the problem was in hand, while local sportsmen mounted a sustained campaign to abate industrial waste discharges. In north Alabama, fish kills and threats to water recreation instigated a citizen reaction to industrial pollution in the Coosa River. Citizen outrage along the Perdido ushered in pollution abatement efforts that were in line with the emerging national environmental movement but still reflected traditional southern concerns with fishing and outdoor recreation.

Along the Chattahoochee, states showed little concern with keeping records of pollution sources and agency personnel expressed disdain toward the federal conference process. Although Atlanta and its suburbs made considerable progress in terms of treating their effluent by the late 1950s, diminishing natural resources became a focus of the proceedings. Rapid population growth in the upper Chattahoochee largely offset sewage treatment gains, and by the 1960s, this basin was experiencing pollution loads similar to more northerly waterways. Little direct evidence of public pressure to reduce pollution appeared in the hearings, but the focus on recreational use of reservoirs suggests public opposition to lingering pollution and the shortages of recreational opportunities it caused.

While uneven, these case studies support the argument that southern state governments tolerated pollution and federal authorities entered most of these cases (except the North Holston), without a downstream state's invitation. At the same time, the proceedings and reports reveal widespread opposition arising from local sportsmen and water users who saw a relationship between diminished water quality and the loss of abundant sport fisheries. Even in the face of increasing populations and expanding industrialization which discharged a growing pollution burden, state agency personnel resisted appeals to control the declining stream conditions. Sportsmen and other water users got the attention of federal officials, who eventually intervened. Their efforts all reflect the loss of water quality or a self-induced shortage of usable water and fish habitat. It is also important to note that drought figured into several of the pollution incidents. And the protracted response to the loss of water quality in those situations should be a concern as we plan for the impending impacts of a changing climate.

Groundwater presented an entirely different situation. State agencies generally participated in seeking remedies for pollution of these subterranean supplies, and public health was a prime concern. Citizen lawsuits did occur when there was an obvious culprit, even though it used practices approved by the state, as in the Velsicol case in Tennessee.

Conclusions

Confronting the Limits to Abundance

The Texas High Plains faces periodic drought, a recurrent climatic variation in this semi-arid grassland. To cope with shortages since World War
II, farmers have increasingly relied on "underground rain" from the Ogallala Aquifer. Even as they increased their dependency on this subterranean
source, a particularly serious drought in the early 1950s, followed by another extended dry period in the 1960s, prompted Texas water planners
to eye "surplus" water in the Mississippi River as a more reliable solution.
After all, the lower Mississippi basin commonly endured horrendous excesses that spilled across the floodplain. Given the damage inflicted by
these episodes, it would be downright neighborly to spare Louisiana the
agony of that surplus and redirect it toward relieving Texas's shortages.
The seeming disparity between water availability and demand mobilized
an extravagant plan to divert water from the fluid spine of the American
South to its westward margins, but this one plan represents a growing
trend made more evident by the combination of increasing pressure on
limited water supplies and periodic droughts that accentuate unsustainable water policies and practices.

This concluding chapter will explore the related issues of surplus and
deficit and the simple imbalance between supply and demand that is driving increasingly shrill claims for water security in a region once thought to
be immune from the water wars more common in the arid West. Indeed,
the most contentious imbroglios have been over proposals and not actual
diversions. Nonetheless, as states stake out battle lines, political rhetoric
becomes ever more combative over the issue of interbasin water diversions.
I will consider a series of Texas plans to divert water from humid regions
with more abundant water supplies and also a water shortage situation in
Georgia that was largely the consequence of socially generated shortages—
made obvious by hydrological drought. These case studies highlight the
steps that southern water managers seek to take as they adapt to climatic
variation and the challenges they face as the region pushes hard up against
its water limits.[1] They also demonstrate that water conservation, a more
sustainable option, has provided the coping capacity during these periodic
shortages.

Surplus–Deficit and Water Policy

Drought, in the simplest terms, is a deviation from normal precipitation that creates a local or regional water deficit. It may be measured in terms of a downward deviation from normal precipitation, diminished stream flow, inadequate soil moisture available to crops, or shortages of water available to society. While these distinct measures are significant to climatologists and hydrologists, they sometimes occur simultaneously, and when that happens drought garners intense public scrutiny. The Dust Bowl of the 1930s was an exceptionally prolonged drought that left streams, soil, vegetation, and communities wanting. Likewise the drought of the 1950s, while not as severe its 1930s predecessor, had multiple impacts over expansive areas and prompted significant social adjustments. Farmers on the High Plains of Texas had deployed pumps to begin lifting water from the Ogallala Aquifer by the 1950s and they believed this underground rain would immunize them from climatic variation. By the 1960s, it had become apparent that intensive water mining was lowering the water table of an aquifer that received precious little recharge. The realization that the Ogallala was a finite resource spawned policy adjustments.[2] In Texas, groundwater conservation districts sought to promote conservation to prolong the viability of the subterranean water source.[3] Confrontations among users and adjustments to shortages are nothing new. Lawsuits against upstream water "theft" were common in colonial Mexico, but sharing or rationing among users illustrates practical adaptations made in the face of shortages.[4] In broad terms, Jacque Emel and Elizabeth Brooks argue that natural resource shortages provide the impetus for policy adjustments, or scarcity drives action to more carefully delineate rights to limited resources. These geographers analyzed administrative adjustments in groundwater policies that supplanted common law approaches in several Great Plains states that recognized impending shortages in the Ogallala in the late twentieth century.[5] Conceptually, social adaptations to water deficit include legal mechanisms imbedded in protections for existing users. Technological solutions, such as diverting water from a basin of surplus to one of deficit, have been used widely in the West, but these are complicated in the humid East, where riparian principles prohibit the diminishment of water quality or quantity to downstream users.[6]

Surplus water prompts different social adaptations. Fending off floods has inspired levee construction.[7] Excess soil moisture has prompted draining of fens and wetlands around the globe.[8] Seasonal excesses, punctuated by periods of shortage, have motivated dam construction to capture surpluses for later use or for diversion of water to deficit areas untouched by seasonal spikes in flow. Social solutions to surplus have been more structural than legal, but legal frameworks still shape social actions, while also reflecting society's expectations. As technology has challenged common legal principles, some judicial precedent and public policy have adjusted to new situations.[9] Nonetheless, destroying a neighbor's levee to protect your crops during a flood is legally unacceptable, just as is flooding a neighbor's property with water captured behind a private mill dam.

In the humid East, diversion of water out of a basin would deny a fellow riparian undiminished supply and therefore would be contrary to those common law principles. There are means to adapt policy to water shortages. Congress has authority over navigable waterways and can approve or forbid interbasin transfers from those streams to address water demands. Typically, when an interbasin transfer is considered, the primary question is whether or not it would have an adverse impact on the basin of origin. To receive approval, an interbasin transfer application must demonstrate that the demand is real and cannot be satisfied economically from within and that the benefits of the receiving basin are greater than the costs to the basin of origin. If a transfer would deny legal users of vested water rights, there is little likelihood the action would receive approval. Both social and economic costs are considered, and increasingly environmental impacts are factored in.[10] States can enact laws that legislatively approve or prohibit interbasin transfer on non-navigable streams—one form of policy adjustment in the face of shortage. Texas has approved interbasin transfers within its boundaries since the 1960s.

Despite legal impediments to interbasin transfer, the practice has taken hold in the American West, where prior appropriation doctrine has made the practice a bit more flexible, although basic protections for areas of origin still apply in theory. In the early twentieth century Los Angeles secured water from the Owens Valley to satisfy its growing demands, and by midcentury Colorado River water was moving beyond its basin to southern California consumers. These western examples redirected water from rural areas, with fewer resources to pay for the water, to urban consumers. In the East, New York City expanded the reach of its public water system to tap a transbasin source. And Texas, to a lesser extent, has allowed interbasin transfers within its state boundaries for decades.[11] In each of these situations, proponents made the case that the benefits to the receiving basin outweighed the costs to the basin of origin.

It was within this legal context that Texas recognized its emerging groundwater shortage on the High Plains in the 1960s and Atlanta, Georgia, faced exhaustion of its major municipal reservoir in the 2000s. To cope with an impending shortage, Texas policy makers crafted a grand solution to assist agriculturists by diverting water from an adjacent urban and industrial region—quite the reverse of western practices. They also sought a solution that they believed would be more enduring and less demanding to consumers than conservation-oriented practices and administrative adjustments. The modern Texas plan sought access to water from basins beyond its own borders and from streams that received precious little input from Texas tributaries. In effect, its policy makers rejected the concept of long-term deficit and replaced it with hope for a long-term supply that would draw on neighboring surpluses. This outlook ignored the potential for climatic variation that might impact the basin of origin. And even though its initial 1960s plans did not materialize, tapping surpluses has remained a central component of subsequent Texas plans. Georgia politicians similarly looked toward abundant rivers outside their state's boundaries to supplement urban demand in times of drought.

Is There a Surplus?

Between 1951 and 1957, the High Plains in general and Texas in particular endured one of their most devastating historical droughts (until the 2011–12 event). In the wake of the first dry period, west Texans embraced a federal plan to build a canal to divert unused water from the eastern and more humid region of the state to the drier southwest.[12] Although this plan did not materialize, it remained a tantalizing option. Following more dry years during the 1960s, along with recognition of falling water tables in the Ogallala Aquifer due to water mining, government planners turned their eyes further east. Viewed from Amarillo, the sheer volume of water that emptied from the Mississippi River into the Gulf of Mexico seemed an extravagant waste—even though Louisiana did not endure significant spring floods in the mid-1960s. So with uncommon foresight along with typical Lone Star hubris, Texas water planners began strategizing how to perpetuate irrigation-dependent agriculture in the face of a rapidly disappearing subterranean supply. As early as 1966, the Texas Water Development Board suggested "importation of water from out-of-state" among the alternatives to address future water shortages.[13] In 1967 Congress authorized the Mississippi River Commission (MRC) to examine the possibilities of exporting any *surplus* Mississippi River water to satisfy Texas's growing water demands—defining and identifying surplus were central to its charge.[14] The following year, the Texas Water Plan projected that the state would need 12 to 13 million acre feet of water from out of state sources each year by 2020 to meet its needs. The plan added, "Reconnaissance studies indicate that under conditions the lower Mississippi River Basin is the most feasible possibility, with the point of diversion below most diversions for consumptive uses in the Mississippi River Basin States." The plan took pains to point out it would only seek to divert any "surplus" from the neighboring basin.[15]

Louisiana, Texas's eastward neighbor, would have to cope with impacts of this diversion and reacted predictably. At a conference convened to discuss the transfer, a Louisiana representative claimed the state was indeed "water rich," but that its economic development hinged on its fluvial fortune. And to sustain its economic progress, it had to guard that wealth.[16] In the same forum Lone Star officials once again stressed that Texas was interested *only* in any surplus from the Mississippi and did not seek to steal water destined for existing uses.[17] An official from the Mississippi River Commission, charged with examining the feasibility of this plan, further emphasized that "surplus" was the key term in its deliberations. If the supply was not greater than the existing demand in the lower Mississippi valley, all other subsequent considerations were moot.[18]

The MRC moved forward deliberately with its study to determine if a surplus existed, along with considering several other elements of the grand scheme's feasibility. That the study received funding suggests there was an assumed surplus—at least on the part of the project's promoters. The general plan called for diverting any surplus from either a point near the Old River Control Structure (near the historical mouth of the Red River) or a second near the mouth of the Atchafalaya River close to the Gulf of Mexico (a distributary of the Mississippi that receives about one third of the larger river's discharge). From either point of diversion the water would be rerouted through a series of canals, existing river channels, and reservoirs up over 3,500 feet to the High Plains of Texas and New Mexico. A portion would also flow through a canal parallel to the Texas coast to users near Corpus Christi (fig. 8.1).[19]

The MRC and its collaborators analyzed the long-term flow of the Mississippi to determine if a surplus existed. They soon came to understand the ecological complexities of the delta region and grasped that diversion was not as simple as skimming millions of acre feet off the top of the spring floods and pumping them to Texas. To keep costs manageable all

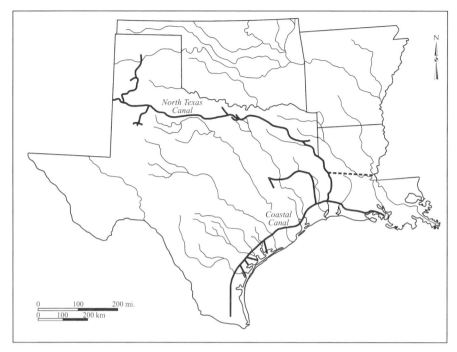

FIG. 8.1. Proposed Mississippi River Diversion, 1968. After Texas Water Development Board, *The Texas Water Plan* (Austin: Texas Water Development Board, 1968). Cartography by Mary Lee Eggart.

the water-moving apparatus would have to be scaled to transporting a modest amount of water year round, which meant tapping the river during both high and low stages. Yet, year-round diversions would impinge on the minimum flow of 150,000 cfs (cubic feet per second) needed by oceangoing ships during the fall low-flow season and a base flow of double this amount required to protect public and industrial water supplies from saltwater intrusion.[20] Furthermore, Louisiana researchers pointed out that the spring high river stage was the worst time to divert water from the Mississippi— that is during the times of greatest surplus. Heavy sediment loads during the annual flood would increase the cost of pumping and also settle out in the canals and reservoirs, rapidly diminishing their effective capacity. So the prime diversion season would be during the minimum low flow in the fall when the lower river region could least afford it.[21] Additionally, scientists were coming to recognize the importance of river sediment in maintaining the coastal wetlands and preventing land loss. The MRC report conceded that its water demand assumptions did not factor in sustaining sufficient flow to offset coastal land loss or estuarine ecologies that were vital to the Louisiana marine fisheries.[22]

The MRC report concluded that any excess flow projected for 2020 would occur only one-third of the year and that deficits would prevail most months of the year. The narrow, and seasonal, margin of excess would demand larger and more costly pumping systems and storage reservoirs in Texas. Ultimately, the reconnaissance report concluded that the project was economically unfeasible unless there were consumers who could pay far more than High Plains farmers.[23] Frustrated by these findings, Texas irrigators turned to conservation practices that have slowed the rate of Ogallala depletion.[24]

During the next two decades, the prime need for water rose in cities like Dallas, San Antonio, Houston, and Corpus Christi. Dallas had already begun to tap water from east Texas by subsidizing the construction of a reservoir on the Sabine River in 1960 in exchange for a regular water allotment.[25] With phenomenal population growth during the 1970s and 1980s (table 8.1), mayors of the other major Texas cities also turned their gaze to the Sabine River—a relatively small waterway that formed a portion of the state's eastern border and that shared its drainage basin with Louisiana. So, in 1992 these cities revisited the idea posited by federal authorities three decades earlier and agreed to conduct a feasibility study to transfer water from the Toledo Bend Reservoir on the Sabine.[26] Under the rubric of the Trans-Texas Water Program, various state, local, and basin agencies carried out a feasibility study which determined that east Texas, including the Sabine River basin, would have water to share.

The program's initial assessment reported that "substantial surplus

TABLE 8.1 Population Growth in Major Texas Cities, 1970–1990

City	1970	1980	1990
Corpus Christi	204,000	232,000	257,000
Dallas	904,000	1,006,000	1,197,000
Houston	1,232,000	1,630,000	2,099,000
San Antonio	654,000	786,000	936,000

Source: Campbell Gibson, *Population of the 100 Largest Cities and Other Urban Places in the United States: 1790 TO 1990* (Washington, DC: U.S. Census, 1998) [http://www.census.gov/population/www/documentation/twps0027/twps0027.html].

water supplies will be available through the next fifty-year period in the Sabine, Neches, and Trinity River Basins." And the Sabine would have the largest relative surplus: "Sabine River supplies will be over eight times larger than projected in-basin demands in the year 2050."[27] In 1998, planners projected demands of 102,000 acre feet annually with supplies of over 1.2 million acre feet, for a net surplus of 826,000 acre feet by 2020. While nowhere near the 12 million acre feet coveted from the Mississippi in the 1970s, this amount would benefit the burgeoning urban populations.[28] Projections suggested that surplus would fall to 791 million acre feet by 2050, but sufficient supplies would exist to augment an otherwise perilous combination of surface and groundwater resources used in growing cities. Ultimately, the feasibility study concluded that "large-scale interbasin transfer of Sabine River supply is the *only* [emphasis added] strategy that could solely meet the long-range Southeast Area demands and the demands of central Texas."[29] Growing cities had increased the demand and thereby reinvigorated the interbasin transfer option. Planners considered population increases, but they did not factor in any climatic variation that might disrupt assumed steady-state stream flows.

Large-scale interbasin transfers have not begun to flow, largely due to the expense of constructing the necessary transport system from the Sabine River reservoirs to Houston. As in the far more grandiose Mississippi River diversion scheme, the costs of moving water to the state's largest city, which is less than 150 miles from the Toledo Bend reservoir, exceeded the projected revenue from water sales. Thus, the city scuttled the plan and began to promote conservation practices to avoid exhausting its water supply.[30]

Even with the Trans-Texas Water Program on the shelf, Texas water planners continue to eye the Sabine and to contemplate options for diversion. Urban demands have not disappeared, and private sector entrepreneurs have jumped into the murky waters of interstate diversions. A private group has proposed buying a portion of Louisiana's water stored in the Toledo Bend Reservoir for use in Texas. Louisiana's Sabine River Authority (SRA) sees this as a potential financial windfall. Currently the authority sells some of its water to downstream power producers and some to hydrocarbon production companies that use it in hydraulic fracturing in the nearby Haynesville Shale formation—both largely within the basin.[31] By diverting sales beyond the basin's boundaries to urban consumers in Texas, the Louisiana SRA reportedly could enjoy a net revenue leap from $4.5 million per year to $54.7 million per year. Proponents of the sale point to a surplus lost, arguing that currently Louisiana is "throwing water down the Sabine River into the Gulf of Mexico."[32] Obviously, the growth of Houston and other Texas cities has amplified the demand for water and this situation portends to drive up the price for water—particularly if competition with the hydraulic fracturing interests continues. While an agreement has not been finalized, the shift from agricultural to urban demands and the financial and political power of huge population centers has altered the calculus used to determine whether or not to construct systems to move water westward from Louisiana to Texas cities. Costs of the transfer may still undo the current plan if not the dream of moving water from areas of excess to areas of shortage.

Redefining Riparians

While the envy of Texas farmers and mayors for water from the more humid East has produced a long-running drama, the more colorful case of water-coveting neighbors is Georgia's interest in obtaining surplus from the Tennessee River. This situation is based largely on Atlanta's urban demands that are complicated by a separate set of water wars over the limited flow in the Chattahoochee—the city's current principal supply. In short, Georgia officials have proposed moving its boundary a short distance northward to intersect a bend in the Tennessee River that would reposition the state as a riparian and entitle Georgia to water in that stream. As preposterous as this may sound, there is a basis for that claim.

First, let me provide some background. The Chattahoochee River rises in northern Georgia, flows in a southerly direction by Atlanta, veers westward and forms a lengthy portion of the Alabama/Georgia border, merges with the Flint to become the Apalachicola, and drains into the Gulf of Mexico through the Florida Panhandle (fig. 8.2). With an average flow of less than 3,000 cfs, it is a relatively modest stream, but one tapped by Atlanta as its principal water supply and also modified and maintained as a navigable stream and hydropower source since the nineteenth century.[33]

Advocates for river improvements brought the Corps of Engineers to the scene, and in the 1940s the federal engineers received authorization to begin work on a series of locks and dams along the lower river. As part of its river "improvements," in 1957 the Corps completed the Buford Dam, which impounds Lake Lanier as a reservoir to sustain sufficient downstream flows to maintain navigational channels and hydroelectric production. Over time, Atlanta became increasingly dependent on this supply,

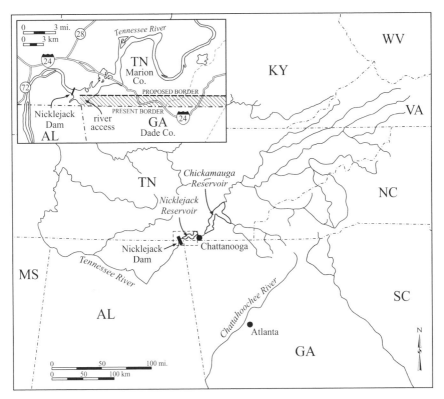

FIG. 8.2. Setting of Tennessee-Georgia Interbasin Transfer Dispute. Compiled from numerous sources. Cartography by Mary Lee Eggart.

and the Corps recommended that a portion of Lake Lanier's water be re-allocated to urban consumers in 1988. This sparked the so-called tri-state water wars that erupted when Alabama and Florida took steps to intercede in what they saw as upstream piracy that was contrary to riparian doctrine (see chap. 5).[34]

Alabama sought to maintain adequate flow for navigation and hydro-power production, the primary uses authorized by Congress in the initial plan—although water supply was part of the plan. Florida's interests lay in maintaining the proper salinity in Apalachicola Bay to protect endangered species and valuable marine fisheries. After filing suits, the states worked within an interstate water compact during the 1990s to craft a mutually agreeable water allocation plan, but they were unable to resolve the complex and contentious claims. As litigation over the water issue resumed in 2003 and lumbered through the courts in the new century, the severe drought of 2007 amplified public attention to Atlanta's precarious water supply. Lake Lanier fell to record low levels, and the reduced flow jeopardized all downstream uses—especially that of Atlanta's water-consuming public. Faced with an uncertain judgment in the court case, Georgia water officials began to seek alternative sources in the event the city might lose access to a portion of the Chattahoochee's flow. With no adequate groundwater supply to offset the drought-induced shortages, Georgia's political leaders salivated over the Tennessee River, which drains one of the country's highest rainfall regions and flows tantalizingly close to the north Georgia border—about one hundred miles from downtown Atlanta (fig. 8.2).[35]

Even before the desirous glances from Georgians, Tennessee officials had long-standing apprehensions about competing claims for Tennessee River water. Possible diversions down the Tombigbee waterway in Alabama and also requests from a growing Birmingham, which had riparian rights to water in the basin, were among the early alarms. After the Atlanta Regional Commission approached the Chattanooga, Tennessee, water company about purchasing Tennessee River water, the Tennessee legislature swiftly passed the Inter-Basin Water Transfer Act in 2000 and effectively blocked the most pressing and largest potential diversion.[36]

Undaunted, supporters of an interbasin transfer constructed an argument that sought to establish that (1) there was a water surplus in the Tennessee River basin and (2) that Georgia had a legal claim to water in the nearby waterway. Transfer advocates cited a 2004 Tennessee River Authority study which asserted that interbasin diversions of up to 1 billion gallons a day would have little effect on reservoir levels in the massive system. With projected demands of only 264 million gallons a day for the Atlanta metropolitan region, Georgians argued that southbound transfers would be inconsequential.[37] Such was the hydrological argument for surplus. The legal claim was not so straightforward.

Georgia's assertion of rights to water in the Tennessee is a grand tale of error and intrigue. Officials in the Peach Tree State argued that the original State of Georgia contained most of what is now Alabama and Mississippi, and hence a sizable stretch of the Tennessee River. According to a confidential memorandum prepared in 2008, diversion supporters claimed that the federal government had agreed that Georgia would retain riparian status even after ceding the Mississippi Territory to the U.S. in 1802.[38] Not long after the territorial subdivision, surveyors laying out the Georgia's northern border in 1818 mistakenly placed markers about one mile south of the 35th parallel, the line of latitude agreed upon by Tennessee and Georgia as the border (fig. 8.2). Despite several efforts in the nineteenth century to shift the border to the position memorialized in the Georgia code and specified in the federal act that admitted Georgia to the Union in 1788, the functional boundary remained south of the intended line. If the border was to be shifted northward to the 35th parallel, a small portion of Nicklejack Lake, an impoundment on the Tennessee River near Chattanooga, would fall within Georgia and thus establish its riparian status. Georgia bolstered its argument by asserting that as a federal agency, the TVA was obligated to develop the Tennessee River for the benefit of the entire region and had to honor the 1802 Cession Agreement that guaranteed Georgia's riparian access to the Tennessee.[39] Furthermore, portions of the TVA's service area lie in Georgia and some 6 percent of the river's flow arises in Georgia.[40]

If the two states can agree to allow some diversion toward Atlanta that would not violate Tennessee's Inter-Basin Transfer Act, riparian common-law principles would impede such actions. Currently, urban and industrial users of the Tennessee's water eventually return most water back to the waterway as sewage. By piping a substantial quantity into the Chattahoochee River basin, users below Chattanooga could object since the water used in Georgia would not return to the Tennessee. This diversion could impact aquatic life in the Tennessee and could deny water consumers of their normal supplies, especially during dry periods.[41] Estimates of the cost of pumping the used water back to Tennessee suggest it would be five times more expensive than pumping the water to Atlanta—making that option economically ridiculous.[42]

After nearly two years of deficit precipitation, Lake Lanier fell to record low levels late in December 2007 and remained low through much of 2008. In the midst of the 2007–8 north Georgia drought, the state legislature passed a resolution to restore the north border to the 35th parallel and supported formation of a boundary-line commission.[43] Some Georgia legislators admitted they did not want the land itself but sought leverage to move forward with negotiations on an interbasin transfer. Tennessee legislators responded by declaring the resolution a "heinous assault on the sovereignty of Tennessee."[44]

In the midst of the drought and as the legal wrangling over the Chattahoochee continued, Georgia officials encouraged conservation as a stopgap measure. The state's water management plan, released in 2008, acknowledged drought as a recurrent climatic situation. To contend with the state's prevailing drought, it recognized conservation as a priority and sought to eliminate waste. Core elements of the plan included public education and also regional water conservation plans.[45]

After rains broke the drought and produced record flooding in 2009, the border commission movement stalled and even conservation seemed less pressing. Yet when a federal judge ruled in 2010 that the Corps of Engineers' diversion of water to Atlanta from Lake Lanier was not permissible, Georgia again focused on the Tennessee River as an alternative source. A water plan for north Georgia asserted that the Tennessee River was a regional water source, not merely a state or riparian basin supply, and that portions of its flow originated in Georgia.[46] Also, diplomacy entered the discussion. Georgia legislators suggested that in exchange for water, it would help establish high-speed rail from Chattanooga to Atlanta's airport and also ensure improved access for Tennessee shippers at the port of Savannah.[47] Georgia legislators also took a more aggressive stance and proposed redirecting water from its headwater tributaries to the Tennessee River toward Atlanta.[48] Tennessee officials have consistently showed little interest in any proposals that would divert water to Atlanta.

Although an appeals court has overturned the 2010 decision and ruled that Atlanta will be able to continue using water from Lake Lanier, city water managers remain uneasy about that water source and continue their interest in the Tennessee River as a possible supply.[49] Strategies currently center on asserting riparian status or purchasing the essential fluid. Either strategy must still contend with the impacts of diversion on downstream users, in addition to the costs of financing such a transfer.

Interbasin transfers loom large in the future of the South's hydrology. With climate variation and long-term climate change, along with growing populations, the region will continue to run into water limits with greater frequency. One of the principal means to cope with shortage in the past has been to seek water from adjacent river basins. The initial schemes in Texas proved too costly in mere economic terms but likely would have encountered major obstacles anyway, when the environmental costs to the Louisiana coastal wetlands were fully factored into the equation. Even the much more modest, and urban-driven, Trans-Texas Program has been too costly to implement. High Plains farmers and Houston's thirsty citizens have turned to water conservation to stretch their existing supplies.

Georgia, when faced with an inadequate supply for its burgeoning metropolis, turned toward the Tennessee River. Political interventions blocked its desire to obtain water from the TVA reservoir. Legal maneuvering to establish riparian rights to the water have stalled, and water planners, as in Texas, have turned to conservation to keep the faucets flowing. Yet Georgia's desire to replumb the Tennessee continues and leaders are seeking some urban amenity that might persuade eastern Tennesseans to relinquish their hold on a portion of their fluid resources.

Concluding Thoughts on Southern Waters

It must have been in the late 1970s when I first noticed a glaring example of new pressures on existing southern water supplies. Driving through a small valley in the Green River watershed of western North Carolina, I passed, to my amazement, irrigation apparatus used to water nursery stock on a rural farm. The southern Blue Ridge is one of the wettest areas in the country, with average annual precipitation of more than sixty inches per year. Even to my novice eye, this equipment suggested farmers did not want to rely on that copious quantity of natural rainfall, but sought to ensure their crops got the moisture when they deemed it necessary. After all, there was plenty of moisture to reallocate at the proper time. In the years since this observation, it has become more and more common to see southern farmers erect irrigation systems in their fields. I have seen this on the Virginia coastal plain near the Dismal Swamp, on the floodplains of the Red River in central Louisiana, and in southern Georgia—areas where natural rainfall had adequately provided for agricultural needs in the past. It represents one of a number of emerging conflicts over water.

The expanding irrigated landscape exposes an emerging competitor for limited water supplies and runs counter to decreases in water used for irrigation in more arid western states where farmers have implemented conservation practices.[50] As early as the 1950s, the U.S. Census began tabulating impressive increases in the number of irrigated farms and farm acreage in several southern states. Virginia, Tennessee, Kentucky, Georgia, and Mississippi accounted for considerable expansion of artificially watered acreage.[51] This trend continued into the early twenty-first century, when there was substantial increase in irrigation acreage in the water-rich states of Arkansas and Mississippi. Georgia and Louisiana also expanded irrigated acreage, albeit more modestly.[52] Estimates for irrigation water use in Georgia suggest that there will be a nearly 20 percent increase in demand by 2050.[53] A warming climate will only accentuate the demand. What is most dramatic about the growing demand for irrigation is that it is expanding in the South as it declines in more arid regions. Additionally, supplemental water now is relied on in areas that have been under successful cultivation for a century or more and where existing precipitation enabled extensive row-crop agriculture to thrive. It is not simply a shortage of moisture that has prompted farmers to sink wells and install irrigation systems, but irregular droughts and a growing expectation of water on demand. Just as rivers were replumbed to synchronize with urban and industrial expectations in the nineteenth century, today agriculture is placing similar requirements on surface and subsurface water supplies once thought to be virtually limitless. If other uses continue to rise as well, particularly expectations from urban consumers and environmental services, the already contentious water issues will become more inflamed.

Conflict is also obvious in other arenas. The Houston metropolitan area has had to cope with extensive land subsidence, in an already low-lying area, due to groundwater pumping in the late 1960s and 1970s.[54] Not only did this cause substantial property damage at the time, but as hurricanes Rita (2005) and Ike (2008) bore down on the region, the lack of elevation accentuated the urban area's susceptibility to sea-level rise and surge driven by larger storms. Subsidence looms large in the survival of New Orleans as well. Also in Louisiana, industrial use of large amounts of high-quality groundwater for industrial purposes that could just as suitably draw water from the Mississippi River has sparked debate. Overpumping of the area's splendid aquifers is lowering the water table and accelerating saltwater intrusion, which could render the groundwater useless for everyone.[55] Saltwater intrusion caused by urban groundwater extraction has also become an issue in South Carolina, Georgia, and Florida.[56]

Overall consumption patterns in the South reflect emerging contrasts in recent years. Irrigation consumption has increased considerably. As urban populations continue to grow (table 8.2), public water supply withdrawals climbed between 1990 and 2005. Thermoelectric demands have followed population increases and reflect continued demand for domestic and commercial needs, most notably air conditioning. Industry, responding to water pollution regulation, has actually reduced its consumption of fresh water—with the distinct exceptions of the two petrochemical giants of Louisiana and Texas. Nonetheless, all but three states in the region withdrew more water for all uses in 2005 than in 1990. As a region, the South tallied the highest percentage population increase (14.3 percent) between 2000 and 2010. This demographic trend points toward increasing consumer demands—both for domestic uses and power generation.[57]

TABLE 8.2 Metropolitan Statistical Area Population for Selected Southern Cities, 1990 and 2010 (1,000s)

City	1990	2010
Atlanta, Georgia	3,068	5,268
Dallas, Texas	3,989	6,371
Houston, Texas	3,767	5,946
San Antonio, Texas	1,324	2,142

Source: U.S. Census (Washington, DC, 1990, 2010).

Conflict over groundwater, surface water within basins, and water from adjacent basins will continue in the South. Navigation interests, wildlife conservationists, public health officials, economic development advocates, recreationists, and water managers have all experienced the sting of inadequate supplies in recent years. In the South, historical shortages have tended to be short-term. But they are becoming more obvious, if not more frequent, with increasing demand and erratic supplies that are not equally elastic or synchronized. Although trends across the region reveal modest precipitation increases, the areas affected by drought have been more frequent. Seasonal disparities characterized by adequate autumn rain and less abundant winter and summer moisture have become well documented across most of the region. Most troubling is the projection that water availability will decline in coming years due to higher temperatures and longer interludes between rainfall events. Disputes over limited and more irregular water supplies, diminished groundwater recharge during droughts, and continued threats of saltwater intrusion due to sea-level rise will exacerbate existing tensions within the region.[58]

Another issue complicating the resolution of regional water issues has been the lack of interstate river basin compacts in the South. One of the earliest such compacts emerged in the Potomac River basin and contributed to reducing the pollution problem there (chap. 7). Yet the compact approach has not been a viable means to foster cooperation in the region. Widely used in the American West and the Northeast, they have produced some long-standing interstate water allocations, but they have received criticism for their inflexibility and inability to adapt to changing circumstances. Their use in the South has been less than satisfactory. Creation of an interstate basin compact to resolve the Chattahoochee-Flint-Apalachicola conflict proved ineffective and stands as a testament to the unwillingness of state leaders to reach accord. Interstate disputes loom on the horizon, not interstate compacts.

The interbasin transfer issues discussed in this chapter offer a telling lesson. These interstate conflicts reflect the reality that the Southeast no longer has reliable surpluses.[59] When considered from a regional perspective, localized surpluses exist, but with drought and increased demand, deficits become ever more common and any surpluses that persist are not always in the right place at the right time to satisfy human or ecological needs. Increasing demand for water will drive up the price, and more water will eventually flow from low-population regions to those with the greater capacity to pay. Locally, increasing costs will impact those least able to pay for safe water. Climate change will likely force the issue as well. As this chapter has illustrated, water planners have repeatedly looked to diversions before conservation, and this scenario likely will continue. Yet what is also obvious from these historical examples is that conservation is the least costly option and has provided a safety valve for both farmers and urban dwellers. Furthermore, it prompts the users in the basin of demand to adapt to shortages, does not displace either short-term or long-term costs to the water surplus areas, and offers an approach that can accommodate a warmer regional climate with more erratic precipitation.

During its great drought of 2011–13, Texas did not mobilize to hijack Mississippi River water despite falling reservoirs and business closings due to inadequate water. According to an editorial in the *New York Times,* Texas reporter Kate Galbraith observed that "a cultural shift seems to be underway. Conserving water is now seen as a priority in a state that dislikes conserving just about anything."[60] Although politicians called for expanded water supplies, cities and their residents endured the extended drought by cutting back consumption. Perhaps, this observed cultural shift is optimistic thinking, but conservation has enabled survival in past droughts. Technical fixes seldom solve all the problems and in fact often create unintended consequences, as we have seen in the cases of drainage, flood control, and pollution abatement. Long-term water management successes in the South have relied on moderation and not excess. Infusing long-term plans with this underlying concept could prove effective.

Notes

INTRODUCTION

1. Mark Twain, *Life on the Mississippi* (1883; New York: Oxford University Press, 1990); and John Barry, *Rising Tide: The Great Mississippi Flood of 1927 and How It Changed America* (New York: Touchstone, 1997).

2. Almon E. Parkins, *The South: Its Economic-Geographic Development* (New York: John Wiley, 1938), 138; and Howard Odum, *Southern Regions of the United States* (Chapel Hill: University of North Carolina Press, 1936), 293.

3. See National Resources Committee, *Drainage Basin Committee Report for the Chesapeake Bay Drainage Basins, Drainage Basin Committee Report for the Carolina Coastal and Savannah Basins, Drainage Basin Committee Report for the Southeastern Basins, Drainage Basin Committee Report for the Peninsular Florida Basins, Drainage Basin Committee Report for the Tennessee and Cumberland Basins, Drainage Basin Committee Report for the Red and Ouachita Basins, Drainage Basin Committee Report for the Lower Mississippi Basins, Drainage Basin Committee Report for the Western Gulf Basins,* and *Drainage Basin Committee Report for the Arkansas, Upper White, and St. Francis Basins.* (For all these reports: Washington, DC: Government Printing Office, 1937.)

4. Thomas R. Karl, Jerry M. Melillo, and Thomas C. Peterson, eds., *Global Climate Change Impacts in the United States* (New York: Cambridge University Press, 2009), 111–16.

5. Robert W. Kates, "What Kind of Science Is Sustainability Science?" *Proceedings of the National Academy of Sciences* 108, no.49 (2001): 19,449–50.

6. See U.S. Study Commission Southeast River Basins, *Plan for Development of the Land and Water Resources of the Southeast River Basins* (Atlanta: U.S. Study Commission, 1963). This series contained plans for river basins across the Southeast.

7. Donald Worster, *Rivers of Empire: Water, Aridity, and the Growth of the American West* (New York: Pantheon Books, 1985), 5. See also Mark Fiege, *Irrigated Eden: The Making of an Agricultural Landscape in the American West* (Seattle: University of Washington Press, 1999). A popular treatment of water is Marc Reisner, *Cadillac Desert: The American West and Its Disappearing Water* (New York: Viking Penguin, 1986).

8. Richard White, *The Organic Machine: The Remaking of the Columbia River* (New York: Hill & Wang, 1995). For a focus on western fisheries, see Arthur McEvoy, *The Fisherman's Problem: Ecology and Law in the California Fisheries, 1850–1980* (New York: Cambridge University Press, 1990).

9. Donald Pisani, *To Reclaim a Divided West: Water, Law, and Public Policy* (Albuquerque: University of New Mexico Press, 1992), 11.

10. Marc Cioc, *The Rhine: An Eco-Biography, 1815–2000* (Seattle: University of Washington Press, 2002); Stefania Barca, *Enclosing Water: Nature and Political Economy in a Mediterranean Valley, 1796–1916* (Cambridge: White Horse Press, 2010); and Sarah Pritchard,

Confluence: The Nature of Technology and the Remaking of the Rhone (Cambridge, MA: Harvard University Press, 2011).

11. Matthew Evenden, *Fish versus Power: An Environmental History of the Fraser River* (New York: Cambridge University Press, 2004); Christopher Armstrong, Matthew Evenden, and H. V. Nelles, *The River Returns: An Environmental History of the Bow* (Montreal: McGill-Queens University Press, 2009); and Shannon S. Bower, *Wet Prairie: People, Land and Water in Agricultural Manitoba* (Victoria: UBC Press, June 2011).

12. Theodore Steinberg, *Nature Incorporated: Industrialization and the Waters of New England* (Amherst: University of Massachusetts Press, 1991), 16.

13. John Cumbler, *Reasonable Use: The People, the Environment, and the State, New England 1790–1930* (New York: Oxford University Press, 2001).

14. Richard Judd, *Common Lands, Common People: The Origins of Conservation in Northern New England* (Cambridge, MA: Harvard University Press, 1997), 5.

15. This basic point is made in Albert E. Cowdrey, *This Land, This South: An Environmental History*, rev. ed. (Lexington: University of Kentucky Press, 1996); and James C. Cobb, *Industrialization and Southern Society, 1877–1984* (Lexington: University of Kentucky Press, 1984).

16. See the essays in Gerald A. Emison and John C. Morris, eds., *Speaking Green with a Southern Accent: Environmental Management and Innovation in the South* (Lanham, MD: Lexington Books, 2010).

17. Historians cite Ulrich Philips as the foremost spokesperson on the subject: *Land and Labor in the Old South* (Boston: Little, Brown, 1929). See also A. Cash Koeniger, "Climate and Southern Distinctiveness," *Journal of Southern History* 54 (February 1988): 21–44.

18. Jeffrey K. Stine, *Mixing the Waters: Environment, Politics, and the Building of the Tennessee Tombigbee Waterway* (Akron, OH: University of Akron Press, 1993); Richard A. Bartlett, *Troubled Waters: Champion International and the Pigeon River Controversy* (Knoxville: University of Tennessee Press, 1995); Martin Reuss, *Designing the Bayous: The Control of Water in the Atchafalaya Basin, 1800–1995* (Alexandria, VA: U.S. Army Corps of Engineers, Office of History, 1998); and Christopher Morris, *The Big Muddy: An Environmental History of the Mississippi and Its People from Hernando de Soto to Hurricane Katrina* (New York: Oxford University Press, 2012).

19. Jack Temple Kirby, *Poquosin: A Study of Rural Landscape and Society* (Chapel Hill: University of North Carolina Press, 1995); David McCally, *The Everglades: An Environmental History* (Gainesville: University Press of Florida, 1999); and Megan Kate Nelson, *Trembling Earth: An Cultural History of the Okefenokee Swamp* (Athens: University of Georgia Press, 2005).

20. A fine outlet for geographical scholarship devoted to the region is the journal *Southeastern Geographer*.

21. Christopher Meindl,"Water, Water, Everywhere? Toward a Critical Water Geography of the South," *Southeastern Geographer* 51, no. 4 (2011): 615–40.

22. A sweeping overview of water management policy co-authored by one of the foremost authorities on water resources is James L. Wescoat Jr. and Gilbert F. White, *Water for Life: Water Management and Environmental Policy* (New York: Cambridge University Press, 2003). Without question, the most common geographic framework for river studies has been the basin. See James L. Wescoat Jr., "Water Resources," in *Geography in America*

at the Dawn of the Twenty-first Century, ed. Gary L. Gaile and Cort J. Willmott (New York: Oxford University Press, 2003), 283–301.

23. William Graf, "Science, Public Policy, and Western American Rivers," *Transactions of the Institute of British Geographers,* new series, 17, no. 1 (1992): 5–19.

24. William L. Graf, "Damage Control: Restoring the Physical Integrity of America's Rivers," *Annals of the Association of American Geographers* 91, no. 1 (2001): 1–27.

25. Martin W. Doyle, "America's Rivers and the American Experiment," *Journal of the American Water Resources Association* 48, no. 4 (2012): 820–37. For a national policy perspective, see Peter Rogers, *America's Waters: Federal Roles and Responsibilities* (Cambridge, MA: MIT Press, 1993).

26. A poignant deviation from colonial-era abundance was the collapse of the Lost Colony in North Carolina and stress at Jamestown during droughts in the early 1600s. See David W. Stahle, Malcolm K. Cleaveland, Dennis B. Blanton, Matthew, D. Therrel, and David A. Gay, "The Lost Colony and Jamestown Droughts," *Science* 280 (1998): 564–67.

CHAPTER ONE

An earlier version of this chapter appeared as "Meaning of Water in the American South: Transatlantic Encounters," *Atlantic Studies* 5, no. 2 (2008): 203–22, and is used here with permission of Taylor and Francis. The Web site for *Atlantic Studies* can be found at: www .tandfonline.com.

1. LaSalle's declaration of possession proclaimed that "I . . . do now take in the name of his Majesty and of his successors to the crown, possession of this country of Louisiana, the seas, harbors, ports, bays, adjacent straits; and all the nations, people, provinces, cities, towns, villages, mines, minerals, fisheries, streams, and rivers comprised in the extent of Louisiana, from the mouth of the great River St. Louis on the eastern side, otherwise called Ohio, Alighinsipou (Alleghany), or Chickagoua, and this with the consent of the Chouanons (Shawanoes), Chicachas (Chickasaws), and other people dwelling therein, with whom we have made alliance; as also along the River Colbert or Mississippi, and rivers which discharge themselves therein, from its source; beyond the country of the Kious (Sioux) or Nadouessions, and this with their consent, and with the consent of the Motantees, Illinois, Mesigameas (Metchigamias), Akansas, Natches, and Koroas, which are the most considerable nations dwelling therein, with whom also we have made alliance." M. Cavalier de LaSalle, "Official account of M. de la Salle's Exploration of the Mississippi (Colbert) River to its Mouth, 1682," in *Historical Collections of Louisiana, Embracing Translations of Many Rare and Valuable Documents Relating to the Natural, Civil and Political History of that State, Vol. 1,* ed. Benjamin Franklin French (New York: Wiley & Putnam, 1846), 24–25.

2. Jacques Marquette, "A Translation of Marquette and Joliet's Account of a Voyage to Discover the Mississippi River, in 1673," in *Historical Collections of Louisiana, Embracing Translations of Many Rare and Valuable Documents Relating to the Natural, Civil and Political History of that State, Vol. 2,* ed. Benjamin Franklin French (Philadelphia: Pitman &Daniels, 1850), 284–85; and Henri de Tonty, *Relation of Henri de Tonty Concerning the Explorations of LaSalle from 1678 to 1683,* trans. Melville B. Anderson (Chicago: Caxton Club, 1898), 64–65.

3. Discussions of the strategic considerations in selecting the site of New Orleans appear in Peirce F. Lewis, *New Orleans: The Making of an Urban Landscape,* 2nd ed. (Santa Fe, NM: Center for American Places, 2003), chap. 2; and Craig E. Colten, "Bayou St. John: Strategic Waterway of the Louisiana Purchase," *Historical Geography* 31 (2003): 21–30.

4. Although I had selected the title of this chapter before discovering the book cited below, I must acknowledge it. The author offers an ethnographic view of the meaning of water. As its author states, "Engagement with the environment provides synaethetic experiences that are integral to the generation of meaning; and instrumental in the development of cultural values and practices." Veronica Strang, *The Meaning of Water* (New York: Berg, 2004), 5.

5. Donald W. Meinig, *The Shaping of America: A Geographical Perspective on 500 Years of History,* vol. 1, *Atlantic America, 1492–1800* (New Haven, CT: Yale University Press, 1986), see esp. 65–76.

6. Andrew Sluyter, *Colonialism and Landscape: Postcolonial Theory and Applications* (Lanham, MD: Rowman & Littlefield, 2002),11–27.

7. Both Meinig's and Sluyter's concepts recognize spatial, temporal, and cultural variations, but they also apply as general concepts and are used in that context here.

8. Tristam R. Kidder, "Making the City Inevitable: Native Americans and the Geography of New Orleans," in *Transforming New Orleans and Its Environs: Centuries of Change,* ed. Craig E. Colten, 9–21 (Pittsburgh: University of Pittsburgh Press, 2000), see 19–20.

9. Charles Hudson, *The Southeastern Indians* (Knoxville: University of Tennessee Press, 1976).

10. Gregory A. Waselkov, "Changing Strategies of Indian Field Location in the Early Historic Southeast," in *People, Plants, and Landscapes,* ed. Kristen Gremillion, 179–94 (Tuscaloosa: University of Alabama Press, 1997), see 179–80.

11. Heidi Altman, *Eastern Cherokee Fishing* (Tuscaloosa: University of Alabama Press, 2006), 37–38.

12. Altman, *Eastern Cherokee Fishing,* 39–52; and Daniel H. Usner Jr., *Indians, Settlers, and Slaves in a Frontier Exchange Economy* (Chapel Hill: University of North Carolina Press, 1992), 151.

13. John Lawson, *A New Voyage to Carolina,* ed. Hugh Talmage Lefler (1709; Chapel Hill: University of North Carolina Press, 1967), 162–64; William Bartram, *William Bartram: Naturalist's Edition,* 18; and Robert Beverley, *The History of Virginia in Four Parts,* reprint edition, ed. Charles Campbell (1706; Richmond: J. W. Randolph, 1855), 119.

14. Buckingham Smith, trans., *Narrative of the Career of Hernando de Soto* (New York: Allerton Books, 1922), 23; and Jean Ribaut, *The Whole and True Discouerye of Terra Florida,* facsimile reprint edition with notes by H. M. Biggar (1563; Deland: Florida Historical Society, 1927), 78.

15. John Swanton, *The Indians of the Southeastern United States* (New York: Greenwood, Press, 1946), 45–46 and 488–89.

16. Lawson, *A New Voyage to Carolina,* 164.

17. Altman, *Eastern Cherokee Fishing,* 45–47.

18. Lawson, *A New Voyage to Carolina,* 164.

19. The best summaries of contact-era ethnography are Hudson, *The Southeastern Indians;* and Swanton, *The Indians of the Southeastern United States.*

20. April L. Hatfield, *Atlantic Virginia: Intercolonial Relations in the Seventeenth*

Century (Philadelphia: University of Pennsylvania Press, 2004), 8–20 and 37. See also Louis de Vorsey, "Amerindian Contributions to the Mapping of North America: A Preliminary View," *Imago Mundi* 30 (1978): 71–78; and Barbara Belyea, "Amerindian Maps: The Explorer as Translator," *Journal of Historical Geography* 18, no. 3 (1992): 267–77.

21. Hatfield, *Atlantic Virginia*, 37; Hudson, *Southeastern Indians*, 315; and Swanton, *The Indians of the Southeastern United States*, 589–630.

22. Jack D. Forbes, *The American Discovery of Europe* (Urbana: University of Illinois Press, 2007), esp. chaps. 3 and 4.

23. Robbie Ethridge, *From Chicaza to Chickasaw: The European Invasion and the Transformation of the Mississippian World, 1540–1715* (Chapel Hill: University of North Carolina Press, 2010), 22.

24. Hudson, *The Southeastern Indians*, 128, 134, 145–46, 172, 322–24, and 326–27. Also see John Lawson, *A New Voyage to Carolina*, 223.

25. John R. Swanton, *Myths and Tales of the Southeastern Indians* (Washington. DC: Smithsonian Bureau of American Ethnology, 1929), see 98, 118, 123, and 151.

26. Hudson, *The Southeastern Indians*, 128, 134, 145–46, 172, 322–24, and 326–27. Also see Lawson, *A New Voyage to Carolina*, 223.

27. Marcia de Castro and Marcia and Burton Singer, "Was Malaria Present in the Amazon before the European Conquest? Available Evidence and Future Research Agenda," *Journal of Archaeological Science* 32, no. 3 (2005): 337–40; and Fred B. Kniffen, Hiram F. Gregory, and George A. Stokes, *Historic Indian Tribes of Louisiana: From 1542 to the Present* (Baton Rouge: Louisiana State University Press, 1987), 110.

28. On the importance of Indian place names see Belyea, "Amerindian Maps," and de Vorsey, "Amerindian Contributions to the Mapping of North America."

29. A critical analysis of the imposition of colonial names on indigenous landscapes is R. D. K. Herman, "The Aloha State: Place Names and the Anti-Conquest of Hawai'i," *Annals of the Association of American Geographers* 89, no. 1 (1999): 76–102. Also see Stuart Horsman, "The Politics of Toponyms in the Pamir Mountains," *Area* 38, no. 3 (2006): 279–91; and Saul B. Cohen and Nurit Kliot, "Place Names in Israel's Ideological Struggle over Administered Territories," *Annals of the Association of American Geographers* 82, no. 4 (1992): 653–80.

30. G. H. Colton, *Colton's Atlas of the World* (Philadelphia: J. H. Colton, 1856) [http://www.davidrumsey.com/maps1427.html].

31. Patricia O Afable and Madison S. Beeler, "Place-Names," in *Handbook of North American Indians, vol. 17, Languages*, ed. Ives Goddard (Washington, DC: Smithsonian Institution, 1996), 185–99; Karen M. Booker, Charles M. Hudson, and Robert Rankin, "Place Name Identification and Multilingualism in the Sixteenth Century Southeast," *Ethnohistory* 39, no. 4 (1992): 399–51; and Patricia Galloway, "Debriefing Explorers' Amerindian Information in the Delisles' Mapping of the Southeast," in *Colonial Enounters: Perspectives on Native American Mapmaking and Map Use*, ed. G. Malcolm Lewis, 223–40 (Chicago: University of Chicago Press, 1998).

32. William P. Cumming, *Mapping the North Carolina Coast: Sixteenth-Century Cartography and the Roanoke Voyages* (Raleigh: North Carolina Department of Cultural Resources, 1988), 39.

33. Hatfield, *Atlantic Virginia*, 8–20. On the overlay of European names on rivers, see Gene Waddell, "Ignorance and Deceit in Renaming Charleston's Rivers; Some Observations about the Reliability of Historical Sources," *South Carolina Historical Magazine* 891 (1988): 40–50.

34. William A. Read, "Louisiana Place Names of Indian Origin," *Louisiana State University Bulletin*, new series, 19, no. 2 (1927): 35–36 and 39.

35. William P. Cummings, *The Southeast in Early Maps* (Chapel Hill: University of North Carolina Press, 1958), 10–12; and Booker, Hudson, and Rankin, "Place Name Identification."

36. William A. Read, *Indian Place Names of Alabama* (Baton Rouge: Louisiana State University Studies, no. 29, 1937), 4.

37. William A. Read, "Indian Stream Names in Georgia," pt. 1, *International Journal of American Linguistics* 15, no. 2 (1949): 128–32, and "Indian Stream Names in Georgia," pt. 2, *International Journal of American Linguistics* 16, no. 4 (1950): 203–7.

38. P. Burwell Rogers, "Indian Names in Tidewater Virginia," *Names* 4 (1956): 155–59; and Hamill Kenny, *The Origin and Meaning of Indian Place Names of Maryland* (Baltimore: Waverly Press, 1961), 11–12.

39. Ribaut, *The Whole and True Discouerye of Terra Florida*, 64, 79, quote at 82; and Paul E. Hoffman, *Florida's Frontiers* (Bloomington: Indiana University Press, 2002), 50.

40. Usner, *Indians, Settlers, and Slaves*, 212–13; Daniel H. Usner Jr., *American Indians in the Lower Mississippi Valley: Social and Economic Histories* (Lincoln: University of Nebraska Press, 1998), 69; and Kniffen et al., *Historic Indian Tribes of Louisiana*, 202–15.

41. Beverley, *History of Virginia*, quotes at 93, also see 117–20.

42. George Percy, "Observations by Master George Percy, 1607," in *Narratives of Early Virginia, 1606–1625*, ed. Lyon G. Tyler (New York: Charles Scribner's Sons. 1907), quotes at 15 and 19. For discussion of the English reliance on Native Americans for food, see Percy, "Observations of Mater George Percy," 21–22; and John Smith, "A True Relation, by Captain John Smith, 1608," in *Narratives of Early Virginia, 1606–1625*, ed. Lyon G. Tyler (New York: Charles Scribner's Sons, 1907), 33–39. David W. Stahle, Malcolm K. Cleaveland, Dennis B. Blanton, Matthew D. Therrell, and David A. Gay, "The Lost Colony and Jamestown Droughts," *Science* 280, no. 5363 (1998): 564–67.

43. Unidentified source quoted in Marc de Villiers, "A History of the Foundation of New Orleans, 1717–1722," *Louisiana Historical Quarterly* 3 (1920): 153–251, quote at 174; and Lewis, *New Orleans: Making of an Urban Landscape*, chap. 2.

44. Thomas Jefferson, *Notes on the State of Virginia*, ed. David Walstreicher (1785; New York: Palgrave, 2002), 81–91.

45. Yi-Fu Tuan, *The Hydrologic Cycle and the Wisdom of God: A Theme in Geoteology.* (Toronto: University of Toronto Press, 1968), 122.

46. LaSalle, "Official Account of M. de LaSalle's Exploration," 48–50.

47. André E. Guillerme, *The Age of Water: The Urban Environment in the North of France, A.D. 300–1800* (College Station: Texas A&M University Press, 1988), 177–223.

48. Read, "Louisiana Place Names," 39.

49. Hatfield, *Atlantic Virginia*, 8–38; and Cumming, *The Southeast in Early Maps*.

50. Mark Thompson, "Locating the Isle of Orleans: Atlantic and American Historiographical Perspectives," *Atlantic Studies* 5, no. 3 (2008): 305–33.

51. The increasing reliance on geometric boundaries introduced tensions between Europeans and indigenous societies as they formalized colonial and Indian territories. See Louis De Vorsey Jr., *The Indian Boundary in the Southern Colonies, 1763–1775* (Chapel Hill: University of North Carolina Press, 1961).

52. Marcel Giraud, *A History of French Louisiana*, vol. 5, trans. Brian Pearce (Baton Rouge: Louisiana State University Press, 1991), 192–98.

53. Le Page du Pratz, *The History of Louisiana*, trans. Joseph G. Tregle Jr. (1774; Baton Rouge: Louisiana State University Press, 1975), 22 and 288.

54. Craig E. Colten, *An Unnatural Metropolis: Wresting New Orleans from Nature* (Baton Rouge: Louisiana State University Press, 2005), esp. chap. 5.

55. Karl W. Butzer, "French Wetland Agriculture in Atlantic Canada and Its European Roots: Different Avenues to Historical Diffusion," *Annals of the Association of American Geographers* 92 (2002): 451–70.

56. Guillerme, *The Age of Water*, 187.

57. Jean Baptiste Bernard de la Harpe, "On the Present State of Louisiana in the Year 1720," ed. Claude Sturgill and Charles Price, *Louisiana Historical Quarterly* 54 (1971): 28–45, quote at 45.

58. Pierre de Charlevoix, *Journal of a Voyage to North America*, facsimile reprint edition (1761; Ann Arbor: University Microfilms, 1966), 276.

59. Du Pratz, *The History of Louisiana*, 22.

60. James Pitot, *Observations on the Colony of Louisiana from 1796 to 1802*, translated from the author's manuscript by Henry C. Pitot (Baton Rouge: Louisiana State University Press, 1979), 110.

61. John Duffy, *Epidemics in Colonial America* (Baton Rouge: Louisiana State University Press, 1953), 204–6; and Timothy Silver, *A New Face on the Countryside: Indians, Colonists, and Slaves in South Atlantic Forests, 1500–1800* (New York: Cambridge University Press, 1990), 155.

62. Both colonial correspondences date from 1671 and are quoted in St. Julien Ravenel Childs, *Malaria and Colonization in the Carolina Low Country, 1526–1696* (Baltimore: Johns Hopkins University Press, 1940), quotes at 150 and 153.

63. Thomas Ashe, "Carolina, or a Description of the Present State of that Country," in *Narratives of Early Carolina, 1650–1708*, ed. Alexander S. Salley Jr. (New York: Charles Scribner's Sons, 1911), 141.

64. Duffy, *Epidemics in Colonial America*, 204–14.

65. Jo Ann Carrigan, *Saffron Scourge: A History of Yellow Fever in Louisiana, 1796–1905* (Lafayette: Center for Louisiana Studies, 1994), 12.

66. Silver, *A New Face on the Countryside*,162; and Carrigan, *Saffron Scourge*, 12.

67. William Darby, *A Geographical Description of the State of Louisiana* (New York: James Olmstead, 1817), 63.

68. Timothy Flint, *Recollections of the Last Ten Years* (1826; New York: Knopf, 1932), 290.

69. Judith A. Carney, *Black Rice: The African Origins of Rice Cultivation in the Americas* (Cambridge, MA: Harvard University Press, 2001), 78–98 and 101–6.

70. Hall, *Africans in Colonial Louisiana*, 122. See also Usner, *Indians, Settlers, and Slaves*, 207; and Morris, *The Big Muddy*, esp. chap. 3.

71. Sam B. Hilliard, *Hog Meat and Hoe Cake* (Carbondale: Southern Illinois University Press, 1992), 201–36.

72. Scott Giltner, "Slave Hunting and Fishing in the Antebellum South," in *"To Love the Wind and the Rain": African Americans and Environmental History*, ed. Dianne D. Glave and Mark Stoll, 21–36 (Pittsburgh: University of Pittsburgh Press, 2006).

73. Solomon Northrup, *Twelve Years a Slave,* reprint edition edited by Sue Eakin and Joseph Logsdon (1853; Baton Rouge: Louisiana State University Press, 1992), 101–7. The notion of swamp as an ominous environment for European Americans and a more familiar sanctuary for African Americans is developed by Conevery Valencius, *The Health of the Country: How American Settlers Understood Themselves and Their Land* (New York: Basic Books, 2002), esp. chap. 5.

74. Lawrence N. Powell, *The Accidental City: Improvising New Orleans* (Cambridge, MA: Harvard University Press, 2012), 266.

75. Walter Pitts Jr., *Old Ship of Zion: The Afro-Baptist Ritual in the African Diaspora* (Oxford: Oxford University Press, 1993), 45; William E. Montgomery, *Under Their Own Vine and Fig Tree: The African-American Church in the South, 1865–1900* (Baton Rouge: Louisiana State University Press, 1993), 293–95.

76. Lawson, *A New Voyage to Carolina,* quote at 163; and Hoffman, *Florida's Frontiers,* 50–61.

77. David Hardin, "Laws of Nature: Wildlife Management Legislation in Colonial Virginia," in *The American Environment: Interpretations of Past Geographies,* ed. Lary M. Dilsaver and Craig E. Colten, 137–62 (Lanham, MD: Rowman & Littlefield, 1992), see 141–43.

78. TheodoreSteinberg, *Nature Incorporated: Industrialization and the Waters of New England* (Cambridge: Oxford University Press, 1991), 25. During the colonial period, the legal concept of riparian, or ownership-based, rights had not come into practice. Thus, waters remained a nonexclusive resource. See Anthony Scott and Georgina Coustalin, "The Evolution of Water Rights," *Natural Resources Journal* 35 (1995): 821–960.

79. Allan Greer, "Commons and Enclosure in the Colonization of North America," *American Historical Review* 117, no. 2 (2012): 365–86, quotes at 368 and 371.

80. Gregory A. Waselkov, "Indian Maps of the Colonial Southeast," in *Powhatan's Mantle: Indians in the Colonial Southeast,* rev. ed., ed. Gregory A. Waselkov, Peter H. Wood, and Tom Hatley, 435–502 (Lincoln: University of Nebraska Press, 2006), esp. 443–46; and Galloway, "Debriefing Explorers," 224–27.

81. Swanton, *The Indians of the Southeastern United States,* 630; and Beverley, *History of Virginia,* 119.

82. Scott and Coustalin, "The Evolution of Water Rights." See also Joshua Getzler, *A History of Water Rights at Common Law* (New York: Oxford University Press, 2004), chap. 3, 117–52; and Alvin T. Embrey, *Waters of the State* (Richmond: Old Dominion Press, 1931).

83. *A Digest of the Civil Laws Now in Force in the Territory of Orleans* (New Orleans: Bradford & Anderson, 1808), 126–30.

84. Betty E. Dobkins, *The Spanish Element in Texas Water Law* (Austin: University of Texas Press, 1959), 120. Also Charles R. Poerter Jr., *Spanish Water, Anglo Water: Early Development in San Antonio* (College Station: Texas A&M University Press, 2009), chap. 6.

85. Hardin, "Laws of Nature," 137–62; Silver, *New Face on the Countryside,* 117 and 135; An Act to Prevent Obstructing the Passage of Fish up the Pedee and Main Yadkin Rivers, Ch. 55, *Acts Passed by the General Assembly of the State of North Carolina* (Raleigh, NC: Bell & Lawrence, 1926), 162–64. For similar developments in Georgia, see T. Downey, *Planting a Capitalist South: Masters, Merchants, and Manufacturers in the Southern Interior, 1790–1860* (Baton Rouge: Louisiana State University Press, 2006).

86. Prohibitions of obstructing navigable waterways include statutes in Alabama and North Carolina. Harry Toulmin, *Digest of the Laws of Alabama* (Chawba, AL: Ginn &

Curtis, 1823), 703; and Frederick Nash, James Iredel, and William Battle, *The Revised Statutes of the State of North Carolina*, vol. 1 (Raleigh, NC: Turner & Hughes, 1837), 533–36. For Virginia, see *The Revised Code of the Laws of Virginia* (Richmond, VA: Thomas Ritchie, 1819), chaps. 235, 247, and 248.

87. Scott and Coustalin, "The Evolution of Water Rights," 854–55; and Oliver Prince, *Digest of the Laws of the State of Georgia* (Athens: Oliver Prince, 1837), 688–89 and 701.

88. Act No. 519, *South Carolina Statues at Large*, vol. 3 (Columbia, SC: A. S. Johnston, 1838), 269–70.

89. Prince, *Digest of the Laws of the State of Georgia*, 701; and Toulmin, *Digest of the Laws of Alabama*, 713.

90. William Saunders, *The Colonial Records of Carolina*, vol. 2 (Raleigh, NC: P. M. Hale, 1886), xxii–xxiii; and Nash et al., *Revised Statutes of the State of North Carolina*, 420.

91. Prince, *Digest of the Laws of the State of Georgia*, 701.

CHAPTER TWO

1. Thomas E. Dahl, *Wetlands: Losses in the United States, 1780's to 1980's* (Washington, DC: U.S. Department of the Interior, Fish and Wildlife Service, 1990), 7.

2. Ann Veleisis, *Discovering the Unknown Landscape: A History of America's Wetlands* (Washington, DC: Island Press, 1997), 71–75; David C. Miller, *Dark Eden: The Swamp in Nineteenth-Century American Culture* (New York: Cambridge University Press, 1989), see esp. chaps. 1–3; Anthony Wilson, *Shadow and Shelter: The Swamp in Southern Culture* (Jackson: University Press of Mississippi, 2006); and Rebecca C. McIntyre, "Promoting the Gothic South," *Southern Cultures* 11, no. 2 (2005): 33–61.

3. On drainage of the midwestern wet prairies, see Hugh Prince, *Wetlands of the American Midwest: A Historical Geography of Changing Attitudes* (Chicago: University of Chicago Press, 1997); and John Thompson, *Wetlands Drainage, River Modification, and Sectoral Conflict in the Lower Illinois Valley, 1890–1930* (Carbondale: Southern Illinois University Press, 2002). A succinct treatment of federal wetlands policy in the United States is Jeffrey K. Stine, *America's Forested Wetlands: From Wasteland to Valued Resource* (Durham, NC: Forest History Society, 2008), 9.

4. Jack Temple Kirby, *Poquosin: A Study of Rural Landscape and Society* (Chapel Hill: University of North Carolina Press, 1995); and Charles Royster, *The Fabulous History of the Dismal Swamp Company* (New York: Knopf, 1999).

5. Sam B. Hilliard, "The Tidewater Rice Plantation: An Ingenious Adaptation to Nature," *Geoscience and Man* 12 (1979): 254–69; Mart Stewart, *"What Nature Suffers to Groe": Life, Labor, and Landscape on the Georgia Coast, 1680–1920* (Athens: University of Georgia Press, 2002); and Judith Carney, *Black Rice: The African Origins of Rice Cultivation in the Americas* (Cambridge, MA: Harvard University Press, 2001).

6. There has been a growing body of literature on Southern wetlands. See Gay M. Gomez, *A Wetland Biography: Seasons on Louisiana's Chenier Plain* (Austin: University of Texas Press, 1998); Megan Kate Nelson, *Trembling Earth: A Cultural History of the Okefenokee Swamp* (Athens: University of Georgia Press, 2005); Mikko Saikku, *This Delta, This Land: An Environmental History of the Yazoo-Mississippi Floodplain* (Athens: University of Georgia Press, 2005; Tycho de Boer, *Nature, Business, and Community in North Carolina's Green Swamp* (Gainesville: University Press of Florida, 2008); and Angela Halfacre, *Constructing a*

Conservation Culture in the South Carolina Lowcountry (Columbia: University of South Carolina Press, 2012); and T. Robert Hart, "The Lowcountry Landscape: Politics, Preservation, and the Santee-Cooper Project," *Environmental History* 18 (2013): 127–56.

7. Marjory Stoneman Douglas, *The Everglades: River of Grass* (New York: Rinehart & Company, 1947), 6; and Nelson M. Blake, *Land into Water—Water into Land: A History of Water Management in Florida* (Tallahassee: University Presses of Florida, 1980), 2.

8. Martin Reuss, *Designing the Bayous: The Control of Water in the Atchafalaya Basin, 1800–1995* (Alexandria, VA: U.S. Army Corps of Engineers, Office of History, 1998), 355.

9. The definitive biography on Douglas is Jack E. Davis, *An Everglades Providence: Marjory Stoneman Douglas and the American Environmental Century* (Athens: University of Georgia Press, 2009), Helen Muir quoted at 5.

10. Douglas, *The Everglades*, 6.

11. Douglas, *The Everglades*, 13.

12. Davis, *An Everglades Providence*, 4.

13. Henry Wadsworth Longfellow, "Evangeline," in *The Poetical Works of Henry Wadsworth Longfellow*, vol. 2 (1847; New York: AMS Press, 1966), 19–105, quote at 67.

14. George A. Coulon, *350 Miles in a Skiff through the Louisiana Swamps* (New Orleans: George Coulon, 1858), 2.

15. Malcolm L. Comeaux, *Atchafalaya Swamp Life: Settlement and Folk Occupations*, Geoscience and Man, vol. 2 (Baton Rouge: Louisiana State University, School of Geoscience, 1972).

16. C. C. Lockwood, *Atchafalaya: America's Largest River Basin Swamp* (Baton Rouge, LA: Beauregard Press, 1982); and Gwen Roland, *Atchafalaya Houseboat: My Years in the Louisiana Swamp* (Baton Rouge: Louisiana State University Press, 2006).

17. John McPhee, *Control of Nature* (New York: Farrar, Straus, & Giroux, 1989).

18. Charles A. Camillo, *Divine Providence: The 2011 Flood in the Mississippi River and Tributaries Project* (Vicksburg, MS: Mississippi River Commission, 2012).

19. U.S. Fish and Wildlife Service, "South Florida Ecosystem," n.d. [http://www.fws.gov/verobeach/MSRPPDFs/SFecosystem.pdf].

20. Buckingham Smith, "Report of Buckingham Smith on his Reconnaissance of the Everglades, submitted to R. J. Walker, Secretary Of the Treasury, June 1, 1848," in *Everglades of Florida*, Senate Document 89, 62nd Cong, 1st sess., 1911, 46–54, quote at 51.

21. Smith, "Report of Buckingham Smith," 50.

22. John Ives, "Memoir by Lieut. J. C. Ives to Accompany Davis Map of the Everglades, 1856," in *Everglades of Florida*, Senate Document 89, 62nd Cong, 1st sess., 1911, 71–72.

23. J. O. Wright, "Report on the Drainage of the Everglades of Florida, submitted to the Secretary of Agriculture, June 25, 1909," in *Everglades of Florida*, Senate Document 89, 62nd Cong, 1st sess., 1911, 149–50.

24. David McCally, *The Everglades: An Environmental History* (Gainesville: University Press of Florida, 1999), 88.

25. "Report of the Florida Joint Legislative Committee on Drainage," in *Everglades of Florida*, Senate Document 89, 62nd Cong, 1st sess., 1911, 121–22.

26. A. C. True, cover letter, June 25, 1909, for "Report on the Drainage of the Florida Everglades by J. O. Wright," in *Everglades of Florida*, Senate Document 89, 62nd Cong, 1st sess., 1911, 140.

27. Chris F. Meindl, Derek H. Alderman, and Peter Waylen, "On the Importance of Environmental Claims-Making: The Role of James O. Wright in Promoting the Drainage of Florida's Everglades in the Early Twentieth Century," *Annals of the Association of American Geographers* 92, no. 4 (2002): 682–701; and McCally, *The Everglades,* 101.

28. McCally, *The Everglades,* 98–105, quote at 98.

29. Secretary of the Army, *Comprehensive Report on Central and Southern Florida for Flood Control Purposes,* House Document 643, 80th Cong., 2nd sess., 1949, 30; and McCally, *The Everglades,* 121–28.

30. Blake, *Land into Water,* 34.

31. Ted Steinberg, *Acts of God: The Unnatural History of Natural Disaster in America* (New York: Oxford University Press, 2000), 59–63; and Michael Grunwald, *The Swamp: The Everglades, Florida, and the Politics of Paradise* (New York: Simon & Schuster, 2006), 217.

32. L. LeMar Stephan, "Vegetable Production in the Northern Everglades," *Economic Geography* 20, no. 2 (1944): 79–101.

33. Secretary of the Army, *Comprehensive Report,* 26–32, quote at 32; and Grunwald, *The Swamp,* 218–19.

34. Secretary of the Army, *Comprehensive Report,* 45–50; Grunwald, *The Swamp,* 222–24.

35. Blake, *Land into Water, 180–90;* and McCally, *The Everglades,* 170–74.

36. Blake, *Land into Water,* 186–94; and M. L. Shelton, "Surface-Water Flow to Everglades National Park," *Geographical Review* 80, no. 4 (1990): 355–69.

37. Blake, *Land into Water,* 290–93.

38. Grunwald, *The Swamp,* 256–57.

39. U.S. Government Accountability Office, *South Florida Ecosystem: Restoration Is Moving Forward but Is Facing Significant Delays, Implementation Challenges, and Rising Costs* (Washington, DC: Government Accountability Office, GA-07–520, 2007), 2–4, quote at 4. See also Matthew C. Godfrey and Theodore Catton, *Rivers of Interest: Water Management in South Florida and the Everglades, 1948–2010* (Washington, DC: U.S. Government Printing Office, 2011).

40. Chris F. Meindl, "Repairing the Damage or Making It Worse? The Everglades since 1980," in Nelson M. Blake, *Land into Water, Water into Land,* rev. ed. (Gainesville: University Press of Florida, 2010), 405–11, quote at 410–11; and Curtis H. Marshall, Roger A. Pielke Sr., and Louis T. Steyaert, "Crop Freezes and Land-Use Change in Florida," *Nature* 426 (November 6, 2003): 29.

41. C. R. Demas, S. R. Brazelton, and N. J. Powell, "The Atchafalaya Basin—River of Trees," U.S. Geological Survey Fact Sheet, 021–02, 2001 [http://la.water.usgs.gov/pdfs/rivertree-web.pdf, accessed January 2013].

42. William Cullen Bryant, ed., *Picturesque America* (New York: D. Appleton & Company, 1872), 372.

43. Samuel H. Lockett, *Louisiana As It Is: A Geographical and Topographical Description of the State* (1869; Baton Rouge: Louisiana State University Press, 1969), 54.

44. William Darby, *A Geographical Description of the State of Louisiana* (New York: James Olmstead, 1817), 59–60, quote at 60.

45. Comeaux, *Atchafalalya Swamp Life,* 31–33.

46. Rachel E. Norgress, "The History of the Cypress Lumber Industry in Louisiana," *Louisiana Historical Quarterly* 30, no. 3 (1947): 1–83, see 12–18.

47. Michael Williams, *Americans and Their Forests: A Historical Geography* (New York: Cambridge University Press, 1989), 244–52; and Norgress, "History of the Cypress Lumber Industry," 10–22.

48. Harold N. Fisk, *Geological Investigation of the Atchafalaya Basin and the Problem of Mississippi River Diversion,* vol. 1 (Vicksburg, MS: Mississippi River Commission, 1952), 23–24; and Reuss, *Designing the Bayous,* 210.

49. D. O. Elliott, *The Improvement of the Lower Mississippi River for Flood Control and Navigation* (Vicksburg, MS: U.S. Waterways Experiment Station, 1932), 321; and Charles A. Camillo and Matthew T. Pearcy, *Upon Their Shoulders: A History of the Mississippi River Commission* (Vicksburg, MS: Mississippi River Commission, 2004), esp. chap. 12.

50. Mississippi River Commission, *The Mississippi River: A Short Historic Description of the Development of Flood Control and Navigation on the Mississippi River* (Vicksburg, MS: Mississippi River Commission, 1940), 32–34.

51. The most comprehensive discussion of this process is Reuss, *Designing the Bayous,* see esp. chaps. 7 and 8. Also Fisk, *Geological Investigation,* 104–20.

52. Grits Gresham, *Atchafalaya Basin Crisis* (New Orleans: Louisiana Wild Life and Fisheries Commission, 1963).

53. Reuss, *Designing the Bayous,* chaps. 9–11. See also U.S. Army Corps of Engineers, New Orleans District, *A Feasibility Report/Environmental Impact Statement on the Atchafalaya Basin Floodway System: Preliminary Draft,* vol. 1 (New Orleans: U.S. Army Corps of Engineers, 1981).

54. U.S. Fish and Wildlife Service, "Atchafalaya National Wildlife Refuge: Comprehensive Conservation Plan, 2011," 53–54 [http://www.fws.gov/southeast/planning/CCP/AtchafalayaFinalPg.html, accessed January 2013].

55. U.S. Fish and Wildlife Service, "Atchafalaya National Wildlife Refuge," 181.

56. National Park Service, "Atchafalaya National Heritage Area Management Plan," 2011 [http://parkplanning.nps.gov/document.cfm?parkID=423&projectID=22438&documentID=46849, accessed January 2013].

57. Edward Chin, John Skelton, and Harold P. Guy, *The 1973 Mississippi River Basin Flood: Compilation and Analyses of Meteorologic, Streamflow, and Sediment Data* (Washington, DC: U.S. Geological Survey, Professional Paper 937, 1975, 1).

58. C. B. Belt Jr., "The 1973 Flood and Man's Constriction of the Mississippi River," *Science* 189, no. 4204 (August 29, 1975): 681–84, quote at 684.

59. Paul S. Trotter, G. Alan Johnson, Robert Ricks, and David R. Smith, *Floods on the Lower Mississippi: An Historical Economic Overview* (Baton Rouge, LA: National Weather Service, SR/SSD 98–9, 1998) [http://www.srh.noaa.gov/topics/attach/html/ssd98–9.htm, accessed January 2013].

60. Charles A. Camillo, *Divine Providence: The 2011 Flood in the Mississippi River and Tributaries Project* (Vicksburg, MS: Mississippi River Commission, 2012), 228–32.

61. Raphael G. Kazman, *If the Old River Control Structure Fails? The Physical and Economic Consequences* (Baton Rouge: Louisiana Water Resources Research Institute, Bulletin 12, 1980).

62. See Thomas Dahl, *Wetlands: Status and Trends in the Coterminous United States,*

1986–1997 (Washington, DC: Government Printing Office, 2000); and Office of Technology Assessment, *Wetlands Their Use and Regulation* (Washington, DC: Government Printing Office, 1984).

CHAPTER THREE

1. Political perspectives appear in John L. Larson, *Internal Improvements: National Public Works and the Promise of Popular Government in the Early United States* (Chapel Hill: University of North Carolina Press, 2001); and Paul F. Paskoff, *Troubled Waters: Steamboat Disasters, River Improvements, and American Public Policy, 1821–1860* (Baton Rouge: Louisiana State University Press, 2007). The role of the Corps of Engineers is traced in Todd Shallat, *Structures in the Stream: Water, Science and the Rise of the U.S. Army Corps of Engineers* (Austin: University of Texas Press, 1994).

2. Considerable areas across east Texas, Louisiana, Mississippi, Alabama, and Florida stand out with more than 9 percent of their total territory in floodplain, with much of Louisiana and Florida exceeding 17 percent. Stephen A. Thompson and Gilbert F. White, "A National Floodplain Map," *Journal of Soil and Water Conservation* 40, no. 5 (1985): 417–19.

3. John M. Barry, *Rising Tide: The Great Mississippi Flood of 1927 and How It Changed America* (New York: Touchstone, 1997); and Rutherford Platt, *Disasters and Democracy: The Politics of Extreme Natural Events* (Washington, DC: Island Press, 1999).

4. See Mark Cioc, *The Rhine: An Eco-biography, 1815–2000* (Seattle: University of Washington Press, 2002). Water control rose to a federal level in the arid West according to Donald Worster, *Rivers of Empire: Water, Aridity, and the Growth of the American West* (New York: Pantheon, 1985).

5. Barry, *Rising Tide*, 399.

6. Michele L. Dauber, *The Sympathetic State: Disaster Relief and the Origins of the American Welfare State* (Chicago: University of Chicago Press, 2013), esp. chaps. 1 and 4. Even though southern states-rights advocates bristled at federal spending authority, they did little to turn back federal investment in flood control in their region. Also, Kevin Rozario, *The Culture of Calamity: Disaster and the Making of Modern America* (Chicago: University of Chicago Press, 2007), 146–47.

7. Dauber, *Sympathetic State*, chap. 4.

8. See American National Red Cross, *The Mississippi Valley Flood Disaster of 1927* (Washington, DC: American National Red Cross, 1929); Albert E. Cowdrey, *Land's End: A History of the New Orleans District Corp of Engineers* (New Orleans: U.S. Army Corps of Engineers, New Orleans District, 1977), esp. chap. 3; Pete Daniel, *Deep'n as It Come: The 1927 Mississippi River Flood* (Fayetteville: University of Arkansas Press, 1996); and Barry, *Rising Tide*.

9. Robert W. Harrison, *Alluvial Empire*, vol. 1, *A Study of State and Local Efforts toward Land Development in the Alluvial Valley of the Lower Mississippi River* (Little Rock, AR: U.S. Department of Agriculture, Economic Research Service, 1961); and Craig E. Colten, *An Unnatural Metropolis: Wresting New Orleans from Nature* (Baton Rouge: Louisiana State University Press, 2005), esp. chap. 1.

10. Benjamin G. Humphreys, *Floods and Levees of the Mississippi River* (Washington, DC: Mississippi River Levee Association, 1914), 34.

11. Arthur D. Frank, *The Development of the Federal Program of Flood Control on the Mississippi River* (New York: Columbia University Press, 1930), esp. chap. 3.

12. The contested positions are discussed in Martin Reuss, "Andrew A. Humphreys and the Development of Hydraulic Engineering: Politics and Technology of the Army Corps of Engineers, 1850–1950," *Technology and Culture* 26, no. 1 (1985): 1–33; and George S. Pabis, "Delaying the Deluge: The Engineering Debate over Flood Control on the Lower Mississippi River, 1846–1861," *Journal of Southern History* 64, no. 3 (1998): 421–54.

13. The definitive history of the MRC is Charles A. Camillo and Matthew T. Pearcy, *Upon Their Shoulders: A History of the Mississippi River Commission* (Vicksburg, MS: Mississippi River Commission, 2004).

14. Frank, *Development of the Federal Program,* 55.

15. Joseph L. Arnold, *The Evolution of the 1936 Flood Control Act* (Fort Belvoir, VA: U.S. Army Corps of Engineers, Office of History, 1988), 13–14; and Karen M. O'Neill, *Rivers by Design: State Power and the Origins of U.S. Flood Control* (Durham, NC: Duke University Press, 2006), 105.

16. Camillo and Pearcy make the argument that Louisiana's delegation was discredited by the failure of the levees in 1927 and that Illinois lawmakers carried the argument for national flood control; see *Upon Their Shoulders,* 142–44. A contemporary critique of the levees-only policy appears in J. P. Kemper, *Floods in the Valley of the Mississippi a National Calamity* (New Orleans: National Flood Commission, 1929).

17. A. J. O'Keefe, mayor of New Orleans, testimony before Congress in U.S. House of Representatives, *Flood Control Hearings,* pt. 1, Mississippi River and Its Tributaries, 70th Cong., 1st sess., 1927, 5.

18. Lee Thomas, mayor of Shreveport, Louisiana, testimony before Congress in U.S. House of Representatives, *Flood Control Hearings,* pt. 1, Mississippi River and Its Tributaries, 70th Cong., 1st sess., 1927, 75–77.

19. William H. Thompson, mayor of Chicago, Illinois, testimony before Congress in U.S. House of Representatives, *Flood Control Hearings,* pt. 1, Mississippi River and Its Tributaries, 70th Cong., 1st sess., 1927, 2–4.

20. Len Small, governor of Illinois, testimony before Congress in U.S. House of Representatives, *Flood Control Hearings,* pt. 1, Mississippi River and Its Tributaries, 70th Cong., 1st sess., 1927, 7–8.

21. W. E. Hull, congressman from Illinois, testimony before Congress, in U.S. House of Representatives, *Flood Control Hearings,* pt. 1, Mississippi River and Its Tributaries, 70th Cong., 1st sess., 1927, 86–88.

22. O'Neil, *Rivers by Design,* 139–40.

23. O'Neil, *Rivers by Design,* 157; and Arnold, *Evolution of the 1936 Flood Control,* 81.

24. General Edwin M. Markham, Chief of Engineers, testimony before Congress, in *Flood Control Act of 1936 Hearings,* 74th Cong., 2nd sess., 1936, 7.

25. U.S. Congress, House of Representatives, *Potomac River and Tributaries including Occaquan Creek: Letter from the Secretary of War,* House Doc. 101, 73rd Cong., 1st sess., 1934, esp. 25–26.

26. U.S. Congress, House, *Potomac River,* House Doc. 101, 349–53.

27. U.S. Congress, House, *Potomac River,* House Doc. 101, 26–27.

28. U.S. Congress, House, *Potomac River,* House Doc. 101, 389–94.

29. U.S. Congress, House of Representatives, *Tennessee River and Tributaries, North Carolina, Tennessee, Alabama, and Kentucky*, House Doc. 328, 71st Cong., 2nd sess., 1930, 2–4 and 78–79.

30. U.S. Congress, House of Representatives, *Control of Floods in the Alluvial Valley of the Lower Mississippi River*, House Doc. 798, 71st Cong., 3rd sess., 1931, 5.

31. A "superflood" was calculated as likely to happen once in two hundred years based on the maximum observed floods of all tributaries occurring simultaneously. U.S. Congress, *Control of Floods*, House Doc. 798, 2 and 42.

32. U.S. Congress, *Control of Floods*, House Doc. 798, 6–10, quote at 6.

33. U.S. Congress, House of Representatives, *Development of Rivers of the United States*, House Doc 395, 73rd Cong., 2nd sess., 1934, esp. 66.

34. Nathan C. Grover, *The Floods of March 1936, Pt. 3, Potomac, James, and Upper Ohio Rivers, Water Supply Paper 800* (Washington, DC: U.S. Geological Survey, 1937).

35. Arnold, *Evolution of the 1936 Flood Control*, 59–67.

36. Herman R. Koppleman, representative from Connecticut, comments before Congress in *Flood Control Act of 1936, Hearings, Part 3*, 74th Cong., 2nd sess., 1936, 181–82.

37. Joseph F. Guffey, representative from Pennsylvania, comments before Congress in *Flood Control Act of 1936, Hearings, Part 3*, 74th Cong., 2nd sess., 1936, 225.

38. National Science Foundation, *A Report on Flood Hazard Mitigation* (Washington, DC: National Science Foundation, 1980), 29; and Federal Interagency Floodplain Management Task Force, *Floodplain Management in the United States: An Assessment Report, V. II* (Washington: Federal Interagency Floodplain Management Task Force, 1992), 3–3. See also Thompson and White, "A National Floodplain Map."

39. U.S. Army Corps of Engineers, National Levee Database [http://nld.usace.army.mil/egis/f?p=471:1, accessed January 2013]. Tabulation by author from query for miles of levee by state.

40. Charles A. Camillo, *Divine Providence: The 2011 Flood in the Mississippi River and Tributaries Project* (Vicksburg, MS: Mississippi River Commission, 2012), 4. Investments in flood reduction for Chattanooga, according to the TVA, have averted $2.6 billion in damages there. Federal Interagency Floodplain Management Task Force, *Floodplain Management in the United States*, 12–17.

41. Ted Steinberg, *Acts of God: The Unnatural History of Natural Disaster in America* (New York: Oxford University Press, 2000), 70.

42. Patricia B. Bixel and Elizabeth H. Turner, *Galveston and the 1900 Storm* (Austin: University of Texas Press, 2000), esp. chap. 3.

43. Secretary of the Army, Mississippi Coast, 90th Cong. 1st sess., 1967, 41–42.

44. Craig E. Colten, *Perilous Place, Powerful Storms: Hurricane Protection in Coastal Louisiana* (Jackson: University Press of Mississippi, 2009), 21–23.

45. Secretary of the Army, *Biscayne Bay, Florida: Letter from the Secretary of the Army*, 89th Cong., 1st sess., 1965, 20.

46. See Jay Barnes, "Scattered by the Winds: The Lost Settlement of Diamond City," *Weatherwise* 60 (November/December 2007): 36–41; Craig E. Colten,"Floods and Inequitable Responses: New Orleans before Katrina," in *Environmental and Social Justice in the City: Historical Perspectives*, ed. Richard Roger and Genevieve Massard-Guilbaud (Cambridge: White Horse Press), 113–29.

47. Secretary of the Army, *Lake Pontchartrain, Louisiana: Letter from the Secretary of the Army*, U.S. Senate Doc. 139, 81st Cong., 2nd sess., 1950. Also see Colten, *Perilous Place, Powerful Storms*.

48. Walter R. Davis, "Hurricanes of 1954," *Monthly Weather Review* 82, no. 12 (1954): 370–73, see esp. 372–73.

49. Neal M. Dorst, "The National Hurricane Research Project," *Bulletin American Meteorological Society* 88, no. 10 (2007): 1566–88.

50. Robert C. Gentry, "The 1955 Hurricane Season," *Weatherwise* 9, no. 1 (1956): 11–29; and H. C. Sumner and Thomas J. O'Connell, "Hurricanes Cause Devastating Floods," *Weatherwise* 8, no. 5 (1955): 124–26.

51. Gordon E. Dunn, Walter R. Davis, and Paul L. Moore, "Hurricanes of 1955," *Monthly Weather Review* 83, no. 12 (1955): 315–26, quotes at 316 and 319.

52. Dorst, "The National Hurricane Research Project," 1568–69.

53. Secretary of the Army, Biscayne Bay, Florida: Letter, House Doc. 213, 89th Cong. 1st sess., 1965, 29–30; Secretary of the Army, Isle of Palms, Sullivan's Island and Charleston, South Carolina: Letter, House Doc. 421, 89th Cong., 2nd sess., 1966, 25; and Secretary of the Army, Coastal Areas, Georgia: Letter, House Doc 37, 88th Cong., 1st sess., 1963, 23.

54. Secretary of the Army, Hurricane Survey of Northwest Florida: Letter, House Doc. 459, 89th Cong., 2nd sess., 1966, 45; Secretary of the Army, Alabama Coast: Letter, House Doc. 108, 90th Cong., 1st sess., 1967, 41; and Secretary of the Army, Mississippi Coast, House Doc. 99, 90th Cong., 1st sess., 1967, 45–46.

55. Secretary of the Army, Galveston Harbor and Channel, Texas: Letter, House Doc. 173, 81st Cong., 1st sess., 1949, 2 and 26–28.

56. Secretary of the Army, *Lake Pontchartrain and Vicinity, Louisiana: Letter* (Washington. DC: Government Printing Office, 1965), 1–2 and 82–86.

57. See Colten, *Perilous Place, Powerful Storms*, 28–50.

58. U.S. Congress, House of Representatives, *Southeast Hurricane Disaster (Hurricane Betsy): Hearings*, 89th Cong., 1st sess., 1965; and U.S. Congress. House of Representatives, *Hurricane Betsy Disaster of September 1965: Hearings*, 89th Cong., 1st sess., 1965.

59. Gilbert F. White et al., *Changes in Urban Occupance of Flood Plains in the United States* (Chicago: University of Chicago, Department of Geography Research Paper 57, 1958).

60. U.S. Congress, House, *Disaster Insurance: Hearings*, 84th Cong., 2nd sess., 1956, see table 1, 38–39. I tabulated flood damages for the Northeast ($1.1 billion), Midwest/Great Plains ($2.1 billion), South ($1.0 billion), and West ($365 million).

61. U.S. Congress, Senate, *Federal Disaster Insurance: Hearings*, 84th Cong., 1st sess., 1956. Hearings were held in Washington, DC; New York City; Goshen, New York; Boston, Massachusetts; Providence, Rhode Island; Hartford, Connecticut; and Raleigh, North Carolina.

62. Antoni N. Sadlak, representative from Connecticut, testimony before Congress, in U.S. Congress, Senate, *Federal Disaster Insurance: Hearings*, 84th Cong., 1st sess., 1956, 730.

63. Thomas J. Dodd, representative from Connecticut, testimony before Congress, in U.S. Congress, Senate, *Federal Disaster Insurance: Hearings*, 84th Cong., 1st sess., 1956, 736–37.

64. Hale Boggs, representative from Louisiana, testimony before Congress, in *Southeast Hurricane Disaster: Hearings*, 89th Cong., 1st sess., 1965, 4–5.

65. Secretary of the Department of Housing and Urban Development (hereafter Secretary HUD), *Insurance and Other Programs for Financial Assistance to Flood Victim* (Washington, DC: Government Printing Office, 1966), 26 and 34–35. Ironically, at the same time Gilbert White was heading up a task force considering flood insurance. See Task Force on Federal Flood Control Policy, *A Unified National Program for Managing Flood Losses: Report by the Task Force on Federal Flood Control Policy,* House Doc. 465 (Washington, DC: Government Printing Office, 1966).

66. Secretary HUD, *Insurance and Other Programs,* 32–33 and 43–44.

67. Val Peterson, administrator, U.S. Disaster Relief Administration, testimony before Congress, in *National Flood Insurance Act of 1968: Hearings,* Senate, 90th Cong., 1st sess., 1967, 1–10.

68. Hale Boggs, representative from Louisiana, testimony before Congress, in *National Flood Insurance Act of 1968: Hearings,* Senate, 90th Cong., 1st sess., 1967, 3–6.

69. Claude Peppers, representative from Florida, testimony before Congress, in *National Flood Insurance Act of 1968: Hearings,* Senate, 90th Cong., 1st sess., 1967, 128–29.

70. Roger A. Pielke Jr., Mary W. Downton, and J. Zoe Miller, *Flood Damage in the United States, 1926–2000: A Reanalysis of National Weather Service Estimates* (Boulder, CO: National Center for Atmospheric Research, 2002), table 7-2.

71. U.S. Army Corps of Engineers, *Flood of 1973: Post Flood Report, Mississippi and Tributaries Flooding* (Vicksburg, MS: U.S. Army Corps of Engineers, 1973), 126–32.

72. U.S. Army Corps of Engineers, National Levee Database, 2012 [http://nld.usace.army.mil/egis/f?p=471:1:1101256715279501::NO].

73. The "Southeast" in this study included Alabama, Florida, Georgia, North Carolina, South Carolina, and Virginia. The "South" included Arkansas, Kansas, Louisiana, Mississippi, Oklahoma, and Texas. See Roger A. Pielke Jr. and Mary W. Downton, "Precipitation and Damaging Floods: Trends in the United States, 1932–1997," *Journal of Climate 13* (2000): 3625–37. This study did not include hurricane wave and surge flood damages.

74. State of Louisiana, *State of Louisiana May 2011 Flood Event Draft After-Action Report* (Baton Rouge: State of Louisiana, 2011), 5; and Federal Emergency Management Agency, Louisiana-Flooding FEMA-4015-DR, 2011 [http://www.fema.gov/pdf/news/pda/4015.pdf, accessed March 2013].

75. Camillo, *Divine Providence,* 233.

76. Thomas R. Karl, Jerry M. Melillo, and Thomas C. Peterson, eds., *Global Climate Change Impacts in the United States* (New York: Cambridge University Press, 2009), 111–16.

77. Raymond J. Burby, "Flood Insurance and Floodplain Management: The US Experience," *Environmental Hazards* 3 (2001): 111–22, see 118.

78. Adama Sainz, "Florida Building Codes, Revamped since Andrew, Still Being Reworked," *Insurance Journal* (May 18, 2007) [http://www.insurancejournal.com/news/southeast/2007/05/18/79827.htm, accessed March 2013]. New Orleans enacted wind-resistance codes in 1995. See New Orleans, City of, 1995, Municipal Code of Ordinances, Ordinance 21145. Legislative action required wind-resistant construction after 2005. See Wanda Edwards, "Five Years after Katrina Gulf Coast Building Codes Still Inadequate," *Insurance Journal* (August 30, 2010) [http://www.insurancejournal.com/news/southcentral/2010/08/30/112857.htm, accessed March 2013].

79. Craig E. Colten and Alexandra Giancarlo, "Losing Resilience on the Gulf Coast:

Hurricanes and Social Memory," *Environment: Science and Policy for Sustainable Development* 53 , no. 4: 6–19. Also see Raymond Burby, "Hurricane Katrina and the Paradoxes of Government Disaster Policy: Bringing about Wise Government Decisions for Hazardous Areas," *Annals American Academy of Political and Social Sciences* 604 (2006): 171–91.

80. Roger A Pielke Jr. and Christopher Landsea, "Normalized Hurricane Damages in the United States: 1925–1995," *Weather and Forecasting* 13 (1998): 621–31.

81. Federal Emergency Management Agency, *Hurricane Ike in Texas and Louisiana: Building Performance Observations, Recommendations, and Technical Guidance*, FEMA P-757, 2009 [http://www.fema.gov/library/viewRecord.do?id=3577, accessed March 2013].

82. Karl, Melillo, and Peterson, eds., *Global Climate Change Impacts*, 111–16.

83. Rutherford H. Platt, *Land Use and Society: Geography, Law, and Public Policy* (Washington, DC: Island Press, 1996), 425–27; and E. T. Pasterick, "The National Flood Insurance Program," in *Paying the Price: The Status and Role of Insurance against Natural Disasters in the United States*, ed. H. Kunreuther and R. J. Roth, 125–54 (Washington, DC: Joseph Henry, 1998).

84. South Carolina Governor's Office, *An Analysis of the Damage Effects of Hurricane Hugo and Status of Recovery One Year Later* (Columbia, SC: Fontaine Company, 1991), table II-1.1, 10–11.

85. U.S. Army Corps of Engineers, Charleston District, *Hurricane Hugo After-Action Report* (Charleston, SC: U.S. Army Corps of Engineers, Charleston District, 1990,7; and South Carolina Governor's Office, *An Analysis of the Damage Effects of Hurricane Hugo*, 57–58 and 73.

86. Federal Emergency Management Agency, Federal Insurance Administration, *Learning from Hurricane Hugo: Implications for Public Policy* (Washington, DC: Federal Emergency Management Agency, Federal Insurance Administration, 1992), 13–14 and 27.

87. Burby, "Flood Insurance and Floodplain Management," 119.

88. Florida Department of Environmental Protection, Bureau of Beaches and Coastal Systems, *Hurricane Ivan: Beach and Dune Erosion and Structural Damage Assessment* (Tallahassee: Florida Department of Environmental Protection, Bureau of Beaches and Coastal Systems, 2004).

89. U.S. Government Accountability Office, *Information on Proposed Changes to National Flood Insurance Program*, GAO-09–420R (Washington, DC: USGAO, 2009), 17.

90. See Rawle O. King, *The National Flood Insurance Program: Status and Remaining Issues for Congress* (Washington, DC: Congressional Research Service, No. 7–5700, 2013), 6. According to the Congressional Research Service, payments by the NFIP for the ten most costly floods sent $23.6 billion to southern policy holders and between $13 and $16 billion (about) to policy holders in the Northeast in the wake of hurricanes Irene and Sandy.

91. U.S. Government Accountability Office, *Flood Insurance: FEMA's Rate Setting Process Warrants Attention*, GAO-09–12 (Washington, DC: USGAO, 2008), 1–2, and *National Flood Insurance Program: New Process Aided Hurricane Katrina Claims Handling* (Washington, DC: USGAO, 2006), 19.

92. Hurricane Sandy in November 2012 inflicted extensive damage on the New York metropolitan area. Estimates of National Flood Insurance Program payouts in early 2013 ranged from $12 to $15 billion, below Hurricane Katrina totals. Nonetheless, this event once again exceeded the funds available in the NFIP and prompted revisions to ensure its solvency. King, *The National Flood Insurance Program*, 5–8.

CHAPTER FOUR

1. Todd L. Savitt and James H. Young, eds., *Disease and Distinctiveness in the American South* (Knoxville: University of Tennessee Press, 1988); and A. Cash Koeniger, "Climate and Southern Distinctiveness," *Journal of Southern History* 54, no. 1 (1988): 21–44.

2. The prominence of typhoid in the South is reported in George C. Whipple, *Typhoid Fever: Its Causation, Transmission, and Prevention* (New York: Wiley & Sons, 1908), see map at 114. The best national overview of urban sanitation is Martin V. Melosi, *The Sanitary City: Urban Infrastructure in America from Colonial Times to the Present* (Baltimore: Johns Hopkins University Press, 2000), see chaps. 6–8.

3. Conevery Bolton Valencius, *The Health of the Country: How American Settlers Understood Themselves and Their Land* (New York: Basic Books, 2002), 133–42.

4. Margaret Humphries, *Yellow Fever in the South* (Baltimore: John Hopkins University Press, 1992); and John Ellis, *Yellow Fever and Public Health in the New South* (Lexington: University of Kentucky Press, 1992).

5. Carville Earle, "Environment, Disease, and Mortality in Early Virginia," *Journal of Historical Geography* 5, no. 4 (1979): 365–90.

6. Darrett B. Rutman and Anita H. Rutman, "Of Agues and Fevers: Malaria in the Early Chesapeake," *William and Mary Quarterly*, 3rd series, 33, no. 1 (1976): 31–60; and H. Roy Merrens and George D. Terry, "Dying in Paradise: Malaria, Mortality, and the Perceptual Environment in Colonial South Carolina," *Journal of Southern History* 50, no. 4 (1984): 533–50. See also Noah Webster, *A Brief History of Epidemic and Pestilential Diseases* (1799; New York: B. Franklin, 1970).

7. Humphries, *Yellow Fever*, 2.

8. Jo Ann Carrigan, "Yellow Fever: Scourge of the South," in *Disease and Distinctiveness in the American South*, ed. Todd L. Savitt and James H. Young (Knoxville: University of Tennessee Press, 1988), 55–78, esp. 58–59.

9. City Council of New Orleans, *Report of the Sanitary Commission of New Orleans on the Yellow Fever Epidemic of 1853* (New Orleans: Picayune, 1954), vii.

10. Edward Barton, "Report on the Sanitary Condition of New Orleans, in City Council of New Orleans, *Report of the Sanitary Commission of New Orleans on the Yellow Fever Epidemic of 1853* (New Orleans: Picayune, 1954), quote at 219 and 388–91.

11. City Council of New Orleans, *Report of the Sanitary Commission of New Orleans*, viii.

12. Andrew M. Bell, *Mosquito Soldiers: Malaria, Yellow Fever, and the Course of the American Civil War* (Baton Rouge: Louisiana State University Press, 2010), see chap. 3; and Humphries, *Yellow Fever*, 26–27. See also Ari Kelman, *A River and Its City: The Nature of Landscape in New Orleans* (Berkeley: University of California Press, 2003), 78–118.

13. Daniel Drake, *Principal Diseases of the Interior Valley of North America* (Philadelphia: Lippincott, Grambo, & Co., 1854), 195.

14. Humphries, *Yellow Fever*, 22–25.

15. Craig E. Colten, *An Unnatural Metropolis: Wresting New Orleans from Nature* (Baton Rouge: Louisiana State University Press, 2005), esp. chap. 2; and New Orleans Auxiliary Sanitary Association, *Report of the Flushing Committee* (New Orleans: Dunn & Brothers, 1881), 7–11. The general progress of sanitation is chronicled in the Louisiana Board of Health, *Annual Report of the Board of Health of Louisiana* (New Orleans: Graham, 1880–94).

16.Margaret Warner, "Local versus National Interest: The Debate over Southern Public Health, 1878–1884," *Journal of Southern History* 50, no. 3 (1984): 407–28, esp. 408.

17. John H. Ellis, *Yellow Fever and Public Health in the New South* (Lexington: University of Kentucky Press, 1992), esp. chap. 3.

18. Margaret Humphries, *Malaria: Poverty, Race, and Public Health in the United States* (Baltimore: Johns Hopkins University Press, 2001), 43.

19. Christopher G. Boone, "Obstacles to Infrastructure Provision: The Struggle to Build Comprehensive Sewer Works in Baltimore," *Historical Geography* 31 (2003): 151–68.

20. Ellis, *Yellow Fever*, chap. 7; and Stuart Galishoff, "Germs Know No Color Line: Black Health and Public Policy in Atlanta, 1900–1918," *Journal of the History of Medicine and Allied Sciences* 40 (1985): 22–41.

21. Harold L. Platt, *City Building in the New South: The Growth of Public Services in Houston, Texas, 1830–1910* (Philadelphia: Temple University Press, 1983), 126.

22. Colten, *Unnatural Metropolis*, 54–71.

23. Warner, "Local versus National," 420.

24. Warner, "Local versus National," 427–28; and Ellis, *Yellow Fever*, esp. chap. 4.

25. Humphries, *Yellow Fever*, 13–15 and 115–23.

26. Eduardo Faerstein and Warren Winkelstein Jr., "William Gorgas: Yellow Fever Meets Its Nemesis," *Epidemiology* 22, no. 6 (2011): 872 [doi:10.1097/EDE.0b013e31822e18fa]; and William C. Gorgas, *Sanitation in Havana* (New York: D. Appleton & Co., 1915), 56–52.

27. Humphries, *Yellow Fever*, 161.

28. Rupert Boyce, *Yellow Fever Prophylaxis in New Orleans, 1905* (London: Williams & Norgate, 1906), 21 and 37–52; and Humphries, *Yellow Fever*, 162.

29. Humphries, *Yellow Fever*, 162–74, quote at 169.

30. Daniel Drake, *A Systematic Treatise, Historical, Etiological, and Practical on the Principal Diseases of the Interior Valley of North America*, Book First (Cincinnati: Winthrop B. Smith & Co., 1850), 866.

31. Drake, *Systematic Treatise*, 704–12, quote at 712.

32. John Duffy, "The Impact of Malaria in the South," in *Disease and Distinctiveness in the American South*, ed. Todd L. Savitt and James H. Young (Knoxville: University of Tennessee Press, 1988), 29–55, see 40–41.

33. John W. Trask, "Malaria: A Public Health and Economic Problem in the United States," *Public Health Reports* 31, no. 51 (1915): 3445–42, see 3449.

34. R. H. von Ezdorf, "Malaria in the United States," *Public Health Reports* 30, no. 22 (1915): 1603–24.

35. "Malaria in North Carolina: Prevalence and Geographic Distribution," *Public Health Reports* 32, no. 29 (1917): 1128–34; and "Malaria in South Carolina: Prevalence and Geographic Distribution, 1915 and 1916," *Public Health Reports* 33, no. 2 (1918): 35–37.

36. H. R. Carter, "The Malaria Problem in the South," *Public Health Reports* 34, no. 34 (1919): 1927–35, see 1929.

37. L. D. Fricks, "Malaria Control in the U.S.: Retrospect and Prospect," *Southern Medical Journal* 17 (1924): 578–82, quote at 580. Cited in Humphries, *Malaria*, 51.

38. M. A. Barber, "The History of Malaria in the United States," *Public Health Reports* 44, no. 43 (1929): 2575–87, see 2577.

39. C. C. Dauer and Ernest C. Faust, "Malaria Mortality in the Southern United States

for 1934 with Supplementary Data for Previous Years," *Southern Medical Journal* 29, no. 7 (1936): 757–64.

40. Most reports for Southern rivers noted the prevalence of malaria. See, for example, National Resources Committee, *Drainage Basin Committee Report for the Southeastern Basins* (Washington, DC: Government Printing Office, 1937). For the Apalachicola River, the report emphasized that "malaria control problems take precedence with those of water supply and pollution in the basin." Quote at 17.

41. Humphries, *Malaria*, 70–71.

42. Stanley Trimble, "Perspectives on the History of Erosion Control in the Eastern United States," *Agricultural History* 59 (1985): 162–80; and Carville Earle, "The Myth of the Southern Soil Miner: Macrohistory, Agricultural Innovation, and Environmental Change," in *Ends of the Earth: Perspectives on Modern Environmental History*, ed. Donald Worster (Cambridge: Cambridge University Press, 1989), 175–210. Trimble attributes erosion control to the influence of the Soil Conservation Service, while Earle claims restoration of traditional practices was influential.

43. Duffy, "The Impact of Malaria on the South," 29–54; and Humphries, *Malaria*, see 55–57.

44. Carter, "Malaria Problem in the South," quote at 1929. Drainage, whether by subsurface tiles or open ditches, was central to USPHS malaria-control initiatives. See J. A. A. LePrince, "Malaria Control: Drainage as an Antimalaria Measure," *Public Health Reports* 30, no. 8 (1915): 536–45.

45. Hugh Prince, *Wetlands of the American Midwest: A Historical Geography of Changing Attitudes* (Chicago: University of Chicago Press, 1997); Hugh Hammond Bennett, *Soil Conservation* (New York: McGraw Hill, 1939), esp. 617–59; and Stanley Trimble, *Man Induced Soil Erosion on the Southern Piedmont* (Ankeny, IA: Soil and Water Conservation Society, 1974), 40–41.

46. Stafford C. Happ, Gordon Rittenhouse, and G. C. Dobson, *Some Principles of Accelerated Stream and Valley Sedimentation*, U.S. Department of Agriculture Technical Bulletin 695 (Washington, DC: U.S. Department of Agriculture, 1940), see 4–6.

47. Hugh Hammond Bennett, "Cultural Changes in Soils from the Standpoint of Erosion," *Journal of the American Society of Agronomists* 23 (1931): 434–54, see 436–37.

48. Happ, Rittenhouse, and Dobson, *Some Principles*, see tables in appendix; Carville Earle, "Into the Abyss . . . Again: Technical Change and Destructive Occupance in the American Cotton Belt, 1870–1930," in *The American Environment: Interpretations of Past Geographies*, ed. Lary M. Dilsaver and Craig E. Colten (Lanham, MD: Rowman & Littlefield, 1992), 53–88, see 80.

49. Stanley Trimble, "The Alcovy River Swamps: The Result of Culturally Accelerated Sedimentation," *Bulletin of the Georgia Academy of Sciences* 28 (1970): 131–41.

50. Trimble, *Man Induced Soil Erosion*, 33–34.

51. Jonathan D. Phillips, "A Short History of a Flat Place: Three Centuries of Geomorphic Change in the Croatan National Forest," *Annals of the Association of American Geographers* 87, no. 2 (1987): 197–217, see 213.

52. Earle, "Into the Abyss," 71. Earle argues that soil conservation practices were not the lone influence on arresting erosion. He looks at macro-economic cycles and also the restoration of traditional practices as having decided roles.

53. H. R. von Ezdorf, "Malarial Fevers: Prevalence and Geographic Distribution in Alabama," *Public Health Reports* 29, no. 18 (1914): 1073–83, quote at 1074.

54. To carry out this analysis, I identified the state region with the highest incidence of malaria shown on the USPHS maps and compared those locations with their historical precipitation patterns. One would expect a dry winter, followed by a wet summer to produce ideal conditions for erosion, sedimentation, and expansion of malaria habitat. United States Public Health Service state reports include: "Malaria in Arkansas: Prevalence and Geographic Distribution—1915 and 1916," *Public Health Reports* 33, no. 4 (1918): 100–104; "Malaria in Florida: Prevalence and Geographic Distribution—April 1915 to December 1916," *Public Health Reports* 32, no. 52 (1917): 2219–22; "Malaria in Louisiana: Prevalence and Geographic Distribution," *Public Health Reports* 32, no. 30 (1917): 1182–86; "Malaria in Tennessee: Prevalence and Geographic Distribution," *Public Health Reports* 32, no. 34 (1917): 1339–45"; "Malaria in Eastern Texas: Prevalence and Geographic Distribution," *Public Health Reports* 32, no. 33 (1917): 1301–6; "Malaria in North Carolina: Prevalence and Geographic Distribution," *Public Health Reports* 32, no. 29 (1917): 1128–34; and "Malaria in South Carolina: Prevalence and Geographic Distribution, 1915 and 1916," *Public Health Reports* 33, no. 2 (1918): 35–37. See also von Ezdorf, "Malarial Fevers." Precipitation graphs are available at U.S. Department of Commerce, National Climate Data Center, Online Climate Information [http://www7.ncdc.noaa.gov/CDO/CDODivisionalSelect.jsp#], select for state, division, and precipitation (accessed September 2012).

55. R. C. Derivaux, H. A. Taylor, and T. D. Haas, *Malaria Control: A Report of Demonstration Studies Conducted in Urban and Rural Sections*, Public Health Service Bulletin 88 (Washington, DC: Government Printing Office, 1917), esp. 1–31.

56. Derivaux, Taylor, and Haas, *Malaria Control*, 34–55.

57. R. C. Derivaux, "The Relation of the Railroads in the South to the Problem of Malaria and Its Control," *Public Health Reports* 33, no. 31 (1918): 1267–71, quote at 1267, and see 1270–71.

58. St. Louis Southwestern Railway Lines, *Malaria Control: A Demonstration of Its Value to Railroads Based on Experience of the St. Louis Southwestern Railway Lines, 1917–1920* (Texarkana, AR: St. Louis Southwestern Railway Lines , 1921), quote at 12.

59. St. Louis Southwestern Railway Lines, *Malaria Control*, 7.

60. St. Louis Southwestern Railway Lines, *Malaria Control*, 19–21 and 27–28. See also Don L. Hofsommer, "St. Louis Southwestern Railway's Campaign against Malaria in Arkansas and Texas," *Arkansas Historical Quarterly* 62, no. 2 (2003): 182–93.

61. Earle, "Into the Abyss," 79–80.

62. Alabama State Board of Health, *Annual Report* (Montgomery, AL: Brown Printing, 1923), 92–99, quote at 97–98.

63. Alabama State Board of Health, *Annual Report* (Birmingham, AL: Birmingham Printing, 1924), see 326–500.

64. Alabama State Board of Health, *Annual Report* (1924), 331, 351–522.

65. S. W. Welch, "Malaria Control Work in Alabama," *Southern Medical Journal* 20 (1927): 482–83, quote at 1.

66. Alabama State Board of Health, *Annual Report* (1924), 351, regulation printed at 378. Impoundment studies appear in J. A. A. LePrince, "Impounded Waters," *Public Health Reports* 30, no. 7 (1915): 473–81; and E. B. Gage, "Studies of Impounded Waters in Relation to Malaria," *Public Health Reports* 40, no. 42 (1925): 2211–19. The courts subsequently threw

out Alabama's regulations on a technicality, but legislators passed a revised version in 1927.

67. W. G. Smillie, "Studies of an Epidemic of Malaria at the Gantt Impounded Area, Covington County, Alabama," *American Journal of Hygiene* 7 (1927): 40–72, esp. 41–47, and, "Further Studies of the Impounded Area at Gantt, Alabama," *Southern Medical Journal* 20, no. 6 (1927): 475–80; Welch, "Malaria Control Work in Alabama," 3.

68. Humphries, *Malaria*, 89–91.

69. Alabama State Board of Health, *Annual Report* (Montgomery, 1931), 122.

70. Tennessee Department of Public Health, *Biennial Report, 1926–1927* (Nashville: Tennessee Department of Public Health [TDPH], 1927), 113–15.

71. Tennessee Department of Public Health, *Biennial Report, 1927–29 (Nashville: TDPH, 1929),* 50–52.

72. Tennessee Department of Public Health, *Biennial Report, 1929–1931* (Nashville: TDPH, 1931), 106–7.

73. Tennessee Department of Public Health, *Biennial Report, 1931–1933* (Nashville: TDPH, 1933), 79. In Louisiana, the board of health also curtailed control programs as the economic crisis deepened, Louisiana State Board of Health, *Biennial Report, 1932–1933* (Baton Rouge: Louisiana State Board of Health, 1933), 91.

74. Dauer and Faust, "Malaria Mortality in the Southern United States," see map at 764; Humphries, *Malaria,* 95–96; and Ernest C. Faust, "Clinical and Public Health Aspects of Malaria in the United States from a Historical Perspective," *American Journal of Tropical Medicine* 25 (1945): 185–201.

75. Humphries, *Malaria,* 98–99.

76. John A. Mulrennan and Wilson T. Sowder, "Florida's Mosquito Control System," *Public Health Reports* 69, no. 7 (1954): 613–18, see 614. The role of the military in Alabama is touted in "Preventive Rules Triumph in Malaria Control," *Alabama Game and Fish News* (November 1939): 7.

77. Extensive updates on the state's malaria-control program appear annually in the Florida State Board of Health, *Annual Reports* (Jacksonville: Florida State Board of Health, 1934–40).

78. See Florida State Board of Health, *34th Annual Report* (1934), 30–31; and "Malaria in Escambia County, 1937–1940," Florida Division of Health, RG 810, Series 899, Box 4, Folders 46–51, Florida State Archives, Tallahassee, Florida.

79. Mulrennan and Sowder, "Florida's Mosquito Control System,"615.

80. Mark F. Boyd, "A Review of Malaria Control in the Southern States during 1934," *Southern Medical Journal* 28, no. 8 (1935): 763–64, see 764.

81. Louis L. Williams, "Civil Works Administration Emergency Relief Administration Malaria Control Program in the South," *American Journal of Public Health* 25 (1935): 11–14, see 11–12.

82. "WPA Workers Fight Mosquitos," *American City* 51 (October 1936): 51–52, see 51.

83. George E. Riley and Nelson H. Rector, "Experiences with Minor Drainage in Relation to Malaria Rates in Some Mississippi Delta Counties," *Southern Medical Journal* 30, no. 8 (1937): 862–66.

84. American Society of Civil Engineers, Joint Committee of the National Malaria Committee through its Sub-committee on Engineering, "Malaria Control for Engineers," *Reports: American Society for Civil Engineers* 65 (1939): 229–73, quote at 258.

85. W. G. Stromquist, "Engineering Aspects of Mosquito Control," *Civil Engineering*

14, no. 10 (1944): 431–34; and Tennessee Valley Authority (TVA), *Malaria Control on Impounded Water* (Washington, DC: Government Printing Office, 1947), see 8–14.

86. E. L. Bishop, "Malaria Control Activities of the Tennessee Valley Authority," *Public Health Reports* 51, no. 29 (1936): 970–75; Stromquist, "Engineering Aspects," 432; and TVA, *Malaria Control*, 93–111.

87. Reports on the numerous reservoirs appear in Tennessee Valley Authority, River Basin Operations, Malaria Control Program Projects, Files and Reports, 1933–1960, RG 142, Box 1, Sanitation Section Malaria Control Engineering Annual Report 1937, National Archives, Atlanta, Georgia.

88. W. G. Stromquist (TVA sanitary engineer) memo to E. L. Bishop (TVA director of health), September 24, 1937, TVA Records, RG 142, River Basin Operations, Malaria Control Program Project, Box 1, National Archives, Atlanta, Georgia.

89. Stromquist, "Engineering Aspects,"434. The TVA carried out investigations to demonstrate the minimal impact of mosquito control on aquatic life. See TVA Technical Committee, *Cooperative Investigation of the Relation between Mosquito Control and Wildlife Conservation* (Chattanooga, TN: TVA, 1940), Alabama State Archives, Montgomery, Alabama.

90. TVA, Health and Safety Department, Sixth Annual Meeting of the Board of Malaria Consultants (Louisville, KY, 1940), 32, TVA Records, RG 142, River Basin Operations, Malaria Control Program Project Files and Reports, Box 5, National Archives, Atlanta, Georgia.

91. W. G. Stromquist, "A Partnership in Malaria Control," paper presented to the National Malaria Committee, Louisville, Kentucky, November 1940, 7, TVA Records, RG 142, Reservoir Group, River Basin Operations, Box 31, National Archives, Atlanta, Georgia.

92. TVA, *Malaria Control on Impounded Water*, 11.

93. Bennett, *Soil Conservation*, 4 and 517; and Paul Sutter, "What Gullies Mean: Georgia's 'Little Grand Canyon' and Southern Environmental History," *Journal of Southern History* 76, no. 3 (2010): 579–616, see esp. 589–92.

94. Trimble, *Man Induced Soil Erosion*, 36–50; Bennett, *Soil Conservation*, chaps. 30 and 31.

95. U.S. Department of Agriculture, Soil Conservation Service, *Report of the Chief of the Soil Conservation Service* (Washington, DC: Soil Conservation Service, 1936), 17.

96. U.S. Department of Agriculture, Soil Conservation Service, *Report of the Chief of the Soil Conservation Service* (Washington, DC: Soil Conservation Service, 1939), 68–69.

CHAPTER FIVE

A previous version of this article appeared elsewhere and appears here with kind permission from Springer Science+Business Media: *Water History*, "Navigable Waters: A Different Course in the American South," Craig E. Colten, 2 (2010): 3–17. I would also like to thank Colgate University for hosting me in 2009 as the A. Lindsay O'Connor Visiting Distinguished Professor. Much of the initial research for this chapter took place at Colgate.

1. Wayland F. Dunaway, "History of the James River and Kanawha Company" (PhD Dissertation, Columbia University, 1922), 15–20.

2. Thomas Jefferson, *Notes on the State of Virginia*, 3rd ed. (New York: M. L. and W. A. Davis, 1801), 8–9.

3. Morton J. Horwitz, *The Transformation of American Law, 1780–1860* (Cambridge, MA: Harvard University Press, 1977); Theodore Steinberg, *Nature Incorporated: Industrialization and the Waters of New England* (New York: Cambridge University Press, 1991); Richard W. Judd, *Common Lands, Common People: The Origins of Conservation in Northern New England* (Cambridge, MA: Harvard University Press, 1997); and John T. Cumbler, *Reasonable Use: The People, the Environment, and the State, New England, 1790–1930* (New York: Oxford University Press, 2001).

4. Louis C. Hunter, *Steamboats on the Western Rivers: An Economic and Technological History* (Cambridge, MA: Harvard University Press, 1949); Todd Shallat, *Structures in the Stream: Water, Science, and the Rise of the Corps of Engineers* (Austin: University of Texas Press, 1994); Ari Kelman, *A River and Its City: The Nature of Landscape in New Orleans* (Berkeley: University of California Press, 2003); and Robert H. Gudmestad, *Steamboats and the Rise of the Cotton Kingdom* (Baton Rouge: Louisiana State University Press, 2011).

5. Erik F. Haites, James Mak, and Gary M. Walton, *Western River Transportation: The Era of Early Internal Development* (Baltimore: Johns Hopkins University Press, 1975); John L. Larson, *Internal Improvement: National Public Works and the Promise of Popular Government in the Early United States* (Chapel Hill: University of North Carolina Press, 2001): and Paul F. Paskoff, *Troubled Waters: Steamboat Disasters, River Improvements, and American Public Policy, 1821–1860* (Baton Rouge: Louisiana State University Press, 2007).

6. Steven Hahn, *The Roots of Southern Populism: Yeoman Farmers and the Transformation of the Georgia Upcountry, 1850–1890* (New York: Oxford University Press, 1983); Lacy K. Ford Jr., *Origins of Southern Radicalism: The South Carolina Upcountry, 1800–1860* (New York: Oxford University Press, 1988); and Thomas Downey, *Planting a Capitalist South: Masters, Merchants, and Manufacturers in the Southern Interior, 1790–1860* (Baton Rouge: Louisiana State University Press, 2006).

7. Jeffrey K. Stine, *Mixing the Waters: Environment, Politics, and the Building of the Tennessee-Tombigbee Waterway* (Akron, OH: University of Akron, 1993); Richard A. Bartlett, *Troubled Waters: Champion International and the Pigeon River Controversy* (Knoxville: University of Tennessee Press, 1995); Martin Reuss, *Designing the Bayous: The Control of Water in the Atchafalaya Basin, 1800–1995* (Alexandria, VA: U.S. Army Corps of Engineers, Office of History, 1998); and Christopher Morris, *The Big Muddy: An Environmental History of the Mississippi and Its Peoples from Hernando de Soto to Hurricane Katrina* (New York: Oxford University Press, 2012).

8. Horwitz, *Transformation of American Law*, 140; and Joshua Getzler, *A History of Water Rights at Common Law* (Oxford: Oxford University Press, 2004), 270–96.

9. Merritt Starr, "Navigable Waters of the United States—State and National Control," *Harvard Law Review* 35 (1921): 154–81.

10. Horwitz, *Transformation of American Law*, 142. See also Daniel J. Hulsebosch, "Writs to Rights: Navigability and the Transformation of Common Law in the Nineteenth Century," *Cardozo Law Review* 23 (2001–2): 1049–1106; and John F. Baughman, "Balancing Commerce, History and Geography: Defining the Navigable Waters of the United States," *Michigan Law Review* 90 (1991–92): 1028–61.

11. Starr, "Navigable Waters of the United States," 157–58. A listing of all streams designated as navigable by the Virginia legislature appears in Alvin T. Embrey, *Waters of the State* (Richmond: Old Dominion Press, 1931), 382–90.

12. "Chapter 235: An Act to Reduce into One the Several Acts Concerning Mills,

Mill-dams, and other Obstructions to Water-courses," *Revised Code of the Laws of Virginia*, vol. 2 (Richmond, VA: Thomas Ritchie, 1819), 225–32; and "Chapter 103: Rivers and Creeks," *The Revised Statutes of the State of North Carolina*, vol. 1 (Raleigh: Turner & Hughes, 1836– 37), 533–36.

13. "Survey of the James River: Letter from the Secretary of War," House Doc. 133, 24th Cong, 2nd sess., 1837, quote at 5, and 6–7.

14. "Committee of Commerce, to whom was referred the petition of the inhabitants of Wilmington, North Carolina," Senate Report 49, 19th Congress, 2nd sess., February 2, 1827, 49–50; and Survey of Cape Fear River, House Doc. 127, 20th Cong, 1st sess., February 8, 1828, 8–10. Residents in Savannah, Georgia, made a similar appeal. See, "Memorial of the Savannah Chamber of Commerce," U.S. Senate, Doc. 36, 29th Cong., 1st sess., January 3, 1846.

15. "Memorial of the Citizens of Wilmington, North Carolina, for a further appropria- tion for improving the Navigation of the Cape Fear River," House Doc. 370, 24th Cong., 1st sess., May 12, 1936, and "Mouth of Cape Fear River: Resolutions of the Legislature of North Carolina," House Misc. Docs. 11, 32nd Cong., 2nd sess., January 17, 1853.

16. "Act. 519: An Act to Preserve the Navigation and Fishery in the Several Rivers and Creeks in this Province" [enacted March 11, 1726]; and " Act 704: An Act for Regulating the Making of Dams or Banks for Reserving Water" [enacted May 29, 1744], *The Statutes at Large of South Carolina*, V. *III* (Columbia, SC: A. S. Johnston, 1838), 269–70 and 609–11.

17. See Witt v. Jeffcoat 10 Rich. 389 (1857) and Jackson v. Lewis 1 Cheves 259 (1840).

18. Thomas Downey, "Riparian Rights and Manufacturing in Antebellum South Caro- lina: William Gregg and the Origins of the Industrial Mind," *Journal of Southern History* 66, no. 1 (1999): 77–108, see esp. 86–90. For a general discussion of the emerging timber industry, see John Eisterhold, "Savannah: Lumber Center of the South Atlantic," *Georgia Historical Quarterly* 57 (1973): 526–43.

19. Oliver Prince, "An Act to Keep Open, Remove, and Prevent Obstruction in Savan- nah River," *Digest of the Laws of the State of Georgia* (Athens: Oliver Prince, 1837), 695. The act was passed in 1809 and amended in 1816 and 1829.

20. Oliver Prince, "An Act to Repeal Act to Authorize John M. Dasher to Keep Open and Improve Navigation on Ebenezer Mill Creek," *Digest of the Laws of the State of Georgia*, 701–2.

21. Starr, "Navigable Waters of the United States," 169.

22. State of Alabama, An Act to Prevent the Obstruction of the Navigable Water- Courses in This State, Alabama Legislative Acts, December 1819 [http://www.legislature. state.al.us/misc/history/acts_and_journals/Acts_Oct_Dec_1819/Page11_pg91–100.html, accessed March 2013].

23. William Barnett to the Acting Secretary of War, correspondence, March 12, 1817, in *The Territorial Papers of the United States, V. XVIII*, ed. Clarence E. Carter, 67–72, see 69 (Washington, DC: Government Printing Office, 1952).

24. "Memorial to Congress by the [Alabama] Territorial Assembly," February 12, 1818, in *The Territorial Papers of the United States, V. XVIII*, ed. Clarence E. Carter, 249–51, see 249 (Washington, DC: Government Printing Office, 1952).

25. "Memorial to Congress by the [Alabama] Territorial Assembly," March 10, 1818, in *The Territorial Papers of the United States, V. XVIII*, ed. Clarence E. Carter, 268–71, see 268–69 (Washington, DC: Government Printing Office, 1952).

26. William Barnett, correspondence, March 12, 1817, see 67–70.

27. An Act to Improve the Navigation of the Coosa River and to Aid in Its Connection with the Tennessee Waters, Alabama Legislative Acts, December 30, 1823 [http://www.legislature.state.al.us/misc/history/acts_and_journals/Acts_1823/Acts_50–60.html, accessed March 2013].

28. An Act to Provide for Examining Certain Rivers, Alabama Legislative Acts, December 13, 1819 [http://www.legislature.state.al.us/misc/history/acts_and_journals/Acts_Oct_Dec_1819/Page11_pg91–100.html, accessed March 2013].

29. An Act Declaring Flint River in Navigation [sic Morgan] County a Public Highway, Alabama Legislative Acts, 15 December 1824[http://www.legislature.state.al.us/misc/history/acts_and_journals/Acts_1824/Acts_101–113.html, accessed March 2013]; An Act to Declare Beaver Creek, in Wilcox County, Public Highway, Alabama Legislative Acts, December 20, 1824 [http://www.legislature.state.al.us/misc/history/acts_and_journals/Acts_1824/Acts_101–113.html, accessed March 2013].

30. Horwitz, *Transformation of American Law,* 148–50.

31. Horwitz, *Transformation of American Law,* 40; Steinberg, *Nature Incorporated,* esp. chaps. 4 and 5. Implicit in Horwitz and Steinberg is uniform application of the instrumental interpretation across the country; however, Christine Rosen found considerable variation among industrial states. See her "'Knowing' Environmental Pollution: Nuisance Law and the Power of Tradition in a Time of Rapid Economic Change, 1840–1864," *Environmental History* 8, no. 4 (2003): 565–97.

32. Downey, "Riparian Rights."

33. I reviewed the nineteenth-century digest of case law under the heading of navigable waters and noted all cases in southern states. See *Century Edition of the American Digest: A Complete Digest of All Reported American Cases form the Earliest Times to 1896,* vol. 37, "Navigable Waters" (Minneapolis, MN: West Publishers, 1904). Consistently, the antebellum courts backed the notion of public highway for rivers designated as navigable waters as discussed below. This procedure follows a method pioneered by Christine Rosen, "'Knowing' Environmental Pollution." For additional use of court records, see John A Kirchner, "Navigability of American Waters: Resolving Conflict through Applied Historical Geography," in *Cultural Encounters with the Environment: Enduring and Evolving Geographic Themes,* ed. Alexander B. Murphy and Douglas L. Johnson, 157–75 (Lanham, MD: Rowman & Littlefield, 2000); and K. Maria D. Lane, "Water, Technology, and the Courtroom: Negotiating Reclamation Policy in Territorial New Mexico," *Journal of Historical Geography* 47 (2011): 300–311.

34. "Memorial to Congress by the [Alabama] Territorial Assembly," February 12, 1818, in *The Territorial Papers of the United States, V. XVIII,* ed. Clarence E. Carter, 249 (Washington, DC: Government Printing Office, 1952).

35. "Memorial to Congress by the [Florida] Legislative Council," December 10, 1825, in *The Territorial Papers of the United States, V. XXIII,* ed. Clarence E. Carter, 378–84 (Washington, DC: Government Printing Office, 1952). This memorial appealed for a cross Florida canal.

36. State of Alabama, "An Act to Prevent the Obstruction of the Navigable Water-Courses in This State"; Prince, "An Act to Keep Open, Remove, and Prevent Obstruction in Savannah River," 695; and Downey, "Riparian Rights."

37. Archibald D. Murphey, *Memoir on the Internal Improvements Contemplated by the Legislature of North Carolina* (Raleigh, NC: J. Glake, 1819), 11.

38. Joseph A. Ernst and H. Roy Merrens, "'Camden's Turrets Pierce the Skies!' The Urban

Process in the Southern Colonies during the Eighteenth Century," *William and Mary Quarterly*, 3rd series, 30, no. 4 (1973): 550–74.

39. Robert D. Mitchell and Warren R. Hofstra, "How Do Settlement Systems Evolve? The Virginia Backcountry during the Eighteenth Century," *Journal of Historical Geography* 21, no. 2 (1995): 123–47.

40. Hunter, *Steamboats on the Western Rivers*, 133.

41. Joseph A. Ernst and H. Roy Merrens, "'Camden's Turrets Pierce the Skies,'" in *The Rise of the Urban South, ed. Lawrence H. Larsen* (Lexington: University of Kentucky Press, 1985), 24–25; Mitchell and Hofstra, "How Do Settlement Systems Evolve?"; and Downey, *Planting a Capitalist South*, 64–65.

42. Jack Temple Kirby, *Poquosin: A Study of Rural Landscape and Society* (Chapel Hill: University of North Carolina Press, 1995), 138–39.

43. For overviews of three examples, see Frederick A. Porcher, *The History of the Santee Canal* (Charleston: South Carolina Historical Society, 1950); Dunaway, "History of the James River"; and Charles C. Weaver, *Internal Improvements in North Carolina Previous to 1860*, Johns Hopkins University Studies in Historical and Political Science, v. 21, nos. 3–4 (Baltimore: Johns Hopkins University Press, 1903).

44. R. Mills, *Statistics on South Carolina* (Charleston, SC: Hurlburt & Lloyd, 1826); and A. Sherwood, *A Gazetteer of the State of Georgia* (Washington, GA: P. Force, 1837).

45. A vigorous discussion has focused on the economic viability of Southern internal improvements. Limited capitalization and a low volume of paying traffic played a role in poor maintenance, which permitted extreme weather events to cause lasting damage to the poorly engineered structures. See Larson, *Internal Improvement*; and J. Majewski, "Who Financed the Transportation Revolution? Regional Divergence and Internal Improvements in Antebellum Pennsylvania and Virginia," *Journal of Economic History* 56, no. 4 (1996): 763–88.

46. Virginia Board of Public Works, *40th Annual Report of the Board of Public Works* (Richmond: Virginia Board of Public Works, 1857); and Kohn, *Internal Improvement in South Carolina, 1817–28*. The impacts are chronicled in Stanley W. Trimble, *Man Induced Soil Erosion on the Southern Piedmont* (Ankeny, IA: Soil and Water Conservation Society, 1974).

47. D. R. Littlefield, "The Potomac Company: A Misadventure in Financing and Early American Internal Improvement Project," *Business History Review* 58, no. 4 (1984): 562–85, see esp. 566 and 583.

48. M. L. Webber, "Col. Snlf's Account of the Santee Canal," *South Carolina Genealogical Magazine* 28, no. 1 (1927); 8–12, and 28, no. 2 (1927): 112–31. Also Porcher, *The History of the Santee Canal*, 6.

49. Mills, *Statistics on South Carolina*; Kohn, *Internal Improvement in South Carolina, 1817–28*; and South Carolina v. Cullum 2 Speers 581 (1844).

50. U.S. Department of the Interior, Census Office, *Reports of the Water-Power of the United States* (Washington: Government Printing Office, 1885), 90–91.

51. A. Murphey, *Memoir on the Internal Improvements Contemplated by the Legislature of North Carolina* (Raleigh: J. Glake, 1819); and Weaver, *Internal Improvements in North Carolina*, 10.

52. U.S. Department of the Interior, *Reports on the Water-power of the United States*, 27–28, and 56.

53. "Memorial to Congress by the [Florida] Legislative Council," December 28, 1924, in *The Territorial Papers of the United States, V. XXIII*, ed. Clarence E. Carter, 378–84, see esp. 381 (Washington, DC: Government Printing Office, 1952).

54. Duke v. Cahawba Navigation Company, 16 Ala 372 (1849); Louisiana v. New Orleans Navigation Company, 11 Mart (O.S.) 309 (1822); N.C. v. Patrick, 14 NC 478 (1832); and Swasey v. The Montgomery, 12 La Ann 800 (1857).

55. See Downey, *Planting a Capitalist South;* and Kirby, *Poquosin.*

56. U.S. Department of the Interior, *Reports on the Water-power of the United States,* 90–91.

57. U.S. Department of the Interior, *Reports on the Water-power of the United States,* 27–37.

58. U.S. Department of the Interior, *Reports on the Water-power of the United States,* 27–28, and 55–58.

59. See Larson, *Internal Improvement.* Also Majewski, "Who Financed the Transportation Revolution?" and Louis C. Hunter, *History of Industrial Power in the U.S. 1780–1930: V. I, Water Power in the Century of the Steam Engine* (Charlottesville: University of Virginia Press, 1979).

60. Downey, *Planting a Capitalist South.*

61. Crenshaw and Crenshaw v. Slate River Co., 27 Va. 245 (1828).

62. Crenshaw and Crenshaw v. Slate River Co., 27 Va. 245 (1828), 25–28.

63. Crenshaw and Crenshaw v. Slate River Co., 27 Va. 245 (1828), 32–35.

64. The classic work on the recovery and renovation of the Southern economy is Gavin Wright, *Old South, New South: Revolutions in the Southern Economy since the Civil War* (Baton Rouge: Louisiana State University Press, 1986); and see Michael W. Fitzgerald, *Splendid Failure: Postwar Reconstruction in the American South* (Chicago: Ivan R. Dee, 2007).

65. The expansion of federally funded river improvements was not limited to the South, but it had an extraordinary impact on the region and directly modified many of the same waterways that local investors had attempted to alter during the antebellum period. Often a first step involved clearing obstructions placed in rivers during the Civil War followed by further channel modifications. These projects are summarized in U.S. Army, *Annual Report, Chief of Engineers for 1880,* pts. 1–3, 46th Cong., 3rd sess., Ex Doc 1, pt. 2, vol. 2 (Washington, DC: Government Printing Office, 1880).

66. U.S. Army, *Annual Report, Chief of Engineers for 1880;* and U.S. Department of Interior, *Reports on Water-power of the United States.*

67. Decisions by the Army Engineers could also leave a river poorly served if they terminated maintenance or declined a local petition. See Hoffman, "The Decline of the Port of Richmond."

68. Morrison v. Coleman, 87 Ala 655 (1888).

69. Goodin's v. Kentucky Lumber Co., 90 Ky 625 (1890).

70. Mills et al. v. U.S., 46 F. 738 (1891), quotes at 745 and 747.

71. The Corps terminated work on the Wateree River in 1889 and resumed navigation maintenance after a successful appeal by local citizens. See, U.S. Army, *Report of the Chief of Engineers,* pts. 1–3, (Washington: DC: Government Printing Office, 1910), 1452.

72. U.S. Army, *Report of the Chief of Engineers,* pts. 1–3 (Washington, DC: Government Printing Office, 1910).

73. Hoffman, "The Decline of the Port of Richmond."

74. National Resources Committee, *Drainage Basin Committee Report, nos. 10–31* (Washington, DC: Government Printing Office, 1937).

75. North Carolina, a state with ample hydropower potential, regularly reported on its emerging hydroelectric capacity. See George F. Swain, J. A. Holmes, and E. W. Myers, *Papers on the Waterpower in North Carolina: A Preliminary Report* (Raleigh: North Carolina Geological Survey, Bulletin No. 8, 1899); North Carolina Department of Conservation and Development, Water Resources Division, *The Power Situation in North Carolina* (Raleigh: North Carolina Department of Conservation and Development, Water Resources Division, Circular No. 16, 1925); also see South Carolina Department of Agriculture, Commerce and Immigration, *Handbook of South Carolina* (Columbia, SC: State Company, 1907), esp. 146–62. A discussion of waterpower laws in Virginia appears in Embrey, *Waters of the State*, 302–77.

76. Robert F. Durden, *Electrifying the Piedmont Carolinas: The Duke Power Company, 1904–1997* (Durham, NC: Carolina Academic Press, 2001).

77. Alabama Power v. Gulf Power, 283 F. 606 (1922).

78. Donald J. Pisani, *Water and American Government: The Reclamation Bureau, National Water Policy, and the West, 1902–1935* (Berkeley: University of California Press, 2002), 222–25; and David P. Billington and Donald C. Jackson, *Big Dams and the New Deal Era: A Confluence of Engineering and Politics* (Norman: University of Oklahoma Press, 2006), 81–85.

79. Michael J. McDonald and John Muldowny, *TVA and the Dispossessed: The Resettlement of Population in the Norris Dam Area* (Knoxville: University of Tennessee Press, 1982); Melissa Walker, "African Americans and TVA Reservoir Property Removal: Race in New Deal Program," *Agricultural History* 72, no. 2 (1998): 417–28; and T. Robert Hart, "The Lowcountry Landscape: Politics, Preservation, and the Santee-Cooper Project," *Environmental History* 18, no. 1 (2013): 127–56.

80. United States v. Appalachian Electric Power, 311 US 377 (1940).

81. U.S. v. Twin City Power Co., 215 F. 592 (1984); and Georgia Power v. Baker, 830 F. 2nd 163 (1987).

82. J. W. Looney and Steven G. Zraick, "Of Cows, Canoes, and Commerce: How the Concept of Navigability Provides an Answer if You Know Which Question to Ask," *University of Arkansas Little Rock Law Review* 25 (2002): 175–89, esp. 177–78.

83. Margaret A. Johnston, "The Supreme Court Scales Back the Army Corps of Engineers' Jurisdiction over 'Navigable Waters' under the Clean Water Act," *University of Arkansas at Little Rock Law Review* 24 (2002): 329–58, see 336–43.

84. While not a case turning on the question of navigability, the series of court decisions allowing the opening of the Tennessee-Tombigbee Waterway represents the priority placed on waterways built by the Corps of Engineers. See Stine, *Mixing the Waters*.

85. U.S. v. Tull, 615 F Supp 610 (1983).

86. U.S. v. West Virginia Power Co., 56 F Supp 298 (1944).

87. Hartman v. U.S., 522 F Supp 114 (1981).

88. U.S. v. Sasser, 738 F Supp 177 (1990).

89. See U.S. Army, *Annual Report, Chief of Engineers* (1880); U.S. Army, *Annual Report of the Chief of Engineers, V. 1–3*, 54th Cong., 1st sess., House Doc. 2, no. 2, 1895; U.S. Army, *Report of the Chief of Engineers*, pts. 1–3 (1910).

90. S. E. Draper, "Legal Issues of Water Allocation for the Apalachicola-Chattahoochee-

Flint River Basin," in *Proceedings of the 1991 Georgia Water Resources Conference* (Athens, GA, 1991), 148–50.

91. Tri-State Water Rights Litigation, 639 F. Supp. 2nd 1308 (2009), 12.

92. Tri-State Water Rights Litigation, 639 F. Supp. 2nd 1308 (2009), 14.

93. Tri-State Water Rights Litigation, 639 F. Supp. 2nd 1308 (2009), 26–27.

94. Tri-State Water Rights Litigation, 639 F. Supp. 2nd 1308 (2009), 49–51.

95. Tri-State Water Rights Litigation, 644 F.3d 1160 (2011), 93–95.

CHAPTER SIX

1. Steven Hahn, *The Roots of Southern Populism: Yeoman Farmers and the Transformation of the Georgia Upcountry, 1850–1890* (New York: Oxford University Press, 1983); Shawn E. Kantor and J. Morgan Kousser, "Common Sense or Commonwealth? The Fence Law and Institutional Change in the Postbellum South," *Journal of Southern History* 59 (May 1993): 201–42; and E. Merton Coulter, *The South during Reconstruction, 1865–1877* (Baton Rouge: Louisiana State University Press, 1947). For a continental treatment, see Allan Greer, "Commons and Enclosure in the Colonization of North America," *American Historical Review* 117, no. 2 (2012): 365–86.

2. Hahn, *Roots of Southern Populism;* and Scott Giltner, *Hunting and Fishing in the New South: Black Labor and White Leisure after the Civil War* (Baltimore: Johns Hopkins University Press, 2008).

3. For New England, see Richard W. Judd, *Common Lands, Common People: The Origins of Conservation in Northern New England* (Cambridge, MA: Harvard University Press, 1997); and for the West, see Louis S. Warren, *The Hunter's Game: Poachers and Conservationists in Twentieth-Century America* (New Haven, CT: Yale University Press, 1997).

4. Joshua Getzler, *A History of Water Rights at Common Law* (New York: Oxford University Press, 2004); and John M. Gould, *A Treatise on the Law of Waters, Including Riparian Rights* (Chicago: Callaghan & Co., 1883).

5. In the American South, "elite" has a much broader definition than in medieval England. Thomas A. Lund, *American Wildlife Law* (Berkeley: University of California Press, 1980), 61.

6. Char Miller, *Gifford Pinchot and the Making of Modern Environmentalism* (Washington, DC: Island Press, 2001), 110–11.

7. Lund, *American Wildlife Law,* 78.

8. Gould, *Treatise on the Law of Water,* 120–47; Morton J. Horwitz, *The Transformation of American Law: 1780–1860* (Cambridge, MA: Harvard University Press, 1977), 140–42; and Craig E. Colten, "Navigable Waters: A Different Course in the American South," *Water History* 2, no. 1 (2010): 3–17.

9. Cases summarized in the various *West's Digests* of state cases through the mid-twentieth century consistently defend state ownership of fish in navigable waters.

10. Lund, *American Wildlife Law,* 27–29; and James A. Tober, *Who Owns the Wildlife? The Political Economy of Conservation in Nineteenth-Century America* (Westport, CT: Greenwood Press, 1981), 26.

11. Arguments that emphasize increasing regulation with resource scarcity appear in Carol M. Rose, "Energy and Efficiency in the Realignment of Common Law Water Rights," *Journal of Legal Studies* 19 (1990): 261–96; and Jacque L. Emel and Elizabeth Brooks,

"Changes in Form and Function of Property Rights Institutions under Threatened Resource Scarcity," *Annals of the Association of American Geographers* 78, no. 2 (1988): 241–52.

12. Louis C. Hunter, *Steamboats on the Western Rivers: An Economic and Technological History* (Cambridge, MA: Harvard University Press, 1949), 145; and David Hardin, "The Laws of Nature: Wildlife Management in Colonial Virginia," in *The American Environment: Interpretations of Past Geographies*, ed. Lary M. Dilsaver and Craig E. Colten, 137–62 (Lanham, MD: Rowman & Littlefield, 1992). Also see Thomas Downey, *Planting a Capitalist South: Masters, Merchants, and Manufacturers in the Southern Interior, 1790–1860* (Baton Rouge: Louisiana State University Press, 2006).

13. Harry Watson, "The Common Rights of Mankind: Subsistence, Shad, and Commerce in the Early Republican South," in *Environmental History and the American South*, ed. Paul S. Sutter and Christopher J. Manganiello, 131–67 (Athens: University of Georgia Press, 2009), see 140–41 and 151–53.

14. Commission of Fisheries of Virginia, *Biennial Report 1924–1925* (Richmond: Virginia Public Printing, 1926), 15–18; and Article 10 of the 1875 compact between Virginia and Maryland provides for mutual protection of fish within Virginia's waters (see Hendricks v. Commonwealth [1882] 75 Va. 934).

15. See Hendricks v. Commonwealth (1882) 75 Va. 934.

16. Tober, *Who Owns the Wildlife?* 23–25.

17. Lund, *American Wildlife Law*, 78.

18. Kentucky Game and Fish Commission, *Report, 1915–1917* (Frankfort, 1917), 5.

19. Commission of Fisheries of the State of Virginia, *Report, 1889–1890* (Richmond: Superintendent of Public Printing, 1890), 4; and Commission of Fisheries of the State of Virginia, *Report for the Year Ending 1895* (Richmond: Superintendent of Public Printing, 1895), 5.

20. Virginia Board of Fisheries, *Report of the Board of Fisheries to the Governor of Virginia, 1901–1902* (Richmond: Superintendent of Public Printing, 1902), 4; and Virginia Commission of Fisheries, *Report of the Commission of Fisheries* (Richmond: Superintendent of Public Printing, 1922), 7.

21. Act 153, State of Louisiana, *Acts Passed by the General Assembly* (Baton Rouge, 1902). A review of this process appears in Gerald Adkins, "From a Little Acorn," *Louisiana Conservationist* (January/February 1988): 4–7.

22. Louisiana Conservation Commission, *Report of the Louisiana Conservation Commission* (Baton Rouge, 1910), 42.

23. Louisiana Board of Commissioners for the Protection of Birds, Game, and Fish, *Report of the Board of Commissioners for the Protection of Birds, Game and Fish* (Baton Rouge, 1912), 9.

24. North Carolina Geological and Economic Survey, *Biennial Report of the State Geologist, 1909–1910* (Raleigh: Edwards and Broughton Printing, 1911), 118–19; and North Carolina Geological and Economic Survey, *Biennial Report of the State Geologist, 1913–1914* (Raleigh: Uzzela & Company 1914), 131–40.

25. North Carolina Geological and Economic Survey, *Biennial Report of the State Geologist, 1909–1910*, 43–44 and 135–37.

26. Commission of Fisheries of Virginia, *Biennial Report 1926–1927* (Richmond, 1928), 6–12.

27. Commission of Fisheries of Virginia, *Report of the Commission of Fisheries of Virginia 1919–1921* (Richmond, VA: Superintendent of Public Printing, 1922), 7–8.

28. Commission of Fisheries of Virginia, *Report of the Commission of Fisheries of Virginia 1926–27*, 11–12.

29. A thorough accounting of the Maryland oyster fishery is Christine Keiner, *The Oyster Question: Scientists, Watermen, and the Maryland Chesapeake Bay since 1880* (Athens: University of Georgia Press, 2009), 64–67, 115–16, and 144–45.

30. Virginia Board of Fisheries, *Report of the Board of Fisheries to the Governor of Virginia, 1902–1903* (Richmond, VA: Superintendent of Printing, 1903), 5–6.

31. Florida Department of Game and Fish, *Second Annual Report* (Tallahassee: Appleyard, 1915), 9–10. The South Carolina Board of Fisheries also complained that lack of appropriations had stymied its effectiveness. South Carolina Board of Fisheries, *Twenty-second Annual Report, 1928* (Columbia: General Assembly of South Carolina, 1928), 3.

32. Florida Department of Game and Fresh Water Fish, *Report of the Department of Game and Fresh Water Fish* (Tallahassee: Department of Game and Fresh Water Fish, 1928), 39–40.

33. Florida Department of Game and Fresh Water Fish, *Report* (1928), 17; Florida Department of Game and Fresh Water Fish, *Biennial Report* (1930), 23; and Florida Department of Game and Fresh Water Fish, *Biennial Report* (1932), 29.

34. Florida Department of Game and Fresh Water Fish, *Biennial Report* (Tallahassee, 1936), 32.

35. Alabama Department of Game and Fish, *Second and Third Biennial Report, 1908–1912* (Montgomery: Brown Printing Company, 1912), 49–51.

36. Alabama Department of Game and Fisheries, *Third Quadrennial Report, 1926–1930* (Montgomery: Wilson Printing, 1930), 90.

37. Alabama Department of Game and Fisheries, *Fourth Quadrennial Report, 1930–1934* (Montgomery, 1934), 29.

38. Florida Department of Game and Fish, *First Annual Report* (Tallahassee: T. J. Appleyard, 1913), 45.

39. South Carolina Chief Game Warden, *Report of A. A. Richardson, 1934–1935* (Columbia: General Assembly of South Carolina, 1935), 14.

40. Tennessee State Game and Fish Commission, *Annual Report, 1950* (Nashville, 1950), 21.

41. Louisiana Board of Commissioners for the Protection of Birds, Game, and Fish, *Report of the Board of Commissioners for the Protection of Birds, Game and Fish* (Baton Rouge, 1912), 8.

42. Louisiana Conservation Commission, *Report of the Board of Birds, Game and Fish 1910* (Baton Rouge, 1910), 1577.

43. Louisiana Department of Conservation, *Biennial Report of the Department of Conservation, 1916–1918* (Baton Rouge, 1918), 139–40 and Louisiana Department of Conservation, *Fourth Biennial Report, 1918–1920* (Baton Rouge, 1920), 80–90. Neighboring states of Texas and Mississippi also accepted federal assistance with hatcheries when offered.

44. Louisiana Conservation Commission, *Report of the Board of Birds, Game and Fish 1910*, 1583–84.

45. Louisiana Conservation Commission, *Report of the Board of Birds, Game and Fish 1910*, 1584.

46. Louisiana Conservation Commission, *Report, 1912–1914* (Baton Rouge, 1914), 80.

47. Louisiana Conservation Commission, *Report, 1914–1916* (Baton Rouge, 1916), 85–98.

48. Robin W. Doughty, *Wildlife and Man in Texas: Environmental Change and Conservation* (College Station: Texas A&M University Press, 1983), 160–65.

49. Texas Game Fish and Oyster Commission, *Report, 1912* (Austin, 1912), 10–11.

50. Texas Game Fish and Oyster Commission, *Report, 1922* (Austin, 1922), 9; Texas Game Fish and Oyster Commission, *Report, 1927* (Austin, 1927), 8; and Texas Game Fish and Oyster Commission, *Report, 1928* (Austin, 1928), 9.

51. North Carolina Department of Natural Resources and Community Development, Division of Parks and Recreation, *State Lakes Master Plan* (Raleigh, 1977), 5.

52. North Carolina Department of Conservation and Development, *Second Biennial Report* (Raleigh, 1928), 37.

53. North Carolina Department of Conservation and Development, *Third Biennial Report* (Raleigh, 1930), 39.

54. North Carolina Department of Conservation and Development, *Third Biennial Report*, 63.

55. North Carolina Department of Conservation and Development, *Fourth Biennial Report* (Raleigh, 1932), 9.

56. North Carolina Department of Conservation and Development, *Fourth Biennial Report*, 9.

57. Tennessee Department of Agriculture, *Biennial Report, 1923–1924* (Nashville: McQuiddy, 1922), 119–21.

58. Tennessee Department of Game, Fish, and Forestry, *Report of the Department of Game, Fish, and Forestry to the Fifty-Seventh General Assembly* (Nashville: McQuiddy, 1911), 13; and Tennessee v. West Tennessee Land Company et al., 127 Tenn. 575 (1913).

59. Tennessee Department of Game and Fish, *Fifth Biennial Report, 1921–1922* (Nashville: Ewing, 1922), 9.

60. Tennessee Department of Game and Fish, *Fifth Biennial Report, 1921–22*, 9–11.

61. Tennessee Department of Game and Fish, *Fourth Biennial Report, 1919–1920* (Nashville: Ewing, 1920), 7–8.

62. Tennessee State Game and Fish Commission, *Annual Report, 1950* (Nashville, 1950), 21–22.

63. Jens Lund, *Flatheads and Spooneys: Fishing for a Living in the Ohio River Valley* (Lexington: University Press of Kentucky, 1995), 20; and Ernest T. Hiller, *Houseboat and River Bottoms People: A Study of 683 Households in Sample Locations Adjacent to the Ohio and Mississippi Rivers, Illinois Studies in the Social Sciences 24, no. 1* (Urbana: University of Illinois), 1939.

64. Mississippi Oil and Gas Board, Game and Fish Commission, and Sea Food Commission, *Biennial Report 1931–1933* (Jackson, 1933), 18.

65. An Act to Create a State Game and Fish Commission (Jackson: American Legion, 1932), 6; and Mississippi Game and Fish Commission, *Biennial Report, 1947–49* (Jackson, 1949), 19.

66. Mississippi Game and Fish Commission, *Eleventh Biennial Report, 1951–53* (Jackson, 1953), 36 and 42.

67. Caddo Parish Police Jury Minutes, Meeting, January 15, 1925, p. 201, WPA Collection, Historical Records Survey Transcriptions of Louisiana Parish Police Jury Minutes, MSS 2984, Reel 274, Louisiana State University, Hill Memorial Library, Baton Rouge.

68. Raymond H. Torrey, *State Parks and Recreation Uses of State Forests in the United States* (Washington, DC: National Conference on State Parks, 1926), 11. See also Ney C. Landrum, *The State Park Movement in America* (Columbia: University of Missouri Press, 2004).

69. Tennessee v. West Tennessee Land Company, 158 S.W. 746 (1913).

70. Edward A. McIlhenny, "The Creating of the Wild Life Refuges in Louisiana," *Ninth Biennial Report of the Department of Conservation of Louisiana, 1928–1929* (Baton Rouge, 1929), 133–39.

71. Trappers refused to pay license fees and threatened to shoot wardens if they were reported for trapping out of season. Correspondence from E. A. McIlhenny to M. L. Alexander (Louisiana Conservation Commission), October 13, 1996, McIlhenny Collection, Accession 3534, box 10, folder 188, Hill Memorial Library, Louisiana State University, Baton Rouge.

72. *Ninth Biennial Report of the Department of Conservation of Louisiana, 1928–1929* (Baton Rouge, 1929), 214–15; and Louisiana State Parks Commission, *Louisiana State Parks: The Problem and the Answer* (New Orleans, 1935), 9–12.

73. Beatrice W. Nelson, *State Recreation: Parks, Forests, and Game Preserves* (Washington, DC: National Conference on State Parks, 1928), 65.

74. North Carolina Department of Conservation and Development, *Fourth Biennial Report*, 64.

75. Virginia Conservation Commission, Division of Parks, *Virginia State Parks* (Richmond, 1938), frontispiece; and Georgia Department of Natural Resources, *Biennial Report, 1937–1938* (Atlanta, 1938), 14–15. States outside the South also addressed similar issues: see Karl Jacoby, *Crimes against Nature: Squatters, Poachers, Thieves, and the Hidden History of American Conservation* (Berkeley: University of California Press, 2001), 39.

76. See Landrum, *State Park Movement in America*, 124–40. Also Neil M. Mahler, *Nature's New Deal: The Civilian Conservation Corps and the Roots of the American Environmental Movement* (New York: Oxford Press, 2008), 70–74.

77. William E, O'Brien, "State Parks and Jim Crow in the Decade before Brown vs. Board of Education," *Geographical Review* 102, no. 2 (2012): 166–79.

78. See James W. Steely, *Parks for Texas: Enduring Landscapes of the New Deal* (Austin: University of Texas Press, 1999); Robert Pasquill Jr., *The Civilian Conservation Corps in Alabama, 1933–1942: A Great and Lasting Good* (Tuscaloosa: University of Alabama Press, 2008); and Bevley R. Coleman, "A History of State Parks in Tennessee" (PhD dissertation, George Peabody College, 1963).

79. Pasquill, *The Civilian Conservation Corps in Alabama*, 114–15.

80. Coleman, *A History of State Parks in Tennessee*, 24–29.

81. Sarah T. Phillips, *This Land, This Nation: Conservation, Rural America, and the New Deal* (New York: Cambridge University Press, 2007), 185–92.

82. Steely, *Parks for Texas*, 28–41.

83. State Parks Commission of Louisiana, *First Biennial Report, 1934–1935* (New Orleans, 1935), 82.

84. State Parks Commission of Louisiana, *Sixth Biennial Report, 1944–45* (New Orleans, 1945), 23.

85. Mississippi State Board of Park Supervisors, *First Annual Report, 1936* (Jackson, 1936), 60–63; *First Biennial Report, 1939* (Jackson, 1939), quote at 66 and 105.

86. Virginia Conservation Commission, Division of Parks, *Virginia's State Parks* (Richmond: n.p., 1938), "fishing" rules.

87. South Carolina, State Forester, *Report of the State Commission of Forestry, 1934–1935* (Columbia: South Carolina General Assembly, 1935), 32–33.

88. Florida Park Service, *Biennial Report, 1946–1948* (Tallahassee, 1948), 8.

89. Texas Parks and Wildlife Department, *Annual Report, 1963–1964* (Austin, 1964), 1–3.

90. William L. Graf, "Damage Control: Restoring the Physical Integrity of America's Rivers," *Annals of the Association of American Geographers* 91, no. 1 (2001): 1–27, see 20–21.

91. Eric H. Lord, "The Obed Wild and Scenic River of Tennessee: Asserting a Federal Reserved Water Right in Riparian Jurisdiction," *Great Plains Natural Resources Journal* 7 (2003): 1–30.

92. Kevin G. Cheri, Buffalo National River, "Superintendents' Compendium," September 2012 [http://www.nps.gov/buff/parkmgmt/upload/2012-Compendium-with-lower-dist-hunting-map-092812.pdf, 11, accessed March 2013]. See also Dwight Pitchaithley, *Let the River Be* (Santa Fe, NM: National Park Service, Southwest Cultural Resources Center, 1978), 95–104.

93. Louisiana Department of Wildlife and Fisheries, "Scenic Rivers" [http://www.wlf.louisiana.gov/scenic-rivers, accessed February 2013].

94. Louisiana Department of Wildlife and Fisheries, "Guidelines and Procedures for the Administration of the Natural and Scenic Rivers and Historic and Scenic Rivers," 1993 [http://www.wlf.louisiana.gov/sites/default/files/pdf/document/36297-scenic-river-regulations/regulations.pdf, accessed February 2013].

95. Virginia Department of Conservation and Recreation, "Scenic Rivers Background," n.d. [http://www.dcr.virginia.gov/recreational_planning/documents/srbkgrnd.pdf, accessed February 2013].

CHAPTER SEVEN

Based upon "Southern Pollution Permissiveness: Another Regional Myth" by Craig E. Colten from SOUTHEASTERN GEOGRAPHER, Volume 48, no. 1. Copyright © 2008 by Southeastern Division, Association of American Geographers. Published by the University of North Carolina Press. Used by permission of the publisher. I would like to thank Cliff Duplechin and Mary Lee Eggart for the cartography. Research assistance for some of the Texas groundwater material in this chapter came from Reno Cecora and Rita Setter at Texas State University.

1. Howard W. Odum, *Southern Regions of the United States* (Chapel Hill: University of North Carolina Press, 1936), 292–93.

2. National Resources Committee, *Water Pollution in the United States*, U.S. Congress, House Doc. 155, 76th Cong., 1st sess., 1939.

3. Avery Craven, *Soil Exhaustion as a Factor in the Agricultural History of Virginia and Maryland, 1606–1860*, University of Illinois Studies in the Social Sciences, 21, no. 1 (Urbana: University of Illinois Press, 1926).

4. Stanley Trimble, "Perspectives on the History of Soil Erosion Control in the Eastern United States," *Agricultural History* 59 (1985): 162–80, and *Man Induced Soil Erosion on the Southern Piedmont* (Ankeny, IA: Soil and Water Conservation Society, 1974).

5. James C. Cobb, *Industrialization and Southern Society, 1877–1984* (Lexington:

University of Kentucky Press, 1984); Albert Cowdrey, *This Land, This South: An Environmental History*, rev. ed. (Lexington: University of Kentucky Press, 1996).

6. Edwin Goodell, *A Review of Laws Forbidding Pollution of Inland Waters in the United States*, U.S. Geological Survey, Water Supply and Irrigation Paper, 152 (Washington, DC: U.S. Geological Survey, 1905). This extensive report provides a discussion of laws, state by state.

7. National Resources Committee, *Water Pollution in the United States*, contains a map depicting "classes of pollution control," 69.

8. Cobb, *Industrialization and Southern Society*, 129.

9. Cowdrey, *This Land, This South*, 198.

10. Craig E. Colten, "Too Much of a Good Thing: Industrial Pollution in the Lower Mississippi River," in *Transforming New Orleans and Its Environs: Centuries of Change*, ed. Craig E. Colten, 141–59 (Pittsburgh: University of Pittsburgh Press, 2000).

11. Richard A. Bartlett, *Troubled Waters: Champion International and the Pigeon River Controversy* (Knoxville: University of Tennessee Press, 1995), 38–39.

12. Martin V. Melosi, *The Sanitary City: Urban Infrastructure in America from Colonial Times to the Present* (Baltimore: Johns Hopkins University Press, 2000), 230.

13. See, for example, Suzanne Marshall, *"Lord, We're Just Trying to Save Your Water"* (Gainesville: University Press of Florida, 2002).

14. Carville Earle, "The Myth of the Southern Soil Miner: Macrohistory, Agricultural Innovation, and Environmental Change," in *The Ends of the Earth: Perspectives on Modern Environmental History*, ed. Donald Worster, 175–210 (Cambridge: Cambridge University Press, 1989), and "Into the Abyss . . . Again: Technical Change and Destructive Occupance of the American Cotton Belt, 1870–1930," in *The American Environment*, ed. Lary M. Dilsaver and Craig E. Colten, 53–88 (Lanham, MD: Rowman & Littlefield, 1992).

15. Georgia v. Tennessee Copper Company, 206 U.S. 230 (1907); Duncan Maysilles, *Ducktown Smoke: The Fight over One of the South's Greatest Environmental Disasters* (Chapel Hill: University of North Carolina Press, 2011); and Craig E. Colten, "Contesting Pollution in Dixie: The Case of Corney Creek," *Journal of Southern History* 72 (2006): 605–34.

16. Colten, "Too Much of a Good Thing"; Bartlett, *Troubled Waters*; Craig E. Colten, "Texas vs. the Petrochemical Industry: Contesting Pollution in an Era of Industrial Growth," in *The Second Wave: Southern Industrialization from the 1940s to the 1970s*, ed. Philip Scranton, 146–67 (Athens: University of Georgia Press, 2001); Zack Delaune, "Unwelcome Neighbors? Industrial Growth and Water Pollution in Lake Charles, Louisiana, 1940–1960" (Unpublished thesis, Louisiana State University, 2007); and Scott Dewey, "The Fickle Finger of Phosphate: Central Florida Air Pollution and the Failure of Environmental Policy," *Journal of Southern History* 65 (1999): 565–603.

17. Although there are many examples of air pollution, this work focuses on the rich record that emerged in response to water pollution concerns nationwide.

18. Colten, "Contesting Pollution in Dixie," and "Too Much of a Good Thing." Southern sportsmen were also less likely to be involved with national conservation groups like the Isaac Walton League that spearheaded efforts elsewhere. See Philip Scarpino, *Great River: The Environmental History of the Upper Mississippi River, 1890–1950* (Columbia: University of Missouri Press, 1985), esp. chap. 4. There were some exceptions (see chap. 6).

19. Michael Williams, *Americans and Their Forests: A Historical Geography* (New York: Cambridge University Press, 1992); and Cobb, *Industrialization and Southern Society*.

20. National Resources Committee, *Water Pollution in the United States, Drainage Basin Committee Reports for the Chesapeake Bay Drainage Basins* (Washington, DC: Government Printing Office, 1937), *Drainage Basin Committee Report for the Southeast Basins* (Washington, DC: Government Printing Office, 1937), *Drainage Basin Committee Report for the Lower Mississippi River Basins* (Washington, DC: Government Printing Office, 1937), and *Drainage Basin Committee Report for the Tennessee and Cumberland Basins* (Washington, DC: Government Printing Office, 1937).

21. National Resources Committee, *Water Pollution in the United States*, 82.

22. National Resources Committee, *Water Pollution in the United States*, 41.

23. National Resources Committee, *Water Pollution in the United States*, 69; and Craig E. Colten, "Cities and Water Pollution: An Historical and Geographic Perspective," *Urban Geography* 26 (2005): 435–58.

24. Geoffrey Buckley, "The Environmental Transformation of an Appalachian Valley, 1890–1906," *Geographical Review* 88, no. 2 (1998): 175–98.

25. National Resources Committee, *Drainage Basin Committee Report for Chesapeake Bay Drainage Basins*, 13–20.

26. Current federal policy recognizes sediments eroding from agricultural land as a pollution concern, but the 1930s report addressed soil erosion as a separate issue (namely loss of farmland and the creation of wetlands that could harbor malaria-carrying mosquitoes), and I will follow their lead. Non-point pollution became a prominent part of the federal pollution legislation only in the 1980s.

27. National Resources Committee, *Drainage Basin Committee Report on the Southeast Basins*. (Washington, DC: Government Printing Office, 1937), 16–17.

28. National Resources Committee, *Drainage Basin Committee Report on the Southeast Basins*, 28.

29. National Resources Committee, *Drainage Basin Committee Report for the Tennessee and Cumberland Basins*, 8.

30. U.S. Public Health Service, *Report on Pollution of Interstate Waters of the North Fork Holston River* (Cincinnati: Robert Taft Sanitary Engineering Center, 1960), 1.

31. National Resources Committee, *Drainage Basin Committee Report for the Southeast Basins*, 22–23.

32. The NRC discussed both the Pearl and the Pascagoula basins in one section of the 1937 report. This treatment considers only the Pearl since it became the object of an interstate hearing.

33. National Resources Committee, *Drainage Basin Committee Report for the Lower Mississippi River Basins*, 29.

34. National Resources Committee, *Drainage Basin Committees' Reports for the Red and Ouachita Basins* (Washington: Government Printing Office, 1937), 21–22.

35. National Resources Committee, *Water Pollution in the United States*, 6.

36. W. D. Weiss, *Industrial Water Pollution: Survey of Legislation and Regulations* (New York: Chemonics, 1951); W. L. Andreen, "The Evolution of Water Pollution Control in the United States: State, Local, and Federal Efforts, 1789–1972," pt. 1, *Stanford Environmental Law Review* 22 (2003): 146–200; "The Evolution of Water Pollution Control in the United States: State, Local, and Federal Efforts, 1789–1972," pt. 2. *Stanford Environmental Law Review* 22 (2003): 216–94; and Colten, "Cities and Water Pollution."

37. Not all locations had adequate alternative water supplies in terms of quantity. FSA (Federal Security Agency), U.S. Public Health Service, *Summary Report on Water Pollution:*

North Atlantic Drainage Basins (Washington, DC: Federal Security Agency, U.S. Public Health Service, 1951); and USHEW (U.S. Department of Health, Education, and Welfare), *1957 Inventory: Municipal and Industrial Waste Facilities, Regions II, III and IV* (Washington, DC: U.S. Department of Health, Education, and Welfare, Public Health Service, 1958).

38. FSA, U.S. Public Health Service, *Summary Report on Water Pollution: Southeast Drainage Basins* (Washington, DC: Federal Security Agency, U.S. Public Health Service, 1951); and USHEW, *1957 Inventory: Municipal and Industrial Waste Facilities, Regions II, III, and IV.*

39. USHEW, *1957 Inventory: Municipal and Industrial Waste Facilities, Regions II, III, and IV.*

40. FSA, 1951. *Summary Report on Water Pollution: Tennessee River Drainage Basins* (Washington, DC: Federal Security Agency, Public Health Service, 1951), 59.

41. "Wild Life Group Meet with Officials," Abingdon *Journal-Virginian*, January 16, 1947, 16; and USPHS (U.S. Public Health Service), *Report on Pollution of Interstate Waters of the North Fork Holston River* (Cincinnati: Robert Taft Sanitary Engineering Center, 1960), 1–2.

42. Virginia Water Control Board, Minutes, February 4, 1947, 25–27, Virginia State Archives, Richmond, Virginia, Minutes June 3–4, 1948, 9–11, Virginia State Archives, Richmond, Virginia, Minutes, 19–20 1953, 157–65, Virginia State Archives, Richmond, Virginia; and Record of Hearing, Olin Mathieson Chemical Corporation, Saltville, Virginia, May 10, 1956, 1–29, Box 1, BC 1030847, Virginia State Archives, Richmond Virginia.

43. USHEW, *1957 Inventory: Municipal and Industrial Waste Facilities, Regions II, III, and IV*; and U.S. Department of the Interior, Federal Water Pollution Control Administration, 1970, *Proceedings: Conference in the Matter of Pollution of the Interstate Waters of Perdido Bay and Its Tributaries*, January 23, 1970 (Gulf Breeze, FL: U.S. Department of the Interior, Federal Water Pollution Control Administration, 1970).

44. USHEW, *1957 Inventory: Municipal and Industrial Waste Facilities, Regions II, III, and IV*; and FSA, *Summary Report on Water Pollution: Southeast Drainage Basins* (Washington, DC: Federal Security Agency, U.S. Public Health Service, 1951).

45. See Colten, "Contesting Pollution in Dixie."

46. Murray Stein, "Federal Water Pollution Control Enforcement Activities," *Proceedings of the Eighteenth Industrial Waste Conference* (West Lafayette, IN: Purdue University, 1963), 264–72.

47. Stein, "Federal Water Pollution Control Enforcement Activities"; Brian Berry, *Land Use, Urban Form and Environmental Quality* (University of Chicago, Department of Geography, Research Paper 155, 1974, Chicago); and Colten, "Contesting Pollution in Dixie."

48. This case is developed more completely in Colten, "Contesting Pollution in Dixie."

49. U.S. Department of the Interior (USDI), *The Nation's River* (Washington, DC: U.S. Department of the Interior, 1968); and USDI, *The Potomac* (Washington, DC: Government Printing Office, 1967).

50. U.S. Congress, Joint Committee on Washington Metropolitan Problems, *Hearings: Washington Metropolitan Area Water Problems*, 85th Cong., 2nd sess., 1958.

51. U.S. Army Corps of Engineers. 1962. *Potomac River Basin Report, V. 5, Water Supply and Water Quality Control Uses, Requirements and Benefits* (Baltimore: U.S. Army Corps of Engineers, Baltimore District, 1962), 126. Also Stein, "Federal Water Pollution Control Efforts."

52. USPHS, *Report on Pollution of Interstate Waters of the North Fork Holston River*, 2–3

and 22–23. See also Virginia Water Control Board, Minutes, February 4, 1947, 25–27, Minutes June 3–4, 1948, 9–11, Minutes, August 19–20, 1953, 157–65, Virginia State Archives, Richmond, Virginia; and Record of Hearing, Olin Mathieson Chemical Corporation, Saltville, Virginia, May 10, 1956.

53. USPHS, *Conference in the Matter of Pollution of the Interstate Waters of North Fork Holston River* (Kingsport, TN: USPHS, 1962), 106–14.

54. USDI, Federal Water Pollution Control Administration. 1963. *Proceedings: Conference on Interstate Pollution of the Pearl River, October 22, 1963* (New Orleans: U.S. Department of the Interior, Federal Water Pollution Control Administration, 1963); and "Hearing Continues," *Bogalusa Daily News*, October 22, 1963, 1.

55. USDI, Federal Water Pollution Control Administration, *Proceedings: Conference on the Pollution of the Interstate Waters of the Pearl River, Mississippi-Louisiana, November 7, 1968* (Bogalusa, LA: U.S. Department of the Interior, Federal Water Pollution Control Administration, 1968), 98, 107, and 132–37.

56. USHEW, *Conference in the Matter of Pollution of the Interstate Waters of the Coosa River and Its Tributaries* (Rome, GA: USHEW, 1963), 5.

57. USHEW, *Conference in the Matter of Pollution of the Interstate Waters of the Coosa River*, 37.

58. The conference dealt only with the Chattahoochee River and not with the Apalachicola River, which is created at the confluence of the Chattahoochee and the Flint rivers. Consequently, there was no Florida participation in the conference. See esp. USDI, *Proceedings: Conference in the Matter of Pollution of the Interstate Waters of the Chattahoochee River, July 14–15, 1966* (Atlanta: U.S. Department of the Interior, Federal Water Pollution Control Administration, 1966), 136–37 and 178–80.

59. USDI, *Proceedings: Conference in the Matter of Pollution of the Interstate Waters of the Chattahoochee River*, 60–62; and Stein, "Federal Water Pollution Control Activities."

60. USDI, *Proceedings: Conference in the Matter of Pollution of the Interstate Waters of the Chattahoochee River*, 25–37 and 62.

61. "Paying for Clean Water," Atlanta *Constitution*, July 15, 1966, 4.

62. USDI, Federal Water Pollution Control Administration, *Proceedings: Conference in the Matter of Pollution of the Interstate Waters of Perdido Bay and Its Tributaries, January 23, 1970* (Gulf Breeze, FL: U.S. Department of the Interior, Federal Water Pollution Control Administration, 1970).

63. Carl Bridenbaugh, "Baths and Watering Places in Colonial America," *William and Mary Quarterly* 3 (1946): 151–81; Henry Lawrence, "Southern Spas: Source of the American Resort Tradition," *Landscape* 27, no. 2 (1983): 1–12; Sharon Shugart, *The Hot Springs of Arkansas through the Years* (Hot Springs, AR: Eastern National Parks and Monuments Association, 1996); and Janet M. Valenza, *Taking the Waters in Texas: Springs, Spas, and Fountains of Youth* (Austin: University of Texas Press, 2000).

64. J. L. Leal, "Legal Aspects of Water Pollution," *Public Health* 27 (1901): 103–12; and Edwin B. Goodell, *A Review of Laws Forbidding Pollution of Inland Waters* (Washington, DC: U.S. Geological Survey, Water-Supply and Irrigation Paper 152, 1905).

65. George C. Matson and Samuel Sanford, *Geology and Ground Waters of Florida* (Washington, DC: U.S. Geological Survey, Water-Supply Paper 319, 1913), 1, 261.

66. Lloyd Stephenson, William N. Logan, and Gerald A. Waring, *The Ground-Water Resources of Mississippi* (Washington, DC: U.S. Geological Survey, Water-Supply Paper 576), 1928), 26.

67. C. W. Stiles, H. R. Crohurst, and G. E. Thomson, *Experimental Bacterial and Chemical Pollution of Wells via Ground Water, and the Factors Involved* (Washington, DC: U.S. Public Health Service, Hygienic Laboratory Bulletin 147, 1927).

68. Elfreda L. Caldwell and Leland W. Parr, "Pollution Flow from a Pit Latrine when Permeable Soils of Considerable Depth Exist below the Pit," *Journal of Infectious Disease* 62, no. 3 (1937): 225–58; and "Direct Measurement of the Rate of Ground Water Flow in Pollution Studies," *Journal of Infectious Disease* 62 (1938): 259–71.

69. "Underground Waste Disposal and Control: Task Group Report," *Journal American Water Works Association* 49, no. 10 (1957): 1334–42; and William E. Stanley and Rolf Eliassen, *Status of Knowledge of Ground Water Contaminants* (Cambridge, MA: MIT, Department of Civil and Sanitary Engineering, 1960).

70. Ruth Patrick, Emily Ford, and John Quarles, *Groundwater Contamination in the United States*, 2nd ed. (Philadelphia: University of Pennsylvania Press, 1987), 29–30.

71. Harold E. Thomas, *The Conservation of Ground Water* (New York: McGraw-Hill, 1951), 285–87.

72. Stanley and Eliassen, *Status of Knowledge of Ground Water*, 24–25.

73. Texas Board of Water Engineers, *Twenty-First Report, 1952–1954* (Austin: Texas Board of Water Engineers, 1954), 52–55.

74. Hugh S. Gorman, *Redefining Efficiency: Pollution Concerns, Regulatory Mechanisms, and Technological Change in the U.S. Petroleum Industry* (Akron, OH: University of Akron Press, 2001), 34–62.

75. For a listing of these reports, see Charlotte Friebele and Herbert Wolff, *Annotated Bibliography of Texas Water Resources Reports* (Austin: Texas Water Development Board, Report 199, 1976).

76. M. R. Scalf, J. W. Keeley, and C. J. LaFevers, *Ground Water Pollution in the South Central States*, Environmental Protection Technology Series 268 (Corvallis, OR: U.S. Environmental Protection Agency, National Environmental Research Center, 1973), 50–57.

77. For a discussion of the river pollution incident, see Colten, "Too Much of a Good Thing."

78. D. R. Rima, E. Brown, D. F. Goerlitz, and L. M. Law, *Potential Contamination of the Hydrologic Environment from the Pesticide Waste Dump in Hardeman County, Tennessee* (Washington, DC: Federal Water Pollution Control Administration, 1967).

79. Sterling v. Velsicol, 647 F. Supp. 303 (1987).

80. Rufus H. Musgrove, Jack T. Barraclough, and Rodney G. Grantham, *Water Resources of Escambia and Santa Rosa Counties, Florida* (Tallahassee: Florida Geological Survey, Report of Investigations 40, 1965), 95–96.

81. P. E. LaMoreaux, *Ground-Water Resources of the South—A Frontier of the Nation's Water Supply* (Washington, DC: U.S. Geological Survey, 1960), 2.

82. Scalf et al., *Ground Water Pollution in the South Central States*, 83–107.

CONCLUSIONS

I would like to thank Samantha Chaisson, whose thesis on drought in Georgia offered insights to this issue, and John McEwen, who assisted with the research.

1. There are numerous interbasin conflicts that will not be discussed here and that raise additional questions about water priorities. See Mark Davis, "Preparing for Apportionment: Lessons from the Catawba River," *Sea Grant Law and Policy Journal* 2 (2009): 44–55.

2. See John Opie, *Ogallala: Water for a Dry Land* (Lincoln: University of Nebraska Press, 1993), esp. chap. 4; and David E. Kromm and Stephen E. White, eds., *Groundwater Exploitation in the High Plains* (Lawrence: University of Kansas Press, 1992).

3. Jacque Emel and Rebecca Roberts, "Institutional Form and Its Effect on Environmental Change: The Case of Groundwater in the Southern High Plains," *Annals of the Association of American Geographers* 85 (1995): 664–83.

4. Georgina H. Endfield, Isabel F. Tejedo, and Sarah O. O'Hara, "Conflict and Cooperation: Water, Floods, and Social Response in Colonial Guanajuato, Mexico," *Environmental History* 9 (2004): 221–48.

5. Jacque Emel and Elizabeth Brooks, "Changes in Form and Function of Property Rights Institutions under Threatened Resource Scarcity," *Annals of the Association of American Geographers* 78 (1988): 241–52.

6. National Water Commission, *Water Policies for the Future* (Port Washington, NY: Water Information Center, 1973), esp. chap. 8.

7. Karen M. O'Neil, *Rivers by Design: State Power and the Origins of U.S. Flood Control* (Durham, NC: Duke University Press, 2006); and Shannon Stunden Bower, *Wet Prairie: People, Land and Water in Agricultural Manitoba* (Vancouver: UBC Press, 2011).

8. H. C. Darby, *The Draining of the Fens* (Cambridge: Cambridge University Press, 1940); and Hugh Prince, *Wetlands of the American Midwest: A Historical Geography of Changing Attitudes* (Chicago: University of Chicago Press, 1997).

9. Theodore Steinberg, *Nature Incorporated: Industrialization and the Waters of New England* (Amherst: University of Massachusetts Press, 1991); Christine M. Rosen, "'Knowing' Industrial Pollution: Nuisance Law and the Power of Tradition in a Time of Rapid Economic Change, 1840–1864," *Environmental History* 8 (2003): 565–97, and "Costs and Benefits of Pollution Control in Pennsylvania, New York, and New Jersey," *Geographical Review* 88 (1988): 219–40.

10. Dargan Cole Sr. and William B. Carver, "Interbasin Transfers of Water," *Proceedings of the 2011 Georgia Water Resource Conference* [http://www.gwri.gatech.edu/uploads/proceedings/2011/3.5.4Cole.pdf], 2 ; National Water Commission, *Water Policies*, 317–21.

11. Frank Quinn, "Water Transfers: Must the American West Be Won Again?" *Geographical Review* 58 (1968): 108–32; and National Water Commission, *Water Policies*, 323–25.

12. John J. Vandertulip, "Texas Water Plan," *Journal of the American Water Works Association* 58 (1966): 1225–30; and Quinn, "Water Transfers," 116.

13. John Vandertulip and Lewis B. Seward, "The Preliminary Texas Water Plan," in *Technical Papers on Selected Aspects of the Preliminary Texas Water Plan*, Report 31 (Austin: Texas Water Development Board, 1966), 22. Opposition by east Texas legislators to in-state interbasin transfer prompted the state to look beyond its borders. Joe G. Moore Jr., "A Half Century of Water Resource Planning and Policy," in *Water for Texas*, ed. Jim Norwine, John R. Giardino, and Sushma Krisnamurthy (College Station: Texas A&M Press, 2004), 10.

14. To garner stronger support for federal involvement, the investigation included New Mexico as a second possible water recipient. U.S. Department of the Interior, Bureau of Reclamation, *West Texas and Eastern New Mexico Import Project* (Washington, DC: U.S. Department of the Interior, Bureau of Reclamation, 1973), 1; and Raphael G. Kazmann and Ottoniel Arguello, "The Mississippi River—A Water Source for Texas?" Louisiana Water Resources Institute, Bulletin 9 (Baton Rouge: Louisiana State University, 1973), 2–1.

15. Texas Water Development Board, *The Texas Water Plan* (Austin: Texas Water Development Board, 1968), II-24.

16. Calvin T. Watts, "Proposed Diversion of Mississippi River Water from the Viewpoint of the Basin of Origin," in *Proceedings of Conference on Aspects of the Diversion of Mississippi River Water to Texas and New Mexico* (Ruston: Louisiana Polytechnic Institute, 1969), 9–20.

17. Howard Boswell, "The Texas Water Plan," *Proceedings of Conference on Aspects of the Diversion of Mississippi River Water to Texas and New Mexico* (Ruston: Louisiana Polytechnic Institute, 1969), 24–29.

18. Fred H. Baley III, "The Role of the Mississippi River Commission in the Mississippi River Water Export Study,"*Proceedings of Conference on Aspects of the Diversion of Mississippi River Water to Texas and New Mexico* (Ruston: Louisiana Polytechnic Institute, 1969), 77–90; and John T. Pegg, Comments in "Export of Mississippi River Water to Texas and New Mexico," *Journal American Water Works Association* 62 (1970): 369–71.

19. U.S. Department of the Interior, Bureau of Reclamation, *West Texas and Eastern New Mexico Import Project*, chap. 5 (Washington, DC, 1973).

20. U.S. Department of the Interior, Bureau of Reclamation, *West Texas and Eastern New Mexico Import Project*, 65.

21. Kazman and Agruello, "The Mississippi River," 1973, 6–1 to 6–2.

22. U.S. Department of the Interior, Bureau of Reclamation, *West Texas and Eastern New Mexico Import Project*, 153. See also Sherwood M. Gagliano and Johannes L. van Beek, *Hydrologic and Geologic Studies of Coastal Louisiana, Report No. 1, Geologic and Geomorphic Aspects of Deltaic Processes, Mississippi Delta System* (Baton Rouge: Louisiana State University, Center for Wetland Resources, 1970), 99–100.

23. U.S. Department of the Interior, Bureau of Reclamation, *West Texas and Eastern New Mexico Import Project*, 153–56.

24. Emel and Brooks, "Changes in Form and Function of Property Rights Institutions"; and Kromm and White, *Groundwater Exploitation in the High Plains*, esp. 204–23.

25. Sabine River Authority of Texas, *Comprehensive Annual Financial Report, 2011* (Orange: Sabine River Authority of Texas, 2011), 39 [http://www.sratx.org/aboutsra/annual_report/FY2011/2011SRAAnnualReport_reduced.pdf, accessed November 2012].

26. Bill Dawson, "New 3-City Plan is Studied; Possible Shortages Targeted in Texas," *Houston Chronicle*, May 7, 1992, 1.

27. Trans-Texas Water Program, *Planning Information Update* (Austin: Trans-Texas Water Program, 1996), 29.

28. Trans-Texas Water Program, *Water Conservation* (Austin: Trans-Texas Water Program, 1998), 13–14, and *Planning Information Update*, 24.

29. Trans-Texas Water Program, *Phase II Report* (Austin: Trans-Texas Water Program, 1998), 42.

30. Julie Mason, "City Goes with Flow to Reduce Water Use," *Houston Chronicle*, 31 May 1997, 3.

31. Shawn Martin, "Water for Sale," *Louisiana Life* (July/August 2011) [http://www.myneworleans.com/Louisiana-Life/July–August-2011/Water-for-Sale, accessed October 2012].

32. Mark Ballard, "Vote on Sale of Water Looms," *Baton Rouge Advocate*, January 3, 2011 [http://theadvocate.com/home/1705700-125/vote-on-sale-of-water.html, accessed November 2012].

33. R.W. Carter and S. M. Herrick, "Water Resources in the Atlanta Metropolitan Area," U.S. Geological Survey Circular 148 (Washington: USGS, 1951), 9; and Secretary of War, Letter: Apalachicola, Chattahoochee, and Flint Rivers, Georgia and Florida, House Doc. 300, 80th Cong., 1st sess., 1948, and Letter: Apalachicola, Chattahoochee, and Flint Rivers, Georgia and Florida, House Doc. 342, 76th Cong., 1st sess., 1939.

34. J. B. Ruhl, "Water Wars, Eastern Style: Divvying Up the Apalachicola-Chatta-hoochee-Flint River Basin," *Journal of Contemporary Water Research and Education* 131 (2005); 47–54; and Robert E. Vest, "Water Wars in the Southeast: Alabama, Florida, and Georgia Square Off over the Apalachicola-Chattahoochee-Flint River Basin," *Georgia State University Law Review* 9 (1993): 689–716.

35. Ruhl, "Water Wars"; Vest, "Water Wars"; Nicole Carter et al., *Apalachicola-Chatta-hoochee-Flint (ACF) Drought: Federal Water Management Issues*, CRS Report for Congress (Washington, DC: Congressional Research Service, 2008); and Dan Chapman, "Georgia's Water Crisis: Could Tennessee River Help Rescue Georgia?" *Atlanta Journal-Constitution* December 1, 2007, 1A.

36. Duncan Mansfield, "Tennessee Taking Steps to Protect Its Water Wealth," April 23, 2001, AP wire story, n.p. [accessed via Lexis-Nexis]; and William Bradley Carver, Dargan Cole Sr., and Chad Wingate, "Tapping the Tennessee River at Georgia's Northwest Corner: A Solution to North Georgia's Water Supply Crisis," Confidential Water Policy Memo (2008), 3–4 [http://media.timesfreepress.com/docs/2008/02/Tapping_the_Tennes-see_River.pdf, accessed November 2012].

37. William Bradley Carver, Dargan Cole Sr., and Chad Wingate, "Tapping the Tennessee River at Georgia's Northwest Corner: A Solution to North Georgia's Water Supply Crisis," *Proceedings of the Georgia Water Resources Conference*, April 11–13, 2011, Athens, Georgia, 1.

38. Carver et al., "Tapping the Tennessee," 5–8.

39. Carver et al., "Tapping the Tennessee," 5.

40. Carver et al., "Tapping the Tennessee," 15–16.

41. David L. Feldman and Julia O. Elmendorf, *Water Supply Challenges Facing Tennes-see: Case Study Analyses and the Need for Long-Term Planning* (Knoxville: University of Tennessee, Energy, Environment and Resources Center, 2000), 52–53.

42. Chapman, "Georgia's Water Crisis."

43. Shaila Dewan, "Georgia Claims a Sliver of the Tennessee River," *New York Times* February 22, 2008 [http://www.nytimes.com/2008/us/22water.html?_r=0, accessed October 2012]; and Daniel Cusick, "Water: Georgia Gets Serious in Pursuit of Tennessee River," *Land Letter*, February 28, 2008, n.p., accessed via Lexis-Nexis.

44. Jay Bookman, "Border War over Water Likely to Fail," *Atlanta Journal-Constitution* February 28, 2008, 21A.

45. State of Georgia, *Comprehensive State-Wide Water Management Plan* (Atlanta: State of Georgia, 2008); and Georgia Department of Natural Resources, Environmental Protec-tion Division, *Georgia's Water Conservation Implementation Plan* (Atlanta: Georgia De-partment of Natural Resources, Environmental Protection Division, 2010).

46. Andy Johns, "Georgia Water Plan Focuses on Tennessee," *Chattanooga Times Free Press,* February 24, 2011 [http://www.timesfreepress.com/news/2011/feb24/georgia-wa-ter-plan-focuses-on-tennessee, accessed October 2012]; Alabama, Alabama Power Com-pany, and Florida v. U.S. Army Corps of Engineers, Tri-State Water Rights Litigation, U.S.

District Court, Middle District of Florida, Memorandum and Order, July 21, 2010 [http://www.atlantaregional.com/File%20Library/Environment/ep_Tri-State_PhaseIIOrder.pdf, accessed November 2012].

47. "Editorial: Serious Steps in Water Waltz with Tennessee," *Athens-Banner Herald* June 16, 2011 [http://www.onlineathens.com/stories/061611/opi_844969143.shtml, accessed October 2012].

48. M. J. Ellington, "Caucus: Don't Tap into River, Georgia," *Decatur [Alabama] Daily*, April 13, 2011 [http.decaturdaily.com/stories/Caucus-Don't-tap-into-river-Georgia,70855, accessed October 2012].

49. Alabama, Alabama Power Company, and Florida v. U.S. Army Corps of Engineers, Tri-State Water Rights Litigation, U.S. District Court, Middle District of Florida, Memorandum and Order, July 21, 2010; and Tri-State Water Rights Litigation, U.S. Court of Appeals, Ruling, June 28, 2011 [http://www.atlantaregional.com/File%20Library/Environment/ep_Tri-State_Ruling_11th_Circuit_June_2011.pdf, accessed November 2012].

50. U.S. Geological Survey, "Irrigation Water Use," 2000 [http://ga.water.usgs.gov/edu/wuir.html, accessed April 2013].

51. U.S. Census Bureau, *Census of Agriculture: Irrigation of Agricultural Lands*, vol. 3, pt. 1 (Washington, DC: U.S. Department of Commerce, 1959), 2 [http://agcensus.mannlib.cornell.edu/AgCensus/getVolumeTwoPart.do?volnum=3&year=1959&part_id=483&number=1&title=Irrigation%20of%20Agricultural%20Lands, accessed March 2013].

52. Steven Evett, Dennis Carman, and Dale Bucks, "Expansion of Irrigation in the Mid South United States: Water Allocation and Research Issues," in *Proceedings, 2nd International Conference on Irrigation and Drainage, Water for a Sustainable World* (Phoenix, AZ: U.S. Committee on Irrigation and Drainage, 2003), 247–60, see 249.

53. Ruohong Cai, Jeffrey D. Mullen, and John C. Bergstrom, "Irrigated Acreage Projections for Georgia," paper presented at the Southern Agricultural Economics Annual Meeting, Orlando, Florida, 2010 [http://ageconsearch.umn.edu/bitstream/56468/1/Irrigated%20Acreage%20Projections%20in%20Georgia.pdf, accessed April 2013].

54. John P. Warren, Lonnie L. Jones, Ronald D. Lacewell, and Wade L. Griffin, "External Costs of Land Subsidence in the Houston-Baytown Area," *American Journal of Agricultural Economics* 57, no. 3 (1975): 450–58.

55. C. J. Taylor and W. M. Alley, *Ground-water Level Monitoring and the Importance of Long-term Water-level Data*, U.S. Geological Survey Circular 1217 (Washington, DC: U.S. Geological Survey, 2001).

56. P. M. Barlow, *Ground Water in Freshwater-Saltwater Environments of the Atlantic Coast*, U.S. Geological Survey Circular 1262 (Washington, DC: U.S. Geological Survey, 2003).

57. U.S. Geological Survey, "Estimated Use of Water in the United States in 1990" [http://water.usgs.gov/watuse/tables/totab.cat.st.html], 1996, and "Total Water Withdrawals by Water-Use Category, 2005 in Million Gallons per Day" [http://ga.water.usgs.gov/edu/wateruse/pdf/wutotal-cat-mgd-2005.pdf], 2005; and U.S. Census Bureau, "Population Change U.S. Regions, States, and Puerto Rico: 2000–2010" [http://www.census.gov/prod/cen2010/briefs/c2010br-01.pdf], 2011.

58. Thomas R. Karl, Jerry M. Melillo, and Thomas C. Peterson, eds., *Global Climate Change Impacts in the United States* (New York: Cambridge University Press, 2009), 111–16.

59. There are numerous other interstate transfer issues. See Bjorn Kjerfve, "The Santee-Cooper: A Study of Estuarine Manipulations," *Estuarine Processes* 1 (1976): 44–56; William E. Cox, "North Carolina-Virginia Conflict: The Lake Gaston Water Transfer," *Journal of Water Resources Planning and Management* 133, no. 5 (2007): 456–61; and Davis, "Preparing for Apportionment."

60. Kate Galbraith, "Getting Serious about a Texas-Size Drought," *New York Times* April 7, 2013, *Week in Review*, 4.

Index